P9-DEY-559

EASY GUIDE TO
AMERICAN
HISTORY

EASY GUIDE TO
AMERICAN
HISTORY

New York

FALL RIVER PRESS

New York

An Imprint of Sterling Publishing Co., Inc.
1166 Avenue of the Americas
New York, NY 10036

FALL RIVER PRESS and the distinctive Fall River Press logo
are registered trademarks of Barnes & Noble, Inc.

© 2005 by Spark Publishing
This 2014 edition published by Fall River Press.

All rights reserved. No part of this publication may be reproduced,
stored in a retrieval system, or transmitted in any form or by any means
(including electronic, mechanical, photocopying, recording, or otherwise)
without prior written permission from the publisher.

ISBN 978-1-4351-5429-2

For information about custom editions, special sales, and premium
and corporate purchases, please contact Sterling Special Sales at
800-805-5489 or specialsales@sterlingpublishing.com.

Manufactured in the United States of America

2 4 6 8 10 9 7 5 3

www.sterlingpublishing.com

Contents

CONTENTS

Introduction

When the United States of America was founded in the late eighteenth century, there was nothing like it anywhere else. True democracy had not been seen since the time of Athens, and the nations of the world were ruled for the most part by unelected monarchs. But America's founding fathers— men such as Thomas Jefferson, Benjamin Franklin, George Washington, and Alexander Hamilton—created a republican system of government that was, for its time, truly unique. This government reflected the political philosophies of the eighteenth-century Enlightenment. Perhaps most important, the American system of government embodied the belief that liberty, equality, and freedom from tyranny were fundamental freedoms held by ordinary Americans.

Of course, things were not that simple. America's founding documents such as the Constitution and Declaration of Independence might have been brief, but they were revolutionary in concept. Furthermore, their framework was left intentionally loose, so that future generations could continually reinterpret what American democracy meant, while remaining true to the founders' basic tenets. How exactly Americans would navigate a changing world without betraying their ideals would prove to be something of a continuing revolution. Radical cultural movements, fierce political debates, mind-blowing inventions, wars at home and abroad; it's been eventful.

In *Easy Guide to American History*, you'll read all about it.

CHAPTER 1

Colliding Cultures: Pre-Columbian Period to 1700

|||||||||||||||||||||||||||||||||||||||||||||||||||||||||||

Columbus's return from his 1492 voyage to the New World sparked an era of exploration throughout Europe. Explorers and settlers traveled to the New World for many reasons. The Spaniards and Portuguese who first arrived in the fifteenth and sixteenth centuries mainly sought to make their fortune. These explorers conquered the natives and plundered ancient cities in search of riches. Later, most settlers came to the New World to seek a new beginning, with the freedom to worship and live as they pleased.

Within 200 years of Columbus's initial discovery, Spain, Portugal, France, England, and the Netherlands had all established colonies and vied for dominance in the Western Hemisphere. Spain eventually gained control of most of Central and South America, while Britain dominated North America. American colonists in British North America enjoyed a relative degree of political autonomy and later grew resentful of Britain's attempts to exert more control.

Pre-Columbian America

About 12,000 years ago, bands of hunters from northeast Asia pursued mammoths and other big game across a frozen patch of land known as **Beringia**, unwittingly becoming the first Americans. This land bridge has since disappeared and become the salty **Bering Strait** that divides Siberia from Alaska. Cold weather and harsh conditions drove these hunters south in search of food and a better climate. Gradually, they spread across North and South America and formed various Native American tribes. Historians have learned about these people from the artifacts they left behind, including stone tools and weapons, bones, pottery, ancient dwellings, and bits of textiles and basketry.

> *Though most historians believe the first Americans arrived from Asia, debate rages among anthropologists and archeologists about how and when the first Americans arrived. Archeological evidence found in 1927 indicated that the first known natives arrived around 12,000 years ago, and no one questioned this evidence for more than fifty years. Since 1980, however, discoveries made at several archeological sites have proven that people lived in the Americas much earlier than 12,000 years ago. These new findings have created a stir in the archeological community.*

CENTRAL AND SOUTH AMERICAN NATIVES

By the time Christopher Columbus first set eyes on the New World, more than 50 million people lived in North and South America. About 4 million of those people lived in what is now the United States. The richest, most complex native civilizations developed near the **Isthmus of Panama**, the thin strip of land that divides North and South America. There were four major civilizations in this area:

- **The Mayas**, who lived just north of the Isthmus of Panama, developed a sophisticated approach to mathematics and astronomy and a calendar more accurate than that of Europe.

- **The Toltecs**, who lived in the center of present-day Mexico, had conquered most of Central America by the tenth century.

- **The Aztecs**, who frequently made ritual human sacrifices, founded **Tenochtitlán** in 1325, now known as Mexico City.

- **The Incas**, or **Quechua** people, who inhabited the Andes Mountains, developed elaborate road systems and a strong central government.

These four civilizations distinguished themselves from other Native American societies in South America. They are considered more advanced civilizations for the following accomplishments:

- Establishing permanent cities

- Developing large-scale agricultural techniques to raise such crops as maize (corn), beans, squash, chili peppers, avocados, and pumpkins

- Building giant pyramids, courts for ceremonial games, and other monumental architecture

- Engaging in complex commercial and military practices

NORTH AMERICAN NATIVES

In North America, three distinct native civilizations emerged:

- **The Adena-Hopewell** culture of the Northeast, which had reached its peak by the seventh century, long before European conquest. European settlers later encountered their distant descendants in the **Iroquois** and **Pequot** tribes.

- **The Mississippian** culture of the Southeast, which developed sophisticated agricultural practices and created temple mounds akin to the pyramids built in South America. The Mississippians thrived until the fifteenth century, when European diseases wiped them out. The **Creeks**, **Cherokees**, **Choctaw**, **Chickasaws**, and **Seminoles** all descend from this culture.

- **The Pueblo-Hohokam** people of the Southwest, who developed elaborate irrigation systems. Their descendants include the **Hopi**, **Zuni**, and **Anasazi** tribes.

None of these native cultures developed to the same degree of sophistication as the Mayas, Aztecs, or Incas. However, most of the native peoples in North America were able to maintain large agricultural systems, as well as build ceremonial mounds or pueblo dwellings, and develop elaborate clan structures.

Early European Exploration

During the fourteenth, fifteenth, and sixteenth centuries, Europe underwent a period of fast-paced change and development known as the **Renaissance**, meaning "rebirth." Rampant disease, political fragmentation, and religious hysteria had plagued Europeans throughout the medieval period between the fifth and the thirteenth centuries. The Renaissance, however, featured:

- The revival of learning, with emphasis placed on ancient Greek and Roman scholarship

- The growth of major European cities

- The development of trade and capitalistic economies

- The rise of new and powerful monarchies

Increased power and wealth in the hands of the monarchies eventually led to an interest in exploration and expansion.

Johann Gutenberg's invention of the movable-type printing press in 1440 made books and knowledge accessible on a scale never before known. The widespread availability of affordable books on various subjects helped fuel the Renaissance, when people began to question their beliefs about the world around them.

COLUMBUS'S VOYAGES

Italian-born **Christopher Columbus** learned to sail from Portuguese seamen. After years of sailing on Portuguese ships, Columbus hatched his own plan to lead an expedition westward in the hopes of finding a faster route to Asia across the Atlantic. He eventually received financial backing from King Ferdinand and Queen Isabella of Spain in exchange for the gold, spices, and silk he promised to bring back from the Orient.

The Voyage of 1492

Columbus and eighty-seven other men set sail aboard three
ships: the *Nina*, *Pinta*, and *Santa Maria*. After a rocky thirty-
three-day voyage, they landed on an island in the Bahamas. They
named it **San Salvador**. Columbus called the friendly island people *los indios* (Indians) because he believed he and his men had
landed on an island in the East Indies.

Columbus then sailed southward down to Cuba and to the island
of **Hispaniola** in search of the mainland. When one of his ships
sank, he decided to return home. Leaving forty men behind,
Columbus seized a dozen natives to give to the King and Queen
of Spain and sailed back across the Atlantic.

> Contrary to popular belief, **Vikings** actually discovered the New
> World before Columbus. They colonized Iceland, Greenland, and
> Newfoundland in the ninth and tenth centuries and then began
> exploring the eastern coast of Canada. Archeological findings
> have confirmed oral historical accounts of their early discovery of
> North America. The Vikings had withdrawn from their colonies by
> the eleventh century, and the details of their early explorations
> remained unknown to later European explorers.

Columbus's Return Trips to America

Columbus returned to Spain a hero and prepared for a second
voyage. He sailed back to the Americas in 1493 with seventeen
ships, more than 1,200 men, and instructions from the king and
queen to treat the Indians well. Unfortunately, the forty men
Columbus had left on Hispaniola after his first voyage had raped
and murdered many Indians and had plundered their villages.
The natives had struck back in return and killed ten Spaniards.
Columbus counterattacked with crossbows and guns and loaded
five hundred natives on a ship bound for the slave markets in
Spain. He made two more voyages to the Caribbean in the next
decade but refused to believe he had discovered anything other
than outlying parts of Asia.

Sixteenth-century mapmaker Martin Waldseemueller published the first map of the New World in 1507. He named the continents "Americas" to honor Italian explorer **Amerigo Vespucci***, who first sailed near the mainland of America in 1499. Vespucci amazed Europeans with a published account of his voyages in 1504, in which he claimed to have discovered an entirely new continent.*

SPANISH EXPLORATION

By the early sixteenth century, Spain had begun an inland conquest of the Americas mainly to search for gold, silver, and other riches. Spanish conquistadors, or "conquerors," penetrated much of present-day Latin America and established a vast new-world empire for Spain by the 1530s. The following men were the most famous of these conquistadors:

- **Hernando Cortés**, who conquered the Aztecs at Tenochtitlán with only 600 men in 1519

- **Francisco Pizarro**, who defeated the Incas in 1532

- **Hernando De Soto**, who explored the present-day southwestern United States with 600 men in 1539

"Biological Exchange"

An enormously influential exchange occurred when the Europeans landed in the Americas, generally to the benefit of Europeans and detriment of the native peoples. Sugar and bananas crossed the Atlantic, while pigs, sheep, and cattle arrived in the Americas. However, European diseases such as influenza, typhus, measles, and smallpox also crossed the Atlantic and devastated the Native American population.

Subjugation of the Native Americans

The Spanish explored all of South and Central America and eventually became the privileged landowners of the newly discovered continent. They created the *encomienda* system, in which favored Spanish officers controlled land and the nearby native villages.

These officers protected the villages but also demanded tributes from the natives in the form of goods and labor.

Not surprisingly, a bipolar society emerged in Spanish America, with affluent Europeans at the top and poor, subjugated natives at the bottom. By the mid-1500s, much of the Native American population had died from disease, guns, or overwork. To replace this labor force, the Spanish began importing slaves from Africa.

CHALLENGES TO SPAIN'S EMPIRE

Spain also dominated much of southern and western North America during the colonial period, but not without serious competition from the French, the Dutch, and the English. The French challenged Spanish claims first, most significantly when explorer **Jacques Cartier** made three voyages into present-day Canada in the 1530s. Religious civil wars in France halted further attempts to colonize North America until **Samuel de Champlain** founded "New France," a territory that covered much of eastern Canada in the 1600s.

Spain also suffered from Dutch and English pirates who plundered Spanish ships as they crisscrossed the Atlantic. War eventually erupted between Spain and England in the mid-1500s, ending with England's defeat of the Spanish Armada in 1588. The defeat of the armada marked the beginning of British naval supremacy and opened the way for English colonization of the New World.

> Historians refer to this time as the *Age of Exploration*, but it has also become known as the *Age of Exploitation* or the *Age of Conquest*. The terms imply different ways of looking at the period and illustrate differences among the historians who use them.

English Dominance in North America

Early English attempts at colonization proved unsuccessful and expensive, but colonists soon managed to establish themselves in the wilderness of North America. By the eighteenth century, England had replaced Spain as the dominant colonial power on the continent.

THE COLONIZATION MOVEMENT

Several factors made the acquisition of New-World colonies a virtual necessity for England:

- Spanish gold and silver from the New World had flooded Europe and created a severely inflated economy.

- England did not have any colonies that produced gold and therefore suffered greatly from the inflation.

- English farmers had begun growing foods in the Americas, such as corn and potatoes, which helped to eliminate starvation but contributed to the population boom.

- The increased population combined with extreme inflation fueled the unemployment rate in England.

With a depressed economy, high unemployment rates, and growing populations, England needed somewhere to send its citizens to discover riches and relieve the cities of their unemployed masses.

"THE LOST COLONISTS"

In 1578, Queen Elizabeth I granted Sir Humphrey Gilbert a royal patent to explore and claim new territories in North America. Gilbert hoped to transplant Britons to the Americas to acquire wealth for himself and for England. On his first voyage in 1583, he managed to claim some land in Newfoundland but had to turn back as winter approached. Tragically, he and his ship vanished on the return trip.

The next year, Gilbert's half-brother **Sir Walter Raleigh** petitioned the queen for a commission in his own name. In 1587, Raleigh sponsored an expedition of 117 men, women, and children, who settled on Roanoke Island off the coast of North Carolina. The Spanish–English War prevented any further ships from sailing to **Roanoke**, and three years passed before another English ship arrived in 1590. Strangely, the sailors found the settlement abandoned. To this day, historians do not know what happened to those "Lost Colonists."

MANAGING THE COSTS OF COLONIZATION

New-World colonization soon became so expensive that no single individual could fund expeditions. Instead, English entrepreneurs formed **joint-stock companies** in which stockholders shared the risks and profits of colonization. These stockholders expected to earn a return on their investments in the form of gold and silver, wines, citrus fruits, olive oil, and other spoils that would result from colonization. Some of the larger companies such as the **Virginia Company** acquired patents from the monarchy and held monopolies on large tracts of land.

JAMESTOWN

In 1607, three ships carrying almost 100 men reached the Chesapeake Bay. These settlers chose a highly defensible site along the James River in present-day Virginia and established the small settlement of **Jamestown**.

First Encounters

The Jamestown settlers faced extreme difficulty from the outset, and many men fell to disease, starved to death, or died in skirmishes with Native Americans. Only the adventurer **John Smith**'s military expertise and leadership saved the colony. By the time another English ship arrived in 1609, only fifty-three of the original 100 colonists remained. Unfortunately, the ship carried 400 more settlers without any supplies. Overwhelmed and suffering from battle injuries, Smith abandoned the colony and returned to England.

The "Starving Time"

Smith's departure and the advent of winter marked the beginning of the **"starving time"** in Jamestown. Weak from disease and hunger, the 450 colonists destroyed the town for firewood and then barricaded themselves inside their fort to evade hostile natives. Once inside the fort, they resorted to eating dogs, rats, and even one another after food supplies disappeared. Only sixty people survived the winter. As the survivors prepared to abandon the colony the following spring, four English ships arrived with 500 more men and supplies. Settlers struggled for two more years until colonist **John Rolfe** discovered a new American treasure: tobacco.

Cash Crop: Tobacco

Rolfe discovered that the soil in and around Jamestown was perfectly suited for growing tobacco, and England and the rest of Europe couldn't buy enough of it. In fact, so many Europeans smoked or sniffed tobacco that Jamestown had exported thirty tons' worth of leaves to England by 1619. As a result, the little colony prospered and so did Virginia Company investors. At last, stockholders and the monarchy found it profitable to fund expeditions to the Americas. More important, the discovery of tobacco solidified England's position in North America.

To glean a share of the wealth, Parliament and the Crown forbade the colonists from shipping their tobacco anywhere but England. Even with the limited market, tobacco generated enough profit that the colonists grew richer too. Women eventually joined the farmers in Virginia as the colony flourished. Some Jamestown settlers also brought back black **indentured servants** (not slaves) who became the first Africans in North America.

Bacon's Rebellion

Historians have long looked on **Bacon's Rebellion** as the first manifestation of "revolutionary" feelings. In 1676, colonists in Virginia, especially on the western frontier of the colony, had come under attack from some of the Native American tribes in the area. The royal governor, Sir William Berkeley, had ordered an investigation into the attacks and arranged several meetings between the colonists and the Indians. **Nathaniel Bacon**, a farmer and landowner—and Berkeley's cousin—was unhappy with these efforts. He and several other farmers felt that the government was not protecting them. They coalesced into a loose army and began attacking largely peaceful Indian camps throughout northern Virginia.

Berkeley, in trying to keep the peace, labeled Bacon a rebel. Bacon and his forces surrounded the government buildings in Jamestown and forced Berkeley to flee the city. Shortly thereafter, Bacon died and Berkeley was able to return to power. He promptly hung several of Bacon's compatriots.

Bacon's Rebellion is the first instance historians point to of an independent spirit in the colonies. Bacon and his compatriots took matters into their own hands, and while the outcome was not what they had intended, the idea that they could change their lot in life by rising up against the government was one that had never before been visible in the colonies.

THE PILGRIMS

The **Pilgrims**, who eventually established **Plymouth Colony**, belonged to an uncompromising sect of Protestant Puritans in England who challenged the Anglican Church's authority. Also known as **Separatists** because they had separated from the Anglican Church, these Pilgrims formed a Puritan church under their own covenant. Doing so was considered treasonous at the time, since the church and state were intertwined. To avoid imprisonment or persecution, the Pilgrims fled to Holland in 1607.

New World Freedom

Although the Dutch tolerated Puritan religious practices and allowed them to worship freely, the Pilgrim separatists found themselves relegated to performing the lowest-paying jobs. Living in poverty and finding that their children were assimilating into Dutch culture, the Pilgrim congregation made a drastic decision to leave Europe and establish a Puritan colony in the New World. Although the King of England didn't relish the idea of a faith-based settlement in North America, he agreed not to interfere.

The Mayflower Voyage

Securing a land patent from the Virginia Company, the Pilgrims created their own joint-stock company and prepared for the trans-Atlantic voyage. In 1620, 102 men, women, and children crowded aboard the *Mayflower* and set sail for America. Several non-Puritan settlers joined them, including a cooper named **John Alden** and a hired soldier named **Miles Standish**, both of whom played a crucial role in the founding of the colony. During the voyage, the Pilgrims were blown off course. Reaching Cape Cod instead of Virginia, they attempted to head south but had to turn back because of rough seas. The Pilgrims decided to stay on Cape Cod at a place they called Plymouth.

Assistance from Native Americans

The *Mayflower* remained in New England that first winter and provided shelter to the Pilgrims while they tried to build houses on land. Exposure to the elements, malnutrition, and illness soon began to take their toll, and more than half of the Pilgrims died that first winter. The settlers made friends with their neighbors, the Wampanoag Indians, who helped the remainder survive. One Wampanoag named **Squanto** helped the Pilgrims grow maize the next year. By the following autumn, the Pilgrims had their own bumper crop of corn and were well on their way to self-sufficiency.

To celebrate their bountiful first harvest, the Pilgrims held a feast and invited their Wampanoag neighbors. This feast served as the inspiration for the modern-day Thanksgiving holiday.

The Mayflower Compact

By the early seventeenth century, the king had divided English territorial claims in North America between two chartered joint-stock companies, the **London Virginia Company**, which had jurisdiction over the land from present-day North Carolina to New Jersey, and the **Plymouth Virginia Company**, which controlled the land from New York to Maine. Each company would then issue patents to groups of settlers, allowing them to establish settlements on company land.

The Pilgrims had settled what is now Massachusetts with their patent from the Virginia Company and were therefore outside the jurisdiction of either company. Since, technically, no one controlled them, the Pilgrims formed their own government under the **Mayflower Compact**. Forty-one men signed the compact, elected a simple government, and agreed to obey its laws.

MASSACHUSETTS BAY COLONY

Within a few years, a new colony of Puritans overshadowed the smaller Plymouth Colony. In 1629, a group of Puritan merchants and country gentlemen obtained a royal charter to found the **Massachusetts Bay Company**. The stockholders elected **John Winthrop**, a prosperous and respected lawyer and landowner, to serve as governor of the new colony. Unlike all previous charters from the king, the articles included the provision that the government of the Massachusetts Bay Colony could be located in the colony itself rather than in England. Winthrop and a group of 1,000 Puritans settled in Boston and Salem, Massachusetts, in 1630.

Reform vs. Separation

Winthrop's settlers were Puritans, but as they were not members of the Separatists' extreme sect, they were not Pilgrims, like the people of Plymouth. Instead, the Puritans in Boston and Salem believed that the Anglican Church just needed to be purified in order to restore strict biblical interpretations. In short, they were **Reformists**, not Separatists.

"City Upon a Hill"

Winthrop remained the leader of the Massachusetts Bay Colony for twenty years until his death in 1649. During this time, the colony grew rapidly, as nearly 20,000 Puritans fled England for the Salem and Boston area within the first ten years of the colony's existence. This contingent of Reformists planned to establish a shining example of Puritanism for the world and change the Anglican Church through the example of their good works and holy lifestyle.

Winthrop laid out this philosophy of setting an example for others to follow in a famous sermon. While still aboard the ship *Arbella* on the way from England, Winthrop delivered the sermon that has since been hailed one of the most famous and influential speeches in American history. Winthrop told the settlers they would be casting off all the evil and past wrongdoings of Europe and starting a new chapter in human history. He also proclaimed that the New World held the potential for greatness, saying, "We must consider that we shall be a city upon a hill. The eyes of all people are upon us." Winthrop's **"City Upon a Hill"** sermon thus pronounced the colony a beacon of godliness for the world.

> *This vision of America as "city upon a hill" for the entire world to see and emulate has been enormously influential in U.S. politics. Many political leaders and presidents have quoted Winthrop's speech at key points in their careers, including John Adams, Abraham Lincoln, John F. Kennedy, Ronald Reagan, and Bill Clinton, among many others.*

Halfway Covenant

The foundation of the Puritans in the New World was shortly thereafter marked by an important change in the church: how membership was conferred. Up until 1677, membership in the Puritan church was restricted to those who could give verbal testimony of their "experience of Grace." Even those baptized had to pass this testimony before being accepted as full members of the church. In 1622, however, came the publication of the **Halfway Covenants**, adopted to allow certain people to retain a limited degree of church privileges, including baptizing their children, without becoming offical members. In 1677, this new practice was adopted and greatly increased the sizes of congregations in the New World.

THE MIDDLE COLONIES

In the seventeenth century, mostly all the colonists believed the church instilled moral behavior and respect for authority and created better citizens. The governments relied on the church and protected its existence in a reciprocal relationship. As a result, each of the early English colonies established its own state-sanctioned church. All the early colonial leaders in the southern Virginian colonies and the northern Puritan colonies believed everyone in the colony should practice the same religion to maintain unity. They also reasoned there would be no religious persecution if there was only one faith to follow. In other words, each colony would be harmonious without any religious or civic disagreements.

The middle colonies, comprising New York, New Jersey, Pennsylvania, and Delaware, however, did not establish state-sanctioned religions. In refusing to do so, they opened the doors to people from a **multitude of nationalities and faiths**.

The mid-Atlantic region, unlike New England or the southern colonies, drew many of its initial settlers from war-torn or intolerant countries in Europe. Those who fled to the middle colonies of the New World included:

- Dutch Mennonites
- French Huguenots
- German Baptists
- Portuguese Jews
- Dutch Reformed
- Lutherans
- Quakers

All of these groups had borne the brunt of religious exclusion in Europe and were not eager to repeat the experience in the New World. They joined Anglicans already living in the middle colonies and simply agreed to disagree. Add to the mix the indigenous people and the African slaves (with their own religious practices), and the middle colonies become a mosaic of nationalities and religious practices.

New York. Originally called New Netherlands, the English renamed the colony New York after defeating the former Dutch owners in 1664. New York City eventually became a port of entry and home for people of all nationalities. In a census taken in 1770, for example, there were eighteen different churches to support a population of 22,000 people: three Dutch Reformed, three Anglican, three Presbyterian, two Lutheran, one French Huguenot, one Congregational, one Methodist, one Baptist, one Quaker, one Moravian, and one Jewish temple.

New Jersey. The colony of New Jersey developed more slowly than New York, but its diversity was just as great. By 1701, the colony had forty-five different congregations. Most were unable to afford individual churches, so they frequently shared houses of worship.

Pennsylvania. William Penn formed the colony of Pennsylvania to provide a safe haven for the persecuted through the old and new worlds. Although a Quaker himself, Penn believed that force would never convert anyone. Many persecuted peoples such as the Amish, Dunkers, Schwenkfelders, and Mennonites found freedom in Pennsylvania.

Delaware. Scandinavian Lutherans and Dutch Reformed were the first to settle Delaware, and English Quakers and Welsh Baptists soon followed. Although Delaware was one of the most diverse colonies, the Anglican Church had a strong following there by the end of the eighteenth century.

Cast out of Puritan Salem and Plymouth for his radical beliefs, Roger Williams founded the colony of Providence, Rhode Island, in 1636. Providence was the first permanent settlement in Rhode Island and one of the first along with Pennsylvania to legislate freedom of religion.

PRE-COLUMBIAN–1700

Timeline

c. 800–900	Vikings colonize Iceland, Greenland, and Newfoundland.
c. 1300–1600	Europe experiences the Renaissance.
1325	The Aztecs found Tenochtitlán (later known as Mexico City).
1440	Johann Gutenberg invents the moveable-type press.
1492	Christopher Columbus lands on an island in the West Indies and names it San Salvador.
1493	Columbus returns to the Americas on his second voyage.
1521	Hernando Cortés conquers the Aztecs.
1532	Pizarro defeats the Incas.
1539–1542	Spanish explorer Hernando De Soto and 600 soldiers trek through what later becomes the southern United States.
1587	Sir Walter Raleigh founds Roanoke, off the coast of North Carolina.
1588	England defeats the Spanish Armada.
1607	The Virginia Company founds Jamestown.
1609–1610	Colonists in Jamestown suffer the "starving time," an extremely harsh winter.
1612	Colonist John Rolfe begins growing tobacco in Virginia.
1620	Pilgrims sail to America on the *Mayflower* and found the colony of Plymouth in Massachussetts. They also sign the Mayflower Compact, establishing their own government.
1629	The Massachusetts Bay Colony obtains a royal charter and elects John Winthrop as governor.
	Winthrop gives his "City Upon a Hill" sermon.
1636	Roger Williams founds Providence in Rhode Island, the first settlement to legislate freedom of religion.
1662	Halfway Covenant enacted.
1664	English settlers conquer the Dutch settlement of New Netherlands and rename it New York.
1676	Bacon's Rebellion occurs.

CHAPTER 2

Colonial Life:
1700–1763

|||||||||||||||||||||||||||||||||||||||||||||||||||||||||||

There were greater opportunities in America than the colonists could have ever hoped for in Europe. Yet as a distinctive "American" identity was being formed, the colonists still held on to many traditions and characteristics of the Old World. Social stratifications, for example, still existed, though to a lesser extent than in Europe. At the same time, there was more potential for social mobility as many Americans had opportunities to change jobs and their position in life.

Although the thirteen English colonies had much in common, factors such as geography and climate soon created distinct differences. These differences would become more and more pronounced as the colonies swelled in size, and, many years later, would eventually threaten to tear the country apart in ways the colonists in 1700 could never imagine.

Southern Colonies

The southern colonies included Maryland, Virginia, North Carolina, South Carolina, and Georgia. These colonies all boasted plenty of good, cleared land and a mild climate conducive to growing staple and exotic cash crops. Tobacco became the staple crop and the economic foundation of Virginia and North Carolina. South Carolinian soil, though unfit for tobacco, was perfect for growing rice and indigo, a dye used to dye textiles blue. The southern colonies also produced lumber, tar, pitch, turpentine, furs, and cattle.

In colonial times, blue paint was a status symbol, as the dye was expensive and hard to come by. Many well-to-do colonists desired to have their houses painted blue.

WORK IN THE SOUTHERN COLONIES

The production of cash crops required large amounts of land and a large work force. Colonists had plenty of land, but not enough labor. **Indentured servants** performed much of the labor during the early years of colonization. These servants, mostly paupers from England, Ireland, and Germany, got their name from the indenture, or contract, they signed, binding themselves to work for a period of four to seven years to pay for their transportation to the New World. Many of northern Europe's poor voluntarily indentured themselves in order to acquire their own land after their contract had been fulfilled. Indentured servants accounted for roughly half of all white settlers living in the colonies outside New England.

Until the latter half of the 1600s, white indentured servants were the dominant source of labor in the Americas, and it was not until the 1680s and 1690s that slave labor began to surpass the use of white indentured servants. Although **African slaves** cost more initially than indentured servants, they served for life and thus quickly became the labor force of choice on large plantations.

LIFE IN THE EARLY COLONIAL SOUTH

In the early 1600s, most southern colonists lived in utter poverty, and men outnumbered women three to one. Southern colonists suffered high mortality rates because of the many mosquito-born illnesses that plagued the land. As a result, the average southern man could expect to live only forty years, while southern women usually did not live past their late thirties. Moreover, one-quarter of all children born in the southern colonies died in infancy, and half died before they reached adulthood. Most southern colonists lived in remote areas on farms or plantations with their families, extended relatives, friends, and slaves. The Anglican religion dominated the region, although most southerners did not attend church regularly, if at all.

By the 1700s, life had settled down for the southern colonists, and more rigid social classes had formed. A gentry, or wealthy upper class, emerged and built large plantation homes in an attempt to imitate the lives of the English upper crust. Many of the plantation owners relied heavily on credit to maintain their leisurely lifestyles.

Northern Colonies

The northern colonies included New Hampshire, Massachusetts, Rhode Island, Connecticut, New York, and New Jersey. Whereas southerners lived in relative isolation from one another, northern colonial life revolved around townships. Villages formed around the church, and a central green area was usually created (often called "the commons") where important business and community activities took place. People built their houses around the town center and then radiated out in concentric circles. As a result, community involvement and activity became a central feature of life in the North.

States and Territories before the Louisiana Purchase

WORK IN THE NORTHERN COLONIES

Most of the land in the North was stony, sloped, and heavily forested, and people in the North couldn't sustain huge plantations as their southern neighbors could. Instead, families farmed small plots with the help of perhaps one or two servants or slaves. Additionally, the weather was too cold and harsh to support large-scale market crops. As a result, northern farmers mainly grew crops for their own consumption and sold any surplus at local markets. Crops like barley, oats, and wheat were mainly grown; the colonists also raised cattle, pigs, and sheep. Many northerners became fishermen. Skilled artisans migrated to the northern colonies, developing industries that ultimately created a foundation for future manufacturing.

Ample water sources made the construction of mills possible to process grain, textiles, and lumber. In time, a strong merchant class emerged, bolstered by the shipping industry that developed in northern ports. As shipping grew, ship building also increased. Eventually, traders and bankers sprang up to run the manufacturing and shipping economy, and northern port cities like Boston became central trading areas for the British in the Americas.

LIFE IN THE EARLY COLONIAL NORTH

The northern climate was free of mosquitoes, so northerners enjoyed longer lives, usually living well into their sixties, as compared with their southern counterparts. Husbands and wives formed teams of production, with children adding to the number of workers. The single life was almost impossible, given both the religious climate and the physical rigors of life in general at the time.

In contrast to the southern colonies, religion permeated the lives of northern colonists and exercised a pervasive influence over the people. Towns and communities were built around the church, and in most colonies, the church and the state remained one, controlling many aspects of life. Puritans settled in New England, both separatists and reformists, and these rigid religions dominated the region.

The Salem Witch Trials

Increasing influences from the outside world, introduced by new immigrants, among other sources, strained northern society, as the tragedy of the 1692 **Salem witch trials** made clear. Salem had been settled by Puritan reformists, and like most people in the North at this time, they still believed in the supernatural. By 1691, nearly 300 primarily middle-aged women in New England had been convicted of witchcraft. Of those, more than thirty were hanged.

The episode in Salem was far more intense than any other witch-hunt in North America. It began during the winter of 1691–1692, when several adolescent girls accused three local women of practicing witchcraft. Similar accusations followed, and within a year, nineteen women had been hanged, one man pressed to death under heavy stones, and more than 100 others jailed.

New Roles for Women

Historians originally thought that local feuds and property disputes between the town of Salem proper and Salem Village caused the unrest. More recently, many historians have begun to believe that the trials resulted from the clash between two different sets of social values. Many of the accused women had in some way defied the traditional roles assigned to females. Some worked outside the home, while others did not attend church. Whatever the reason, no other similar outbreaks of mass hysteria occurred in New England.

Colonial Cities

The thirteen British colonies developed separately and distinctly throughout the seventeenth century. In fact, the large cities of Boston, New York, Philadelphia, and Charleston had more contact with London than they did with one another. Traveling between cities on crude roads was both difficult and dangerous, which contributed to the isolation. However, taverns provided safe havens, overnight rest stops, and refueling stations. Colonists gathered in taverns to relax, drink, and gossip about politics and business. Many years later, these tendencies would prove vital to both the exchange of information about British injustices and to promoting the efforts of the revolution.

Despite the fact that 90 percent of all colonists lived in townships and small villages in the countryside, the minority of city dwellers controlled commerce, dominated politics, and defined the cultural norms. Society was rigidly stratified in cities, with merchants at the top of the order; craftsmen, retailers, and innkeepers below them; and sailors, unskilled workers, and small artisans at the bottom. Over time, class stratification became more pronounced, and wealth became concentrated among a select few. All of the colonists, however, hungered for English luxury goods. Imports increased through the years as the Americans purchased more and more goods such as mirrors, silver-plated items, spices, linens, wigs, clocks, tea sets, books, and other household items.

Slavery

Slavery had virtually disappeared in Western Europe by the 1500s, and only Spain and Portugal still practiced slavery. Unfortunately, they brought slavery with them to the New World, where it established a strong foothold.

THE FIRST SLAVE TRADERS

The Portuguese were the first Europeans to trade with Africa and the first to reap the enormous profits to be made in the slave trade. By the time Columbus sailed for the Americas, the Portuguese had taken about 25,000 Africans to work on sugar plantations. The Spanish recognized the labor potential of slaves and began importing them to the New World to mine for gold and silver.

THE MIDDLE PASSAGE

Other European countries also became involved in the slave trade. In addition to the Spanish and Portuguese, the English, French, and Dutch actively bought and sold Africans into slavery. These Europeans used extreme violence and brutal tactics to acquire their slaves.

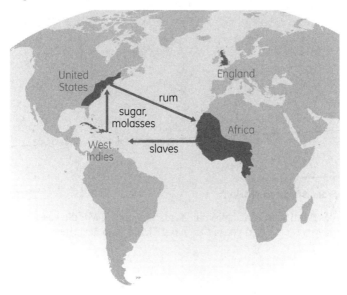

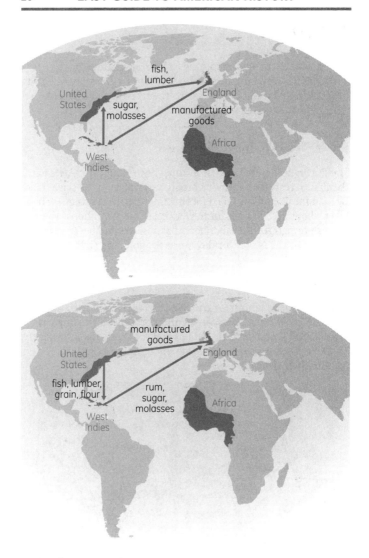

From Africa to Market

Slaves suffered unimaginable hardships on the Middle Passage. Slave traders often packed as many Africans aboard their ships as

*The trans-Atlantic voyage from Africa to the Americas was known as the Middle Passage and was part of a larger shipping pattern known as the **Triangular Trade**, linking Africa, the Americas, and Europe. Slaves traveled from Africa to the Americas; sugar and raw materials would be shipped to Europe; tobacco, timber, and foodstuffs would be shipped from North America to the West Indies.*

possible in order to maximize profits. In addition to depression, slaves suffered from smallpox, measles, gonorrhea, syphilis, yellow fever, scurvy, and dysentery. On average, about 12.5 percent of the captive slaves died during the voyage.

Once they had arrived in the New World, slaves had to endure the **"seasoning"** process, or the period ranging from a few months to a year in which slavers prepared them for sale and life as a slave. Historians estimate that 30 percent of imported Africans died of disease or maltreatment during "seasoning."

Growth of Slavery in the Americas

Between 1492 and 1808, slave traders brought roughly 10 million Africans to the New World, mostly to Spanish or Portuguese plantations in South America and the West Indies. Even though only 400,000 of these slaves traveled to North America, all thirteen colonies had legalized slavery by 1750. Many colonial farmers came to prefer slavery as rising wages in England made it more and more difficult to find indentured servants.

In time, slavery became more acceptable and developed into a key aspect of the economy and American society. States developed laws to keep African Americans under control: whipping, branding, dismembering, castrating, or killing a slave became legal under certain circumstances. Laws also stripped slaves of the freedom of movement, freedom of assembly, and the right to earn money or pursue an education. White Americans feared a slave rebellion above all else, especially considering that slaves outnumbered whites in some areas. Slave revolts in Charleston, South Carolina (1739) and New York City (1741) fueled these fears.

1700–1763

The Enlightenment

During the flurry of exploration and colonization in North America in the seventeenth and eighteenth centuries, Europe was experiencing a scientific revolution known as the **Enlightenment**. Scientists had abandoned the old Ptolemaic view of an earth-centered universe in favor of Copernicus's heliocentric (sun-centered) model. Isaac Newton had published his theory of gravitation, which laid the foundation for a scientific vision of the universe and argued that events occur in accordance with natural laws. More important, people were using reason and the study of mathematics to understand the working of the universe and the world around them.

Philosophers of the Enlightenment like John Locke believed that the American experience embodied the ideas of the Enlightenment. The old barriers of birth and wealth did not apply as much in the New World as they did in Europe, and people of all classes could succeed if they worked hard.

JOHN LOCKE'S CONTRACT THEORY OF GOVERNMENT

John Locke applied the new scientific understandings of the world first presented in the Enlightenment to the study of society and government. Locke came up with an idea he called the **Theory of Contract under Natural Law**, in which he argued that kings and queens did not hold their positions because of God's divine will but because of an accident of birth. In other words, kings had simply gotten lucky. Locke further explained that all humans had certain natural rights such as the rights to life, liberty, and property, and that no government could deny its constituents these rights.

Locke's theory on government had an enormous influence on American political thought. Locke argued that the people "contracted" with the government to protect their interests. If the government failed to do so, then the government had broken the contract and should be disbanded. Colonists quickly picked up on this idea, eventually using it to justify the American Revolution against England. In fact, Thomas Jefferson used very similar language in the Declaration of Independence when he wrote that everyone had the right to "life, liberty, and the pursuit of happiness."

BENJAMIN FRANKLIN

Benjamin Franklin, one of the "founding fathers" of the country, personified the ideas of the Enlightenment. Franklin owned his own print shop, published his own newspaper, and had published his *Poor Richard's Almanac* all by the time he had turned twenty-six. Franklin's business was so successful that he retired when he was only forty-two, and he devoted the rest of his life to science and public service. Among other things, Franklin:

- Founded a library and invented a new kind of stove
- Started an academy that eventually became the University of Pennsylvania
- Formed a debating club that eventually became the American Philosophical Society
- Wrote a treatise entitled *Experiments and Observations on Electricity*, based on his own electrical experiments
- Studied medicine, meteorology, geology, astronomy, and physics
- Served his country as the colonial agent in London and then as the American ambassador to France during the Revolutionary War

Franklin was a living example of Locke's ideas of the possibilities that society and government had to offer.

1700–1763

The Great Awakening

With so many new scientific and philosophical ideas springing out of the Enlightenment, many American colonists turned away from religion. In the 1730s, however, a renewed spirit of evangelism swept through the colonies in the **Great Awakening**. In an attempt to reassert the doctrines of Puritanism, the leading preachers and theologians of the Great Awakening appealed very strongly to colonists' emotions.

GEORGE WHITEFIELD

The Great Awakening began in different cities in the colonies, but all the revivals shared a high level of emotionalism. Preachers such as **George Whitefield** tried to replace the cold and unfeeling doctrines of Puritanism with a religion more accessible to the average person. The twenty-seven-year-old Wesleyan minister noted upon arriving in the colonies from England that American congregations lacked passion because "dead men preach to them."

Planning to reignite the fires of religion in the New World, Whitefield settled in Philadelphia in 1739 and began attracting crowds of more than 6,000 people. Before long, he was holding revivals from as far south as Georgia all the way up to New England. Young and charismatic, Whitefield staged performances for his audiences by acting out the miseries of hell and the joys of salvation. People flocked from miles around to hear him speak, and he urged them to experience a "new birth," or a sudden, emotional moment of conversion and forgiveness of sin. Audiences swooned with anticipation of God's grace, some people writhing, some laughing out loud, and some crying out for help.

JONATHAN EDWARDS

Jonathan Edwards was another noteworthy preacher and theologian during the Great Awakening. He believed that his parishioners, especially the young, lived too freely, spending their time drinking and carousing while the older churchgoers had become preoccupied with making and spending money. Edwards wanted to touch the hearts of those in his congregation and "fright persons away from hell." He would therefore fill his sermons with vivid descriptions of the torments of hell and the pleasures of heaven. By 1735, he reported that "the town seemed to be full of the presence of God; it never was so full of love, nor of joy."

Unlike Whitefield, Edwards never resorted to theatrics, and instead entranced audiences with the seriousness of his message, as in his most famous sermon **"Sinners in the Hands of an Angry God,"** which marked the pinnacle of the Great Awakening movement and is recognized as one of the most famous sermons in American history.

IMPACT OF THE GREAT AWAKENING

The Great Awakening had an enormous impact in the American colonies, especially along the western frontier and in the South. Common folk responded with great enthusiasm, and the Baptists and the Methodists, two popular Protestant denominations, grew enormously as a result.

Ironically, even though revivalists like Whitefield and Edwards had hoped they would encourage a more pious lifestyle, the colonists concluded that salvation was available to all, not merely to a few chosen elect as the Puritans had always claimed. Consequently, the Great Awakening helped democratize religion in the colonies and ultimately took power away from churches and ministers. Moreover, the Great Awakening renewed interest in intellectualism and prompted the founding of new universities and the distribution of books.

Some historians argue that the American Revolution could not have happened without the Great Awakening. They believe that the Awakening encouraged spiritual diversity and emphasized the personal dimensions of salvation, undermining the dogmatic religious institutions of the day. In turn, this spiritual diversity paved the way for the eventual separation of church and state, which became a crucial component of the American conception of freedom.

British Rule

By the 1750s, the American colonists, feeling more unified by such intellectual currents as the Enlightenment and the Great Awakening, had developed a unique culture of their own. Although the individual colonies developed distinctive religious, social, and demographic characteristics, they all shared a basic sense of unity that grew stronger through the coming years of economic and political upheaval.

The colonists had effectively governed themselves throughout most of the seventeenth and eighteenth centuries. For the most part, the British government had left the colonists to fend for themselves during this **Age of Salutary Neglect**, neither imposing new taxes nor enforcing those on the books. Therefore, the colonists resented Britain's attempts to exert more influence over the colonies in the mid-1700s.

BRITISH TRADE WITH THE COLONIES

Although the British had granted the colonies a fair amount of autonomy, they had always attempted to control trade to and from North America. The British imposed laws and taxes to ensure that all trade with the colonies would benefit Britain, and to ensure that the colonists did not take trade matters into their own hands.

The Mercantile System

Under the **Mercantile System**, power and wealth went hand in hand. In other words, the leaders of mercantilist countries (countries with large import and export operations) believed that power derived from a full national treasury. To acquire and keep gold and silver, the mercantilist powers had to limit foreign imports and preserve a favorable balance of trade. To do this, England, France, Spain, Portugal, and the Netherlands:

- Encouraged their domestic manufacturers to produce as many goods as possible

- Developed and protected their own shipping industry

- Acquired colonies to provide raw materials

- Sold finished manufactured goods to the colonists

Under mercantilism, great powers needed to acquire colonies to produce raw materials such as grain, sugar, rice, timber, and tobacco. Each colony also provided the mother country with an exclusive market for its manufactured goods. To safeguard its monopoly in North America, Britain began regulating colonial trade in the 1660s and declared that Americans could only ship their products directly to England. Royal officials could then levy taxes on those goods before shippers sent them elsewhere.

Navigation Acts

The **Navigation Act of 1660** marked England's first real attempt to regulate colonial trade by stipulating that all goods exported from the colonies had to be carried on English ships. The act also declared that colonists could only trade certain raw materials such as sugar, cotton, tobacco, wood, pitch, and tar with England or other British colonies. The **Second Navigation Act of 1663** required that colonial ships unload their cargo upon arriving in England so that each item could be taxed.

Restraining Acts

The **Restraining Acts of 1699** followed the Navigation Acts and protected manufacturers in England by banning factories in the colonies. Although colonial industry hadn't even begun to develop by this point, Britain didn't want colonial manufacturers to compete with domestic manufacturers in England. The Restraining Act also banned the export of woolen products in order to protect the English wool industry and later forbade the export of beaver hats and processed iron.

The Colonists' Response

Most colonists willingly complied with the Navigation and Restraining Acts, simply happy they had achieved a relatively high standard of living in such a short amount of time. More important, the restrictions on manufacturing affected few Americans because manufacturing hadn't ever taken root.

Moreover, the mercantile system showered the colonists with benefits. Even though the British levied taxes on American raw materials, they also kept prices on those materials high by eliminating foreign competition. Britain even paid subsidies to American shipbuilders and tobacco and rice farmers. In short, both sides benefited handsomely from the arrangement.

The Molasses Act

Despite economic benefits, some colonists had begun to complain about their subservient position within the mercantile system by the 1730s. The Navigation and Restraining Acts hit those who conducted trade in the West Indies hardest. In 1733, Britain passed the **Molasses Act** to curtail colonial trade with the West Indies by imposing a huge tax on sugar and molasses imported into the colonies. The act would have seriously disrupted colonial trade, but the royal officials in North America never strictly enforced it. This wavering policy led many Americans to question Britain's intentions and wisdom regarding the regulation of colonial trade.

COLONIAL GOVERNMENTS

King George III owned all the colonies, but Americans enjoyed an unprecedented degree of autonomy. All but one of the colonies had erected their own government with a bicameral legislature comprising an upper and lower house. The king appointed a governor and the members of the upper house in eight of the thirteen colonies. Wealthy land-owning colonists chose the members of the lower house. The colonies of Pennsylvania, Delaware, and Maryland were owned by individuals. These individuals, such as William Penn in Pennsylvania, held the royal charter and appointed legislators. In the corporate colonies of Rhode Island and Connecticut, owned by joint stock companies, wealthy land-owning white men elected all government officials.

Voting and Representation

Colonial governments modeled themselves after the English system with two exceptions:

- A greater percentage of the population could vote in the colonies than in England.

- The colonists rejected the British concept of **"virtual representation."** In England, elected members of Parliament claimed to represent all their constituents because they supposedly represented the interests of all royal subjects no matter where they lived. The colonists disagreed; they felt that delegates should represent only those who had elected them.

All in all, the representative colonial legislatures enjoyed a great deal of freedom, and the king permitted the autonomy as long as colonial laws didn't interfere with Parliament's.

The French and Indian War

For most of the colonial period, Britain and France remained at peace with each other, their colonial empires developing in relative isolation. Beginning in the 1680s, however, the European powers waged several wars for control of North America:

- The War of the Palatinate (King William's War) from 1689–1697 in New England and Canada

- The War of the Spanish Succession (Queen Anne's War) from 1702–1713 throughout the western frontier of the colonies from St. Augustine in Florida to New England

- The War of the Austrian Succession (King George's War) from 1744–1748 in Canada

- The Seven Years' War (the French and Indian War, which actually lasted nine years in the colonies) from 1754–1763 throughout New England and Canada

The British and the American colonists fought side by side against the French in all four wars, gaining much western land and parts of Canada as a result.

> The colonists referred to the Seven Years' War as the French and Indian War because they fought the French and Indians. The British called the war the Seven Years' War, because they didn't count the first two years that the war was fought only in the colonies.

THE FRENCH IN AMERICA

The French established their presence in the New World in the 1670s. Their mercantilist empire spanned from India to Africa to the Americas. The French king expected his North American settlers to export furs and grains back to France and then purchase French manufactured goods. By 1682, the French had sailed from Canada down the Mississippi, claiming land on both sides of the river, and founding the city of New Orleans.

By 1743, the French had reached the Rocky Mountains and claimed the entire interior of North America for themselves. To consolidate their claim, they built a string of forts that ran from Quebec to Detroit and down to New Orleans. The British, however, refused to recognize French territorial claims or the legality of the forts.

Indian Alliances

Both the British and the French knew that they would need the help of the local Native Americans with the skirmishes in the Americas. The British had established effective trading practices with the native tribes, but the French promised them friendship and equality and demonstrated a greater sensitivity to the Native Americans' cultures. French fur trappers, for example, frequently married Indian women and adopted native customs, while the Jesuit priests refrained from using force when trying to convert them to Catholicism.

THE WAR BEGINS

The **French and Indian War** began in 1754 when the governor of Virginia sent a young lieutenant colonel in the Virginia militia named **George Washington** to warn the French that the disputed Ohio Valley territory had been settled at France's peril. Washington carried the message to a French fort but was rebuffed. Soon afterward, he organized a force of volunteers, defeated a small French garrison, and built a modest outpost he called Fort Necessity. The French returned in greater numbers and attacked the fort, eventually forcing Washington to surrender and withdraw to Virginia. Washington's surrender triggered a series of Indian raids along the frontier, in which the Native Americans sought revenge for 150 years of bad treatment by the British.

The Fighting

Fighting raged for two years between the British and the French in the colonies before the war erupted in Europe. In 1756, the colonial war finally spilled over into Europe, when Austria and Russia and eventually Spain formed an alliance with France. Britain allied with Prussia in return. King George II named William Pitt the head of the war ministry, and Pitt tried to keep the focus of the war in North America. He sent large numbers of British troops to the colonies but also encouraged the colonists to enlist, demanding that they defend themselves against the French. Pitt's tactics worked, and the British eventually gained the upper hand. France simply couldn't match Britain's powerful navy or the number of troops stationed in North America.

The French and Indian War climaxed in 1759 when the British defeated the French at Quebec and effectively eliminated France's influence in North America. News of the battle reached London along with news of a similar victory in India, in which British forces had significantly reduced the number of French outposts. Outgunned and outnumbered, France formally surrendered in the Americas in September 1760. It took three more years before Britain could declare victory in Europe.

THE WAR ENDS

The **Treaty of Paris**, or Peace of Paris, ended the French and Indian War and gave Britain undisputed control over all of Canada and almost all of present-day United States, from the Atlantic to the Rockies. Britain decided to keep everything east of the Mississippi and gave Spain everything west of the Mississippi, including the key port city of New Orleans in exchange for Florida. Britain also gained control of several former French colonies in the Caribbean. In short, Britain reigned supreme over North America east of the Mississippi after the conclusion of the war.

IMPACT ON THE COLONIES

The French and Indian War had a tremendous impact on the colonists and on England. Britain's debt skyrocketed because it had had to borrow so much to fund the war, and Parliament decided to raise colonial taxes to pay off that debt. At the same time, Pitt's insistence that the colonists defend themselves added to the colonists' sense of independence from England. Success on the battlefield contributed to the colonists' belief that their reliance on England was coming to an end. Ultimately, the war boosted the new Americans' sense of unity and distinctiveness from Britain.

*At the beginning of the French and Indian War, Benjamin Franklin proposed a plan to link all thirteen colonies in a loose union. Although the colonists rejected this **Albany Plan**, it nevertheless represented one of the first steps toward a unified colonial America.*

1700-1763

Timeline

1692	Several people are tried and convicted of witchcraft in Salem, Massachusetts.
1699	Britain passes the Restraining Act to restrict manufacturing in the North American colonies.
1730–1740	The Great Awakening spreads a renewed spirit of evangelism throughout the American colonies.
1733	Britain passes the Molasses Act of 1733 to tax sugar and molasses imported into British colonies.
1739	British minister George Whitefield comes to North America from England to become a leading figure in the Great Awakening.
1741	Jonathan Edwards, a leading theologian, preaches his famous sermon, "Sinners in the Hands of an Angry God."
1750	Slavery is legalized in all thirteen colonies.
1755	French, English, Americans, and Native Americans begin fighting for control of North America in the French and Indian War.
1763	The Treaty of Paris ends the French and Indian War.

CHAPTER 3

Seeking Independence: 1763–1783

||||||||||||||||||||||||||||||||||||||||||||||||||||||

Prior to the French and Indian War, Britain had essentially left its American colonies to run themselves, a time often referred to as the age of "salutary neglect." Given relative freedom to do as they pleased, the North American settlers established unique forms of government to match their rugged sense of adventure and developing identity as Americans. But after the French and Indian War, Britain's relations with the colonies changed dramatically. Hoping to refill its empty treasury, Parliament levied more taxes on the Americans and tightened regulations governing trade.

Americans were outraged and offended at what they considered encroachments on their liberties. Over time, this indignation grew into a strong desire for rebellion. In just twelve years, between the end of the French and Indian War and the outbreak of the Revolutionary War, Americans transformed from loyal colonists into revolutionary patriots.

Emergence of American Nationalism

The American colonists were jubilant at the end of the French and Indian War in 1763, celebrating both their defeat of the French and the resulting access to the unexplored western frontier. With a new sense of confidence as they looked out across the vast and fertile new territory, Americans saw their future. But obstacles remained in the colonists' path as they sought to claim the land, and the freedom, that they believed was rightfully theirs.

PONTIAC'S REBELLION

Although Britain and the colonists had defeated the French and Native American forces in 1763, they continued to fight Native Americans along the western frontier for several more years. Many of the tribes in the Ohio Valley banded together under the leadership of Ottawa Chief **Pontiac**, a former ally of the French who resented American colonial encroachments on Indian lands.

By October, Pontiac's men had killed more than 2,000 British soldiers and American settlers and had destroyed all but three British outposts in the region. Pontiac eventually signed a peace treaty in 1766, but the British knew that more conflict would arise as long as colonial farmers kept pushing westward in search of new land.

> *Having lost the French and Indian War, Native American tribes hated the idea of having to deal with the aggressive and often arrogant, untrustworthy British. In contrast, the French had been respectful, did not try to remove them from their land, and did not pose a threat to the Native American way of life. Native Americans therefore called Pontiac's Uprising against the British the "War of National Liberation."*

The Proclamation of 1763

To prevent further bloodshed between whites and Indians, Britain issued the **Proclamation of 1763**, which prohibited colonists from settling west of the Appalachian Mountains. Only licensed trappers and traders would be allowed to venture farther, while those colonists who'd already settled beyond the mountains would have to relocate.

Although Britain had hoped the proclamation would help and protect Americans, most colonists were outraged at the policy, especially after they had shed so much blood during the war to win the land in the first place. In addition, many Americans believed that despite the proclamation, they had the right to expand westward. Feeling bitterly betrayed, many hardy colonists ignored the proclamation and crossed into the Ohio Valley anyway.

BRITISH WAR DEBT

Britain's victory in the French and Indian War had cost a fortune, nearly bankrupting the government. To refill the treasury and pay off debts owed to creditors, Prime Minister **George Grenville** convinced Parliamentarians to raise taxes both at home and in the colonies. Even though Britons paid significantly higher taxes than the Americans, colonists balked at the thought of higher taxes. They also resented **King George III**'s decision to permanently station 10,000 British regulars in North America to control his newly acquired territories.

The Sugar Act The first tax hike came in 1764 when Parliament passed the Sugar Act to tax molasses and other imports like textiles, wines, coffee, indigo and sugar. Colonists, of course, hated the Sugar Act because it was the first tax Parliament had ever levied on them solely to raise revenue.

The Currency Act Parliament also passed the Currency Act in 1764, which prohibited the colonists from printing their own cheap paper money. The Currency Act, combined with new taxes and stricter enforcement, shocked the American economy.

The Stamp Act Crisis of 1765 Although the Sugar and Currency Acts did increase revenue, Britain needed much more money in order to pay off war debts and keep troops posted in the colonies. To make up the difference, Grenville next proposed the Stamp Act to tax printed matter and legal documents in the colonies like newspapers, pamphlets, almanacs, bonds, licenses, deeds, diplomas, and even playing cards. Americans despised the Stamp Act more than the Sugar Act or the Currency Act because it taxed items they deemed necessities. More important, they also hated the tax because it challenged colonial assemblies' exclusive power to levy internal taxes.

Quartering Act Parliament passed the **Quartering Act** in 1765, forcing colonists to supply, feed, and house the unwanted British soldiers, even in their own homes if necessary. Colonists resented this act as a direct affront to their civil rights and personal liberties.

THE ISSUE OF REPRESENTATION

Many Americans protested under the cry of **"No taxation without representation!"** Prime Minister Grenville shot back that all members of Parliament represented the interests of all British subjects in the empire no matter where they lived. Colonial critics ridiculed this doctrine of **"virtual representation,"** believing that a small body of men could never satisfactorily represent people they knew nothing about.

In reality, colonists didn't want representation in Parliament, because a few minor representatives in London would've been too politically weak to accomplish anything for the colonies. Rather, the slogan merely symbolized and explained the colonists' distaste for paying taxes they themselves hadn't legislated. Most believed that only locally elected legislatures had the right to levy taxes, not a government thousands of miles and an ocean away.

The Sons of Liberty

A group of educated colonists known as the **Sons of Liberty** began to hold meetings in public places under trees they dubbed "Liberty Trees" to discuss the Stamp Act and possible courses of action. They eventually organized a massive **Stamp Act Protest** in Boston in August 1765 and burned Boston's stamp agent in effigy as it swung from the city's Liberty Tree. Riotous mobs later destroyed the stamp office and ransacked the homes of the local customs officer and the royal governor, Thomas Hutchinson. Colonists also terrorized royal tax collectors to the point that many of the collectors fled the colonies to return to England.

BUILDING COLONIAL UNITY

Opposition to the Stamp Act united colonists, who initiated a widespread **boycott** of British goods in the hopes that desperate British manufacturers would pressure Parliament to repeal the tax. Mutual opposition to the Stamp Act also made colonists realize that they had more in common with each other than they did with Britons. To foster colonial unity, the Massachusetts House of Representatives issued a letter inviting the different colonial assemblies to a meeting. Nine of the colonies responded and sent delegates to New York to attend the **Stamp Act Congress** in October of 1765.

The twenty-seven men who gathered at the congress registered their complaints in the **Declaration of the Rights and Grievances of the Colonies**, petitioning King George III and Parliament to repeal the Stamp Act. Under pressure from British manufacturers and unwilling to enforce the collection of an incredibly unpopular tax, Parliament ultimately consented and repealed the Stamp Act. At the same time, however, it quietly passed the **Declaratory Act**, asserting Parliament's right to tax the colonies in "all cases whatsoever." The Declaratory Act allowed Parliament to save face and provided a temporary solution to the brewing crisis.

Resistance Becomes Rebellion

In 1767, Parliament passed the **Townshend Acts**, which levied taxes on virtually all imports entering the colonies from Great Britain. Although the taxes did increase revenue, they sparked another round of fiery protests from the colonists.

SAMUEL ADAMS FUELS THE REVOLUTION

The ardent Bostonian revolutionary and Son of Liberty **Samuel Adams** launched a citywide propaganda campaign to protest the Townshend taxes. He distributed pamphlets, letters, and essays on the injustices of British rule, all of which quickly spread throughout the colonies. Within just a few years, colonists in most every major city and town from the South to New England had formed their own campaigns.

THE BOSTON MASSACRE

Bostonians hated royal encroachments on colonial liberties, and took their resentment out on the British soldiers garrisoned in the city. Crowds taunted and jeered at the troops for months until the tense situation finally exploded. On March 5, 1770, several British soldiers fired into a crowd of rock-throwing colonists, killing five Bostonians. News of the **Boston Massacre** spread rapidly through the colonies. Hoping to avoid further bloodshed, Parliament repealed all the Townshend duties except for the tax on tea, mostly as a symbol of royal authority.

TAXING TEA

The new Prime Minister, Frederick Lord North, eventually, even drastically, reduced this last tax on tea in order to help the failing East India Company unload its surplus of tea. North also believed that the tax reduction would appease the Americans and restore good relations between Britain and the colonies. Yet colonists resented the reduced tax because they believed it was a British trick to bribe the colonies, grant a monopoly to the East India Company, and ultimately control all colonial trade. Many worried that if Britain successfully regulated the tea trade, they might also try to control other commodities in the future.

> Colonists hated the tax on tea because most considered it an essential for daily, civilized life. While other taxes imposed by Parliament, like those on sugar and stamps, only affected a few segments of society, the tax on tea affected everyone.

THE BOSTON TEA PARTY

Rebels like Sam Adams churned out more propaganda in response to the reduced tax and urged colonists to boycott tea. Port officials throughout the colonies refused to allow East India Company tea ships to unload their cargoes, forcing them to sail back to England. In Boston, however, Governor Hutchinson wouldn't allow the tea ships to return, either, forcing them to remain in port.

The Bostonian Sons of Liberty ended the stalemate on the night of December 16, 1773, when, disguised as Mohawk Indians, they boarded the tea ships and threw several hundred chests of tea into the harbor. Several hundred spectators watched the **Boston Tea Party** unfold and wondered how Britain would respond to such blatant defiance of royal authority.

THE INTOLERABLE COERCIVE ACTS

Outraged, King George III and Parliament immediately passed the **Coercive Acts** to punish Bostonians and exact payment for the thousands of pounds of lost tea. These acts included:

- **The Boston Port Act**, which closed Boston Harbor until the city had repaid the East India Company for the tea. The act paralyzed Boston's maritime economy.

- A new **Quartering Act** requiring Bostonians to house and feed several thousand British soldiers sent to enforce the Coercive Acts.

- **The Massachusetts Government Act**, which cancelled city elections and indefinitely closed town meetings.

Britain hoped their harsh punishment would make an example of Boston and convince Americans in the other colonies to obey the Crown in the future. Instead, the Coercive Acts fostered a greater sense of unity among the thirteen colonies because many thought the punishment too great for the crime. Colonists everywhere rallied to Boston's aid, delivering food and winter supplies from as far away as Georgia.

1763-1783

*Colonists called the Coercive Acts the **"Intolerable Acts"** because they found the new restrictions so unbearable. While taxes on sugar, stamps, and tea were one thing, the closing of a port and invasion of colonial homes was something quite different. The acts directly led the colonists from thoughts of rebellion to the actual planning of an insurrection.*

British Acts and Colonial Response

British Act	Colonial Response
Writs of Assistance, 1760	Challenged laws in Massachusetts Supreme Court, lost case
Sugar Act, 1764	Weak protest by colonial legislatures
Stamp Act, 1765	Virginia Resolves, mobs, Sons of Liberty, Stamp Act Congress
Townshend Duties, 1767	*Letters from a Pennsylvania Farmer*, boycott, Boston Massacre
Tea Act, 1773	Boston Tea Party
Intolerable Acts, 1773	First Continental Congress

THE FIRST CONTINENTAL CONGRESS

Most colonial leaders agreed that the Coercive Acts required a unified response from all of the colonies. Twelve colonies (Georgia abstaining) sent a total of fifty-five delegates to the **First Continental Congress** in Philadelphia in 1774 to draft an official protest. A few of the delegates hoped the Congress would become a colonial parliament of sorts, and proposed measures that would lead to colonial government, but the majority rejected their proposals. Most delegates wanted Congress only to resolve the brewing crisis in Boston, not establish a colonial government or start a rebellion.

Declaration of American Rights

Delegates at the First Continental Congress drafted the **Declaration of American Rights** in 1774, which declared Parliament had no authority over internal colonial affairs. They also created the **Continental Association** to coordinate a stricter boycott on all British goods throughout the colonies. Association committees eventually became the backbone of the Revolution.

An infuriated King George III heard of the colonial meeting and Declaration of American Rights and remarked, "New England colonies are in a state of rebellion," and that "blows must decide whether they are to be subject to this country or independent."

The Revolution Begins

By 1775, resentment toward Britain had calcified into the desire for rebellion. Many cities and towns organized volunteer militias that drilled openly in public common areas while King George III grew increasingly intolerant of American resistance to royal authority.

LEXINGTON AND CONCORD

On April 15, 1775, a British commander dispatched troops to arrest Samuel Adams and John Hancock and seize the arsenal of weapons cached in Concord, Massachusetts. Militiamen from nearby Lexington intercepted them and opened fire. Eight Americans died as the British sliced through the line and moved on to Concord. The **redcoats** arrived in Concord, however, only to find the Concord militia waiting for them. Militiamen fired their muskets from the protection of the forest trees and stone walls into the organized columns of bright red uniforms, killing seventy British soldiers and forcing the British to retreat back to Boston.

> *Colonial militiamen were often referred to as "minutemen" for their supposed ability to dress and prepare for battle in under sixty seconds. Bostonian silversmith and Son of Liberty **Paul Revere** made his famous "Midnight Ride" on April 14, 1775, from Boston to Lexington and Concord to warn the minutemen of the redcoats' approach.*

THE SECOND CONTINENTAL CONGRESS

Almost immediately after the **Battle of Lexington and Concord**, thousands of militiamen surrounded Boston to prevent the British troops from leaving. Meanwhile, delegates from all thirteen colonies gathered once again in Philadelphia at the **Second Continental Congress** to discuss the battle and its consequences. Because most delegates still desired reconciliation with King George III and Parliament, they agreed to sign a petition professing their love for King George III in a document called the **Olive Branch Petition**. They beseeched the king to recall the troops in Boston to restore peace between the colonies and Britain. King George III ultimately rejected the petition. After the British defeat at the Battle of Bunker Hill, King George III officially declared the colonies in a state of rebellion. Any hope of reconciliation and a return to the pre-1763 status quo had vanished.

Washington Takes Command

Even though delegates at the Second Continental Congress had signed the Olive Branch Petition, they also agreed to bolster colonial defenses in case of war. They set aside funds to organize an army and a small navy and also selected **George Washington** to command the newly christened **Continental Army** surrounding Boston.

> While all colonists now believed that their rights had been infringed upon and were ready for action, many feared that not all colonies would support armed revolution, especially those in the South. The delegates hoped that Washington's stature as a highly respected Virginian plantation owner would further unite the northern and southern colonies.

INDEPENDENCE

Their Olive Branch petition rejected, delegates at the Second Continental Congress finally elected to declare independence from Britain on July 2, 1776. They then selected **Thomas Jefferson** to draft the congress's official **Declaration of Independence**.

Life, Liberty, and the Pursuit of Happiness

Jefferson kept the Declaration relatively short because he wanted it to be direct, clear, and forceful. He wrote:

> We hold these truths to be self-evident, that all men are created equal, that they are endowed by their Creator with certain unalienable rights, that among these are Life, Liberty, and the pursuit of Happiness.

Drawing from the writings of John Locke, Jefferson argued that governments exist in order to protect the rights of the people, and that the people have a right and even a duty to overthrow governments that fail their mandate.

A Long Train of Abuses

Jefferson further justified the Revolution by detailing King George III's "abuses and usurpations" against the American colonies, including:

* Shutting down representative colonial legislatures

* Refusing to allow the colonies to govern themselves

* Assuming judicial powers and manipulating the court system

* Conspiring with Native Americans against the colonists

* Restricting trade

* Imposing unjust taxes

* Coercing American sailors to work on British ships

* Taking military actions against Americans

* Refusing to allow colonists to redress grievances

Jefferson argued that the colonists should establish a new government as the United States of America in order to protect their rights.

> John Locke's Second Treatise of Civil Government *had an enormous impact on the thought of American revolutionaries. The foundation of Locke's theories lay in the belief that all people had natural and irrevocable rights to life, liberty, and property, and that governments existed solely to protect those rights. Consequently, if the government violated its contract with the people, then the people had the right to rebel and establish a better government.*

Americans in Revolt

All thirteen colonies immediately prepared for war after the Battle of Lexington and Concord. New militias formed throughout America, usually for the sole purpose of defending local communities from British aggression. Other units, however, rushed to join their comrades, who were cornered by British troops in Boston. Under the strict command of George Washington, Nathaniel Greene, and the German Baron von Steuben, this ragtag collection of undisciplined militiamen eventually became the well-trained **Continental Army**.

> Historians estimate that approximately 350,000 soldiers, or two-thirds of eligible American men in the colonies, served in the Continental Army, local militias, or a combination of both during the Revolutionary War.

COMMON SENSE

The radical English author and philosopher **Thomas Paine** helped turn American public opinion against Great Britain and solidify the emerging colonial unity. In January 1776, he published *Common Sense*, a pamphlet that denounced King George III as a tyrannical "brute." He called on Americans to unite and overthrow British rule so that they could usher in an era of freedom for humanity. Within only a few months of its first printing, Americans had purchased more than 100,000 copies of the pamphlet.

WOMEN IN THE WAR

Most American women supported the war effort as well. Some particularly daring women chose to serve as nurses, attendants, cooks, spies, and even as combatants on the battlefields. The majority of women, however, fought the war at home by managing the family farms and businesses. Making yarn and homespun necessities like socks and underwear to send to militiamen and supporting the boycott on British goods were significant contributions by female Americans.

Sadly, the Founding Fathers never recognized women's tremendous wartime efforts. Despite Abigail Adams's private plea to her husband, John Adams, to "remember the ladies" when making new laws, women didn't receive the right to vote or to even own property at war's end.

THE LOYALISTS

Although most Americans supported the decision to break away from Great Britain and declare independence, about one-fifth of the colonists chose to remain loyal to the Crown. Some, including many lawyers, Anglican clergymen, and royal officials felt that challenging British rule was unconscionable, while others simply wished to maintain the status quo. Although **Loyalists** lived throughout America, the majority lived in the lower southern colonies. Over 100,000 Loyalists fled to Canada, England, and the West Indies before and during the war. Loyalists who stayed in the colonies faced persecution and even death.

NATIVE AMERICANS

Most Native Americans were particularly afraid of future American expansion onto their lands and therefore sided with Great Britain in the war. The influential Mohawk chief **Joseph Brant**, for example, successfully convinced the Iroquois, Creek, Cherokees, and Choctaw, among others, to raid American settlements and outposts in the West.

AFRICAN AMERICANS

Blacks generally supported the British because an American victory would only keep them enslaved. Although approximately 5,000 blacks did serve in militias for the United States, most fled to British encampments and Loyalist areas to escape bondage. As a result, both northern and southern colonies lost tens of thousands of slaves during the war. Those blacks who didn't have the opportunity to escape remained enslaved despite Jefferson's belief that "all men were created equal."

THE UNDECIDED

Finally, some men and women neither supported nor opposed the revolution and opted instead to wait and see what would happen. Because civilian casualties remained low throughout the war, sitting on the fence proved to be a good alternative to fighting for those who didn't much care which side won or lost. Patriotic colonies often tried to reduce the number of free riders by passing laws that essentially ordered, "you're either with us or against us," and many townships prosecuted able-bodied men who failed to join militias.

Washington Wins the War

The odds stood in favor of the British at the beginning of the war since they had the world's most powerful navy, a huge standing army in North America, and a large force of German Hessian mercenaries ready to fight. They soon discovered, however, that fighting in North America was exceedingly difficult. Though George Washington had to rely on a small, inconsistent volunteer force, he could also rely on local militias that used hit-and-run guerilla tactics to confuse the orderly columns of British regulars.

Washington wisely understood that he only needed to outlast the British—not defeat them in every engagement. He knew that Britain would eventually grow tired of fighting an unpopular war so far away from home. Washington focused primarily on outrunning the British, forcing his adversary to chase his Continental Army from colony to colony. This tactic worked brilliantly, considering the Americans didn't have any key strategic areas they needed to defend.

BATTLE OF SARATOGA

The first military success for the colonists came at **Saratoga** in upstate New York in October 1777, when more than 5,700 British troops surrendered to American forces. This victory turned the war around for the Americans because it demonstrated to France that Britain might actually lose the war. By the following year, the two sides had formed the **Franco-American alliance** and agreed to fight the British together until the United States achieved independence.

FRENCH INTERVENTION

Many historians believe that the colonists could not have won the war without French assistance. France, for example, sent fresh troops and supplies to North America to take pressure off the outnumbered Continental Army. More important, however, France's participation expanded the scope of the war. Before long, Britain found itself pitted against the Spanish and the Dutch as well as the French and the Americans and fighting battles in North America, Europe, the Mediterranean, Africa, India, and the West Indies.

BATTLE OF YORKTOWN

Washington, meanwhile, continued to engage the British in North America, first in a series of western campaigns and then in Georgia and South Carolina. Eventually, he moved back northward to join French forces surrounding Britain's General Cornwallis at **Yorktown**, Virginia. Cornered and greatly outnumbered, Cornwallis surrendered to Washington on October 19, 1781, and thus ended the Revolutionary War.

THE TREATY OF PARIS

Once the fighting had stopped, the Continental Congress sent John Adams, John Jay, and Benjamin Franklin to negotiate a permanent settlement. They eventually signed the **Treaty of Paris** on September 3, 1783, in which Great Britain recognized the United States as an independent nation and established a western border along the Mississippi River. The last British troops left New York, and the Continental Army disbanded.

1763-1783

Timeline

1763	Peace of Paris ends French and Indian War.
	Pontiac's Rebellion occurs.
	Parliament issues the Proclamation of 1763.
1764	Parliament passes the Sugar and Currency Acts.
1765	Parliament passes the Quartering and Stamp Acts.
	The Stamp Act Congress convenes in New York.
	Stamp Act riots and protests spread throughout colonies.
1766	Parliament repeals the Stamp Act and passes the Declaratory Act.
1767	Parliament passes the Townshend Acts and suspends the New York legislature.
1768	British soldiers occupy Boston.
1770	Boston Massacre occurs.
	Parliament repeals Townshend Acts but keeps the tax on tea.
1772	Samuel Adams forms the committee of correspondence.
1773	Boston Tea Party occurs.
1774	Parliament passes the Coercive or "Intolerable" Acts.
	The First Continental Congress convenes and drafts the Declaration of American Rights.
1775	Battle of Lexington and Concord occurs.
	The Second Continental Congress convenes.
	Battle of Bunker Hill occurs.
	Paul Revere warns minutemen of redcoats' approach in his Midnight Ride.
1776	Thomas Paine writes *Common Sense*.
	Congress votes for independence; Thomas Jefferson writes the Declaration of Independence.
1777	Battle of Saratoga brings first military success for the colonists.
1778	France and the United States form the Franco-American alliance.
1781	Washington accepts Cornwallis' surrender at Yorktown.
1783	The Treaty of Paris ends the Revolutionary War.

CHAPTER 4

Building a Nation: 1781–1800

||||||||||||||||||||||||||||||||||||||||||||||||||||||||

Shortly after Thomas Jefferson penned the Declaration of Independence, the delegates at the Second Continental Congress drafted the Articles of Confederation, the first constitution of the United States. The Articles, however, failed to truly bind the states together, and as a result, the congress had very little real power. Less than a decade later, congressional leaders decided to scrap the Articles in favor of creating a new and stronger federal government.

Political philosophers around the world have hailed the Constitution as one of the most important documents in world history. It established the first stable democratic government and inspired the creation of similar constitutions around the world. For this reason, past historians have waxed lyrical about the Founding Fathers' incredible foresight when writing the Constitution. Many contemporary historians, however, tend to see the Constitution more as a bundle of compromises rather than a document they knew would change the world. Either way, the Constitution established a much stronger federal government and has since become the oldest living written constitution in the world.

The Articles of Confederation

Delegates at the Second Continental Congress drafted the **Articles of Confederation** to create the first national government of the United States. The Articles loosely bound the thirteen states in a confederacy that eventually proved incredibly weak.

A WEAK NATIONAL GOVERNMENT

Wary of strong central governments after their interactions with Britain, delegates at the Second Continental Congress made certain that the new national congress created under the Articles of Confederation would have very little authority over state legislatures. Instead, drafters hoped that the congress would act as a collective substitute for a monarch, or a multiperson executive. The Articles stipulated that the Congress could do the following:

- Negotiate treaties, declare war, and make peace

- Coin money

- Issue loans

- Maintain an army and a navy

- Operate a postal service

- Negotiate treaties with Native Americans

- Resolve disputes among the states

- Govern western territories for the benefit of all states

The Articles clearly stated that the individual states reserved all powers not specifically granted to congress. Representative governments in the states would levy their own taxes, for example, and then use a percentage of the duties collected to pay their share of national expenditures. Over time, this unfolded as an ineffective way of bankrolling a federal government, primarily because many of the states refused to pay their fair share.

Moreover, Congress had been granted no rights to control interstate commerce. States were thus given a free hand to draft conflicting and confusing laws that made trade across borders difficult. Finally, any changes to the Articles of Confederation required unanimous agreement from all states in the Union, an event that was unlikely to occur even on the smallest issue.

GOVERNING WESTERN LANDS

After the Articles of Confederation went into effect, Congress passed two landmark laws to govern American territories in the West:

- **The Land Ordinance of 1785**, which helped the government survey western lands. The law created townships, each six miles square, that were divided into thirty-six square-mile sections and auctioned to the highest bidder so that any American could settle in the West.

- **The Northwest Ordinance of 1787**, which stipulated that a western territory could apply for full statehood as soon as it had the same number of people as the least populous of the original thirteen states. The ordinance made certain that new states would receive equal footing with older states and that all citizens of the territories would have the same rights as the citizens of the states.

CONTINENTAL DOLLARS AND DEPRESSION

The new Congress immediately set to printing paper currency in order to pay for the Revolutionary War. The money became the standard currency in the United States during the war, but when hard times hit and inflation skyrocketed, these Continental dollars became "not worth a Continental." Many Americans, especially farmers, faced hardship as the economy slid into depression. Congress requested that states increase taxes to help pay for a new national currency, but most states refused and printed their own paper money instead. This, too, quickly succumbed to inflation, and by the end of the war Americans had fistfuls of a variety of worthless money.

Shays's Rebellion

Frustration with the economic depression boiled over in 1786. Farmers throughout the colonies were suffering intensely after the revolution, mainly due to the worthless Continentals they were forced to use as money. Most of the state legislatures refused to provide any assistance to these impoverished farmers and, in some cases, even raised taxes. Unable to find any relief, and still intoxicated from their success in the Revolution, many farmers grabbed their muskets once again and marched on the various state capitals to demand new governments.

The most notorious of these small uprising was **Shays's Rebellion**. Led by the Revolutionary war hero **Daniel Shays**, protesters attacked Massachusetts's courthouses to prevent local judges from foreclosing on farms. The state legislature ultimately used militia troops to crush the uprising. Still, Shays's Rebellion awakened legislators in Massachusetts and throughout the states to the inadequacies of the existing political system.

Forming a More Perfect Union

With Congress's permission, delegates met in Annapolis, Maryland, in 1786 and again in Philadelphia in 1787 to discuss revising the Articles of Confederation. The delegates, however, soon realized that the Articles needed to be scrapped entirely to create a stronger central government.

> *Although Shays's Rebellion had certainly prompted many Americans to question the effectiveness of the federal government, leaders ultimately decided the Articles of Confederation needed amending primarily because the national congress had no power to control interstate commerce or interstate disputes. States' rights versus the power of the federal government would be an issue throughout the next century in the United States.*

1781–1800

THE FRAMERS

The fifty-five men who gathered at the **Constitutional Convention** in Philadelphia came from the upper echelons of society. Most had attended college and had become wealthy planters, lawyers, and merchants but generally understood that they served all classes of Americans. On the other hand, the delegates did want the new government to protect individuals' rights to acquire and hold wealth.

Interestingly, most all of the attendees had not been heavily involved in the revolution: **Thomas Jefferson**, **John Adams**, Samuel Adams, and Patrick Henry were all absent. Nevertheless, most did have experience writing their own state constitutions. Delegates unanimously selected **George Washington** to chair the convention.

CREATING A NEW GOVERNMENT

The men gathered in Philadelphia quickly realized the Articles of Confederation should be scrapped and replaced with a new constitution to create a stronger national government. Even though this decision violated Congress's mandate to merely *revise* the Articles, most delegates feared the Union would collapse without a stronger central government. The delegates drafted a new **Constitution** to create a republican government consisting of three distinct branches: a legislative branch (Congress), an executive branch (the president), and a judicial branch (headed by the Supreme Court). The delegates felt that this **separation of powers** into three different branches would prevent tyranny over the states.

VIRGINIA VS. NEW JERSEY

Both Virginia and New Jersey submitted proposals for a new national legislature, plans that divided delegates and nearly deadlocked the convention. The **Virginia Plan** called for the creation of a bicameral national legislature, or a new Congress with an upper and lower house, in which the number of representatives per state would be apportioned based on that state's population. Many of the more populous states supported this **"large state plan"** because it would give them more power.

New Jersey, on the other hand, proposed the creation of a unicameral legislature in which all states large and small would have the same number of representatives. This **"small state plan"** or **New Jersey Plan**, would have tipped the balance of power to favor the smaller states over the larger ones.

The framers of the constitution did not create a true democracy, which would have been based only on a popular vote, because they didn't trust the "rabble" of uneducated commoners. Instead, they created a republic, a system based on the consent of the governed, where representatives exercised power for the public.

The Great Compromise

Eventually, the delegates settled on a "Great Compromise" to please both Virginia and New Jersey. They decided that the new Congress would have two houses, a Senate in which all states would be equally represented by two senators, and a lower House of Representatives in which the number of delegates would be apportioned based on state population. State legislatures would appoint senators every six years, while the people would elect representatives to the House every two years. The new congress retained all the powers it had under the Articles of Confederation but also had the power to levy taxes.

The Three-Fifths Compromise

Even at this early date, the slavery issue divided the northern and southern states. States with large slave populations wanted slaves to count as people on the official census so that they could have more representatives in the House. States with smaller populations wanted to exclude slaves altogether. Delegates finally made the so-called **Three-Fifths Compromise** to count slaves as three-fifths of a person. They also agreed to discuss banning the slave trade in 1808.

THE PRESIDENCY

After they had created the legislative branch, the delegates moved on to creating a strong executive branch. Most agreed that the Articles of Confederation had left Congress too weak to maintain unity among all thirteen states. To amend this, delegates outlined the powers of a new executive or president of the United States. Elected to a term of four years, the president had the following authority:

- To serve as commander in chief of the army and navy

1781–1800

- To appoint judges to all federal courts
- To veto legislation passed by Congress

Just as important, the House of Representatives could also impeach the president for treason, bribery, and other "high crimes and misdemeanors," because the delegates wanted to make sure the president never became a king.

> *Some delegates, such as **Alexander Hamilton**, officially proposed creating a constitutional monarchy headed by an American king. Although few supported his proposal, many delegates agreed that a strong executive would be necessary to maintain stability.*

THE ELECTORAL COLLEGE

Fearing that the democratic "rabble" would elect an uneducated man to the presidency, the Constitution's framers stipulated that the people would only indirectly elect presidents. Instead, state legislatures would choose a select body of educated men to cast the final votes for the president in the **Electoral College**.

In theory, voters in the college would vote according to the outcome of the popular vote in their states; however, should the people elect a person deemed unqualified for the presidency, electoral voters could change the vote to ensure that only the "best man" become president.

THE JUDICIARY

Finally, the delegates turned to creating a judicial branch. They created a system of federal circuit courts headed by a Supreme Court that outranked all other courts in the nation. The Senate had to approve of all presidential appointments to the Supreme Court, particularly since justices would serve life terms. The Constitution also stipulated that Congress's first duty would be to create the federal court system.

CHECKS AND BALANCES

Despite separation of powers, most delegates wanted to include other safeguards in the Constitution to prevent tyranny. They therefore created a system of **checks and balances** so that each branch of government had the ability to check the powers of the others in order to prevent one branch from dominating the others. The president, for example, has the right to appoint Supreme Court justices, cabinet members, and foreign ambassadors, but only with the approval of the Senate. On the other hand, he reserves the right to veto all congressional legislation. Congress, too, could override a presidential veto with a two-thirds majority vote.

Separation of powers and checks and balance were truly revolutionary. Up to this point in history, government had mainly been composed of single ruling monarchs who decided what was best for their country. This monarch's rule was law, unchecked and without question. Never before had anyone proposed controlling government by setting it against itself, as the Americans proposed with the checks and balances system.

Ratifying the Constitution

Even though the delegates at the Constitutional Convention in Philadelphia had succeeded in drafting a new Constitution to replace the Articles of Confederation, they still had to convince state legislatures to approve the radically different document.

The Articles of Confederation stipulated that all thirteen states must unanimously ratify the Constitution in order for it to take effect. To circumvent this undoubtedly impossible task, the Philadelphia delegates included in the Constitution a section outlining a new plan for ratification. When only nine of the states ratified the document at special conventions with elected representatives, the Constitution would replace the Articles in those nine states. The delegates figured correctly that the remaining states would be unable to survive on their own and would therefore have to ratify the Constitution as well. In effect, the framers of the Constitution chose to appeal to the American people to ensure ratification.

FEDERALISTS VS. ANTI-FEDERALISTS

Debates immediately erupted throughout the thirteen states as to whether or not the new Constitution should replace the Articles of Confederation. The Federalists, or those who supported ratification, generally came from the more educated and wealthier classes and included leaders like John Adams, George Washington, Benjamin Franklin, **James Madison**, and **Alexander Hamilton**, among others.

The Anti-Federalists favored a weaker central government in favor of stronger state legislatures. Not all of them liked the Articles of Confederation, but none of them wanted the new Constitution either. Generally from the poorer classes in the West, but also with the support of patriots like Samuel Adams and Patrick Henry, the Anti-Federalists feared that a stronger national government would one day destroy the liberties Americans had won in the Revolutionary War. They particularly didn't like the fact that the new Constitution didn't delineate any specific rights for the people.

A FEDERALIST VICTORY

Elected conventions in several of the smaller states quickly ratified the Constitution because it gave these states more power in the new legislative branch than they currently enjoyed under the Articles of Confederation. Other ratifying conventions didn't end so quickly or peacefully. Riots broke out in several cities throughout the United States in 1787, and public debates between Federalists and Anti-Federalists became heated. By the summer of 1788, nine of the states had ratified the Constitution, thus making it the supreme law of the land according to the ratification rules. Legislators in the four remaining states—New York, Virginia, North Carolina, and Rhode Island—hated the new Constitution but knew that they couldn't survive without the other nine.

The Federalist Papers

Debate continued to rage in the Anti-Federalist stronghold of New York. To support the Constitution, Alexander Hamilton, James Madison, and **John Jay** published a series of anonymous essays now known as *The Federalist Papers*. Written as propaganda, these essays extolled the benefits of a strong central government and allayed fears about any loss of civil liberties. Historians and political scientists now regard the essays, well written and extremely persuasive, as some of the finest writings on the Constitution and republicanism.

The Bill of Rights

Anti-Federalists in New York finally agreed to ratify the Constitution as long as the new Congress would amend the Constitution to outline specific rights and liberties reserved for the people. Madison himself wrote these ten amendments, collectively known as the **Bill of Rights**. Congress ratified the bill as the first ten amendments to the Constitution, including:

- **The First Amendment**, which protects freedom of religion, speech, and the press

- **The Second Amendment**, which guarantees the right to bear arms

- **The Fifth Amendment**, which guarantees due process of law in criminal cases

- **The Sixth Amendment**, which guarantees the right to a speedy trial by an impartial jury

- **The Ninth Amendment**, which stipulates that the people have other rights besides those specifically mentioned in the Constitution or Bill of Rights

- **The Tenth Amendment**, which awards all powers not specifically given to Congress to the individual states

Washington's Presidency

Voters in the Electoral College unanimously elected George Washington the first president in 1789 and made John Adams the vice president. Washington proved a firm, dignified, and conscientious leader. He felt his responsibility acutely, tried to remain within his branch of power, and never interfered with Congress. Washington created the first presidential cabinet to advise him. He named Alexander Hamilton secretary of the treasury, Thomas Jefferson secretary of state, and Henry Knox secretary of war.

CREATING THE JUDICIARY

Even before ratifying Madison's Bill of Rights, Congress had to create the judiciary branch of government as stipulated in the Constitution. To do so, congress passed the **Judiciary Act of 1789**, establishing a federal court system with thirteen district courts, three circuit courts, and a Supreme Court presided over by six justices. Congress, however, did not want the federal court system to have too much power over local communities and therefore designated that federal courts would primarily serve as appeals courts for cases already tried in state courts.

HAMILTON AND THE ECONOMY

Hamilton hoped to use his position as secretary of the treasury to stabilize the economy and establish a solid credit. His sound fiscal policies enabled him to achieve these goals and strengthen the national government at the expense of the individual states.

Establishing Public Credit

Hamilton knew that the United States needed capital to develop economically and to convince the rest of the world that the new government would honor debts incurred during the Revolution and under the Articles of Confederation. By 1789, the United States owed roughly $51 million, and Hamilton argued that the government should pay back the entire sum as soon as possible. He also wanted the central government to assume all the states' debts and repay creditors "at par," or with interest.

Hamilton believed that the new government should sell bonds to encourage investment from citizens and foreign interests. Congress initially fought **assumption** and **funding-at-par** but eventually conceded. These policies gave the United States a sound credit rating, allowed foreign capital to flow into the country, and stabilized the economy.

1781–1800

> *Alexander Hamilton thought a sizeable national debt would become a "national blessing," reasoning that federal debts would prevent states from drifting from the central government.*

The Excise Tax

In order to raise money to pay off these debts, Hamilton suggested Congress levy an **excise tax** on liquor. Because farmers often converted their grain harvests into alcohol before shipping to save cost, many of the congressmen from agrarian states in the South and West opposed the plan and denounced it as an attempt to make northern investors richer. Congress eventually compromised and agreed to assume all federal and state debts and levy an excise tax in exchange for making the southern city of Washington, D.C., the nation's capital.

The National Bank

Next, Hamilton proposed to create a privately funded **Bank of the United States** to safely store government funds and tie wealthy Americans' interests to the stability of the federal government. Although the Constitution said nothing about creating a national bank, Hamilton argued that the document's **"elastic clause"** allowed the government to pass all laws "which shall be necessary and proper." Moreover, as a **"loose constructionist,"** he generally believed that the Constitution permitted everything it did not expressly forbid. Washington agreed and authorized creation of the bank.

Hamilton's Economic Vision

Hamilton went on to create a broad economic plan, which was primarily designed to encourage industrial growth. He asked congress to issue protective tariffs on foreign goods, subsidies, and bestow awards to encourage the formation of new businesses. Hamilton's goal was to change an essentially agricultural country into a nation with a self-sufficient industrial economy.

JEFFERSONIAN OPPOSITION

Secretary of State Thomas Jefferson opposed nearly every measure Hamilton proposed. As a **"strict constructionist,"** Jefferson believed that the Constitution forbade everything it didn't expressly permit. He therefore vehemently opposed the formation of a Bank of the United States, particularly since it seemed to benefit only the wealthy in the Northeast. He also argued against the excise tax because it unfairly punished southern and western farmers.

The Birth of Political Parties

Hamilton and Jefferson had diametrically opposed visions for the United States. Whereas Hamilton wanted a diversified industrial economy, Jefferson wanted a self-sufficient, agricultural nation. Jefferson in particular despised the thought of large cities and instead wanted a republic consisting of small farmers. These philosophical debates between Hamilton and Jefferson, combined with their own personal animosity for each other, split Washington's cabinet and even Congress during Washington's presidency. Eventually, two distinct political parties emerged from the feud: Hamiltonian **Federalists** and Jeffersonian **Democratic-Republicans**.

Federalists	Democratic-Republicans
Led by Adams, Hamilton, and Marshall	Led by Jefferson and Madison
Associated with aristocracy	Associated with the masses
Encouraged the development of industry	Encouraged the development of agriculture
Favored an alliance with Great Britain	Favored an alliance with France
Championed a strong central government at the expense of individual states	Championed a weak central government in favor of strengthening the states

THE INDIAN INTERCOURSE ACT

Congress passed the **Indian Intercourse Act** in 1790. The Intercourse Act stipulated that Congress would regulate all trade with Native Americans and that the United States would only acquire new western lands via official treaties. Not surprisingly, most American farmers ignored this bill and continued to steal Indian lands in the Ohio Valley. Native Americans naturally fought back in several particularly bloody skirmishes on the frontier. The fighting ended only after American forces routed the most powerful tribes at the **Battle of Fallen Timbers** in 1794.

THE WHISKEY REBELLION

A small band of Pennsylvania farmers marched toward the national capital in Philadelphia to protest Hamilton's injurious excise tax, causing rumors of another revolution to spread throughout the countryside. In response, Washington organized an army of 13,000 and marched to western Pennsylvania to end the so-called **Whiskey Rebellion** before it grew. The farmers quickly disbanded in awe of the massive display of federal force.

> *Washington knew it was important to show the American people that while they may have gained their independence by revolting against the crown, they could not simply revolt against any government when the mood struck them. Washington's willingness to send such an enormous force after merely hearing rumors of rebellion demonstrated the resolve of the new federal government.*

THE FRENCH REVOLUTION

Washington also had many foreign crises to address, most notably the **French Revolution**. In 1789, the French overthrew King Louis XVI to the exultation of Americans. Thomas Jefferson and his supporters in particular believed that a firm friendship with a republican France would only benefit both peoples. When the revolution turned bloody, however, and war erupted between France and Great Britain, American support for France waned.

Many of the Jeffersonian Democratic-Republicans continued to back the French and believed that the United States should honor the 1778 Franco-American alliance. More conservative Americans, such as Hamilton and the Federalists, believed that the United States should ally itself with Britain.

Neutrality and Citizen Genêt

Washington finally ended the debate when he issued his **Neutrality Proclamation of 1793**, which pledged mutual friendship and the desire to trade with both nations. France's ambassador Genêt, however, ignored Washington's proclamation and continued to pursue an alliance anyway. The **Citizen Genêt Affair** outraged Federalists and Democratic-Republicans alike because it illustrated France's blatant disregard for Washington. Jefferson, though also displeased and embarrassed, eventually resigned his cabinet post for having initially supported the ambassador.

JAY'S AND PINCKNEY'S TREATIES

To prevent another war with Britain, Washington also dispatched Supreme Court Chief Justice John Jay to London in 1794 to negotiate a settlement concerning British troops still stationed on American soil. Britain eventually agreed to withdraw its troops from the Ohio Valley and pay damages for American ships the Royal Navy had illegally seized in the year after the Revolutionary War. In exchange, the United States agreed to pay outstanding pre-Revolutionary War debts to British creditors. **Jay's Treaty** angered many Democratic-Republicans who viewed the agreement as a solid first step toward a new Anglo-American alliance, which they opposed. A year later in 1795, Washington's diplomats also ended border disputes with Spain. Known as **Pinckney's Treaty**, the agreement gave Americans access to the Mississippi in exchange for promises of nonaggression in the West.

WASHINGTON'S FAREWELL

Tired of the demands of the presidency, Washington refused to run for a third term, and in 1796 he read his **Farewell Address** to the nation. In the speech, he urged Americans not to become embroiled in European affairs, and, in response to the growing political battles between Jefferson and Hamilton, warned against the dangers of factional political parties, which could ruin a nation.

> Vermont, Tennessee, and Kentucky all joined the Union during Washington's presidency. When Washington left office, there were sixteen states in the Union.

Adams and the Federalists

By the end of George Washington's second term, the ideological and personal differences between Thomas Jefferson and Alexander Hamilton had expanded beyond the cabinet to divide politicians throughout the country. By 1796, these two factions had coalesced into two distinct political parties. Unfortunately, neither party realized that both had the best interests of the country at heart. Debates quite often became heated and even violent as the two parties battled for control of the government.

THE ELECTION OF 1796

Two strong candidates emerged in the months prior to the election of 1796:

- Vice President John Adams for the Federalists
- Former secretary of state Thomas Jefferson for the Democratic-Republicans

Adams won the most electoral votes and thus became president, while runner-up Thomas Jefferson became vice president. The presence of a Democratic-Republican in the upper echelons of the Adams administration made it difficult at times for the new president to promote his strongly Federalist agenda.

> *Before the passage of the Twelfth Amendment in 1804, the Constitution stipulated that the presidential candidate who received the second highest number of electoral votes would become vice president.*

UNDECLARED WARFARE WITH FRANCE

The first test of Adams's mettle came from France in 1796, when Paris ended all diplomatic relations with the United States in response to improved Anglo-American relations outlined in Jay's Treaty with Britain. Washington's Neutrality Proclamation and Jay's Treaty had both stunned France, which had expected the United States to honor the Franco–American alliance made during the Revolutionary War. Consequently, French warships began seizing hundreds of American merchant ships and millions of dollars' worth of cargo without cause or compensation.

The XYZ Affair

Hoping to avoid war with France, Adams sent ambassadors to Paris to normalize relations in 1797. When the emissaries arrived, however, the French officials, nicknamed by the American press X, Y, and Z, demanded a bribe of a quarter of a million dollars before they would even speak with the Americans. The **XYZ Affair** outraged Congress and the American public, and prompted many to cry, "Millions for defense, but not one cent for tribute!" Adams's popularity skyrocketed when he refused the request and prepared for war. Although Congress never officially declared war with France, both countries waged undeclared naval warfare in the Atlantic for several years.

1781–1800

The war ended shortly before Adams left office, when he signed the **Convention of 1800**, in which he promised U.S. merchants would not seek payment for seized cargo in exchange for the annulment of the Franco–American alliance.

THE ALIEN AND SEDITION ACTS

Adams's sudden boost in popularity in the wake of the XYZ Affair gave Federalists in Congress the confidence to boldly strengthen the federal government. In 1798, Congress passed the **Alien and Sedition Acts** in part to prevent French revolutionaries from entering the United States but also to cripple the Democratic-Republicans:

- **The Alien Act** extended the time required for foreigners to become American citizens from five years to fourteen years and gave Congress the power to expel aliens. This act was aimed directly at Irish and French immigrants, who mainly supported the Democratic-Republicans.

- **The Sedition Act** banned public criticism of the president and Congress and was used to silence Democratic-Republican newspapers.

The Virginia and Kentucky Resolutions

Instead of weakening the Democratic-Republicans, the Alien and Sedition Acts only made them stronger. For the first time, Jeffersonians organized as a true opposition party in Congress: they formed caucuses, selected party leaders, and promoted a platform. They also challenged Federalists for the previously nonpartisan position of Speaker of the House.

Democratic-Republicans throughout the country vehemently protested the Sedition Act as a violation of their First Amendment right to free speech. Vice President Jefferson and James Madison even anonymously drafted the **Virginia and Kentucky Resolutions** later that year, in which they proclaimed the Alien and Sedition Acts null and void in those states. The resolutions argued that because the states had formed a compact in creating the Union, the states therefore reserved the right to nullify any congressional laws they deemed unconstitutional.

Jefferson and Madison's Virginia and Kentucky Resolutions were two of the most influential American works written before the Civil War. Arguing that member states had the authority to nullify unconstitutional acts of Congress, the resolutions effectively claimed the power of judicial review for the states, not the Supreme Court. The resolutions also sparked the first debate over whether the states or the federal government had the final authority. Future Democrats—the political descendents of the Democratic-Republicans—would continue this line of reasoning.

Timeline

1781	The Second Continental Congress ratifies the Articles of Confederation.
1785	Congress passes the Land Ordinance of 1785.
1786	Shays's Rebellion occurs.
	Protesters attack courthouses in Massachusetts.
	Delegates meet to discuss revising Articles of Confederation in Annapolis, Maryland.
1787	Congress passes the Northwest Ordinance of 1787.
	The Constitutional Convention is held in Philadelphia, Pennsylvania.
	Alexander Hamilton, John Jay, and James Madison begin writing the *Federalist Papers*.
1788	Nine states ratify the new Constitution.
1789	George Washington becomes the first president.
	Congress passes the Judiciary Act of 1789.
1790	Congress passes the Indian Intercourse Act.
1791	The Bill of Rights is ratified.
	The Bank of the United States is created.
	Congress levies an excise tax.
1792	Washington is reelected.
1793	Washington issues the Neutrality Proclamation.
	The Citizen Genêt affair outrages the American public.
1794	A band of farmers march the capital to protest the excise tax in the Whiskey Rebellion.
	Fighting between Native Americans and American farmers finally ends in the Battle of Fallen Timbers.
	Jay's Treaty angers Democratic-Republicans who oppose an Anglo-American alliance.
1795	Pinckney's Treaty gives Americans access to the Mississippi.
1796	Washington reads his Farewell Address.
	John Adams is elected president.

1797	French officials demand a bribe in the XYZ Affair.
1798	Congress passes the Alien and Sedition Acts.
	U.S. wages undeclared naval war with France.
	Jefferson and Madison write the Virginia and Kentucky Resolutions.

CHAPTER 5

Republican Agrarianism: 1800–1824

||||||||||||||||||||||||||||||||||||||||||||||||||

Many historians argue that the election of 1800 had as much impact on American and world history as the Declaration of Independence and the Revolutionary War because it proved democracy worked. With the election, or "revolution," in 1800, the Federalist party lost the White House to the Democratic-Republicans. This transfer of power without bloodshed was a remarkable feat at the time, and one that brought Thomas Jefferson to the presidency.

Although Jefferson had planned to decrease the size and influence of the federal government and return power to state legislatures, he ironically strengthened the government by bending the Constitution to purchase land. Moreover, his plans to punish Britain and France for unprovoked naval attacks floundered, and his foreign policy ultimately caused a nationwide depression. Britain and the United States eventually fought another war over sovereignty issues that finally ended in a stalemate two years later. Still, Americans emerged from the war with a newfound sense of national pride and unity that helped them focus on improving national infrastructure in the early nineteenth century.

The Election of 1800

As the presidential election of 1800 approached, problems mounted for President Adams and the Federalists. The Alien and Sedition Acts, Jay's Treaty, and the suppression of the Whiskey Rebellion by federal troops had all soured Americans' opinion of the Federalists. Still, Federalists nominated both **John Adams** and Charles C. Pinckney, while Democratic-Republicans selected **Thomas Jefferson** and Aaron Burr to run for president.

JEFFERSON ELECTED

Although Adams received a significant number of electoral votes, he still won fewer than both Jefferson and Burr. Both Democratic-Republican candidates, had tied with seventy-three votes each, thus forcing the House of Representatives to determine the next president. Most Federalists lobbied representatives to elect Burr, but Alexander Hamilton succeeded in convincing his colleagues to vote for his arch-nemesis Jefferson because he hated Burr even more. As a result, Jefferson became the nation's third president and Burr his vice president.

> Until 1804, the presidential candidate who received the most votes became president, and the second-place candidate was vice president, even if they represented different parties. The **Twelfth Amendment** to the Constitution stipulated that candidates for the respective positions would run together on the same party ticket instead of against each other for the presidency. Congress ratified the amendment to avoid a tie in the Electoral College similar to that in the election of 1800.

THE REVOLUTION OF 1800

Historians often refer to the election of 1800 as the **Revolution of 1800** because the Federalists ceded power to the Democratic-Republicans entirely without violence, a truly significant accomplishment given the fact that so many wars in Europe had begun when one party had refused to relinquish control to another. For this reason, the Revolution of 1800 was just as momentous as the Revolution of 1776. Whereas the American Revolution had established the United States as an independent nation, the election of 1800 proved that the new nation would survive.

The election also proved, contrary to George Washington's belief, that political parties would not rip apart the republic. Rather, they actually served as a vehicle for peaceful discussion and exchange without bloodshed.

Adams's Midnight Judges

Shortly before they transferred power to the Democratic-Republicans, Federalists in congress passed the **Judiciary Act of 1801** to ensure that Federalists would continue to control the courts during Jefferson's presidency. Adams even used his last remaining hours as president to appoint a new chief justice to the Supreme Court and forty-two other **"midnight judges"** to lower federal courts.

Republicans in Power

Jefferson came to power promising to reduce the size of the federal government and deemphasize industry in favor of agriculture. Jefferson argued that these actions would set the United States back on its "rightful" course toward agrarian republicanism and redefine the role of the government so it would be less intrusive in the lives of American citizens. He slashed federal spending, virtually disbanded the army and navy, and repealed almost all taxes except those on the sale of federal lands. By selling public lands, Jefferson hoped to encourage the creation of more small farms and rid the government of debt.

MARBURY V. MADISON

Soon after taking office, the Democratic-Republicans proceeded to repeal the bulk of Federalist legislation, including the Alien and Sedition Acts and the Judiciary Act of 1801. Jefferson and his secretary of state, **James Madison,** also refused to honor the appointments of Adams's "midnight judges." Outraged, one Federalist

justice named William Marbury sued Madison, and in 1803 the
Supreme Court heard the case. Chief Justice **John Marshall** sympa-
thized with fellow Federalist Marbury but ruled in the landmark
decision *Marbury v. Madison* that even though the president
should have honored Adams's appointments, the Supreme Court
had no power over Jefferson in this matter because the Judiciary
Act of 1789 was unconstitutional. This decision allowed Marshall
to simultaneously give Jefferson his victory and strengthen the
Supreme Court with the power of **judicial review**, or the right to
declare laws passed by Congress unconstitutional.

THE LOUISIANA PURCHASE

Jefferson overstepped his authority as president again in 1803
when he purchased the vast tract of land between the Mississippi
River and the Rocky Mountains from Napoleon in France.
Although Jefferson knew the Constitution didn't authorize presidents to purchase land, he also realized he had to act on the
unprecedented opportunity to double the size of the country for
only 15 million dollars. The **Louisiana Purchase** gave Americans control of most of the Mississippi River and ended French
dreams of a North American empire.

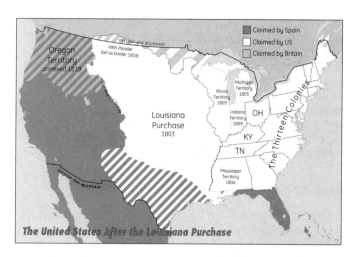

The United States After the Louisiana Purchase

Ironically, Jefferson, a Democratic-Republican who despised taxes, purchased the Louisiana Territory with money earned from Federalist taxes collected during Washington and Adams's presidencies. However, Napoleon had just offered him more land than he had ever hoped to be able to purchase from France. How could he refuse?

LEWIS AND CLARK

In 1803, Jefferson asked Congress to fund an exploratory expedition to the Pacific Northwest, ostensibly "for the purpose of extending the foreign commerce of the United States" mainly by finding a water route to the Pacific Ocean. Jefferson also wanted to map the unexplored Louisiana Territory and foster trade relations with the indigenous Native Americans. With Congress's approval, Jefferson assigned his secretary Meriwether Lewis and army captain William Clark to lead the **"Corps of Discovery"** expedition.

Lewis and Clark embarked on their journey from St. Louis with approximately fifty men in 1804 and returned more than two years later in 1806. They found no easy water route to the Pacific, but returned with maps and information about the terrain, people, and natural resources that would fuel the pioneering spirit of countless Americans.

EMBARGO ACT

France sold the Louisiana Territory to Jefferson primarily because Napoleon needed money to fund his war with Great Britain as he continued to try to conquer the whole of Europe. Although far removed from the fighting, the war nevertheless hurt American trade across the Atlantic. Both the French and English navies frequently seized American ships looking for arms, supplies, and other contraband even though the United States had declared neutrality. Unable to convince either side to respect American neutral shipping rights, Congress and Jefferson decided that American merchants would simply not trade with Europe any more, and passed the **Embargo Act** in 1807, prohibiting trade with the United States. Democratic-Republicans hoped that the embargo would cripple both France and England and force them to respect American shipping rights.

Impressment

Britain complicated the situation by forcing American sailors from seized ships into military service on British warships. Although Royal Navy officials claimed they only impressed their own deserters, records have shown that British officers illegally impressed more than 5,000 American men. Americans at home viewed Britain's policy of **impressment** as an affront to their hard-won liberties and as a violation of the Treaty of Paris that had ended the Revolutionary War.

In what was to become known as the **Chesapeake Affair**, war fever raged once again in the United States when on June 22, 1802, a British ship attacked a U.S. warship, the *Chesapeake*, and then impressed four American sailors. Jefferson wanted to avoid war, but also knew that he couldn't simply ignore Britain's blatant violations of American sovereignty. Congress passed Jefferson's Embargo Acto of 1807 on December 22, six months to the day after the British attacked the *Chesapeake*.

The Embargo's Impact

The Embargo Act crippled the American economy far more than it hurt Britain or France, as American exports fell from $109 million to $22 million in the first year alone. Depression followed soon after, when farmers in the West and South couldn't sell any grain, cotton, or tobacco to the lucrative markets abroad. Rumblings of secession even spread throughout the hardest-hit areas in the northern states. Still, Jefferson refused to lift the embargo, and it remained in effect until Congress finally repealed it in 1809.

ELECTION OF 1808

The depression caused by Thomas Jefferson's Embargo Act weakened the Democratic-Republican Party in the 1808 national elections. Although **James Madison** still managed to defeat the Federalist candidate Charles Pinckney for the presidency, the party lost seats in Congress. As Jefferson's chosen successor,

Madison carried out his fellow Virginian's policies throughout both of his presidential terms.

TECUMSEH AND THE PROPHET

One of Madison's greatest challenges during his first term involved the growing Native American threat to American settlers in the West. American farmers had eagerly pushed westward into the Mississippi River basin since Jefferson's Louisiana Purchase, despite Congress's promise to respect Native American territory in the Indian Intercourse Act of 1790. Frustrated, two Shawnee brothers named **Tecumseh** and Tenskwatawa, nicknamed the Prophet for reportedly having a series of "visions," succeeded in creating a pan-Indian alliance called the **Northwest Confederacy** (including the Shawnee, Cherokee, Choctaw, Chickasaws, and Creeks, among other tribes), which sought a return to traditional ways of Native American life. Fearing another Native American uprising, Madison ordered Indiana Territory Governor **William Henry Harrison** to destroy the Confederacy, which he did in 1811 at the **Battle of Tippecanoe**.

> *Harrison's success at the Battle of Tippecanoe made him famous throughout the United States. He would later capitalize on his fame by running for the presidency in 1836 and 1840, using the rallying cry "Tippecanoe and Tyler, too!" Tyler was Harrison's running mate in the election.*

The War of 1812

By 1810, many of the older and experienced statesmen in Congress had retired, leaving their seats open to a young and passionate new generation. Most of these young congressmen came from the southern and western states and yearned for action. These **"War Hawks,"** like **John C. Calhoun** and **Henry Clay**, had ordered Harrison to defeat Tecumseh and the Prophet and clamored for a new war against Great Britain. Although President Madison hoped to avoid war, he eventually caved to pressures from the War Hawks and requested that Congress declare war against Britain in June of 1812.

NON-INTERCOURSE ACT AND MACON'S BILL NUMBER 2

Because the Embargo Act had failed, Congress passed the **Non-Intercourse Act** in 1809 to reopen trade with every country *except* France and Britain. When this too failed, Congress then passed **Macon's Bill Number 2** in 1810 to entice Britain and France into recognizing American shipping rights. The bill stipulated that the United States would reward the first of the two to respect American shipping by reinstating the embargo on the country that did not.

Hoping to bring the Americans into the war, Napoleon ordered French ships to respect American merchants, thus forcing Madison to reinstate the embargo on trade with Britain. After two more years of British aggression on the Atlantic and in the West, Madison eventually had no choice but to heed War Hawk demands and ask Congress to declare war on Britain.

CAUSES OF THE WAR OF 1812

Americans clamored for war with Britain in 1812 for two reasons: to defeat the British-backed Native Americans in the Ohio Valley and to defend American shipping rights and end the practice of impressments. Despite these goals, many Americans in the West also wanted war in order to seize more land, particularly in British Canada.

A STALEMATED WAR

The war itself went badly for the United States. Thanks to Jefferson's belief in frugal government, the U.S. Navy consisted of just a few ineffective gunboats, and the army had very few men, weapons, or supplies. American forces had some success in the Northwest but couldn't manage to punch through the British blockade of the eastern ports or prevent the burning of Washington, D.C. The war, for all practical purposes, was a stalemate, and both countries signed the **Treaty of Ghent** in 1814 to end it. The treaty essentially stipulated that neither side had gained or lost any territory, and neither side mentioned impressment or the illegal seizure of American ships. Ironically, American troops under the command of General **Andrew Jackson** won a resounding victory in early January 1815 at the **Battle of New Orleans**, just days after diplomats had signed the peace treaty.

THE HARTFORD CONVENTION

While the American and British delegations negotiated the treaty in Ghent, Federalist delegates from five New England states met in Hartford, Connecticut, to discuss their dissatisfaction with "Mr. Madison's War." In fact, some felt so outraged that they proposed secession from the Union. After meeting for several weeks, delegates at the **Hartford Convention** settled on merely petitioning Congress with a list of four major grievances:

- The federal government should compensate New England shippers for profits lost during the war.

- The Constitution should be amended so that states can vote on important decisions that affect the entire Union, such as the admission of new states and declaring war.

- The executive office should be changed so that presidents can only serve one term and cannot come from the same state as the previous president.

- The Three-Fifths Clause should be stricken from the Constitution.

The Hartford Convention's list of demands reflected northern dissatisfaction with the federal government and with the war. Of the first five presidents, only one of them—John Adams—had not been a member of the so-called **Virginia Dynasty**, which consisted of Washington, Jefferson, Madison, and Monroe, all from Virginia. This strong southern representation in the White House frustrated many New Englanders, who felt that they had been left out of the political loop. This frustration was the true driving force behind the delegates' list of demands.

Unfortunately for the Hartford delegates, their petition arrived in Washington, D.C., just as news of Jackson's victory in New Orleans arrived and the Treaty of Ghent was signed. The effect on the Federalists was devastating as the country voiced its support of the war and of the government. The Federalist Party never recovered from the stigma of disloyalty.

> Although Americans today usually associate secession with the South, New Englanders at the Hartford Convention were actually the first to threaten to leave the Union. Talk of secession among states in the early part of the nineteenth century was much more common than in mid-century, though.

The Era of Good Feelings

Despite the fact that the United States had gained nothing from the War of 1812, Americans felt intensely patriotic when the conflict ended in 1814. Jackson's victory at the Battle of New Orleans made Americans particularly proud, as if they had won a "second war for independence" against the most powerful army in the world. This newfound American spirit also boosted the popularity of the War Hawks, like Clay and Calhoun, who emerged as the nation's new congressional leaders in the postwar era.

Democratic-Republican **James Monroe** easily defeated his weak Federalist opponent, Rufus King, in the election of 1816, and in doing so not only effectively killed the Federalist Party, but also ushered in an era of domestic tranquility and single-party rule. One newspaper in Boston, the *Columbian Centinel,* dubbed these virtually controversy-free years the **Era of Good Feelings**. The name stuck.

CLAY'S AMERICAN SYSTEM

As the leader of the War Hawks, Speaker of the House Henry Clay proposed a three-pronged **"American System"** to improve the national infrastructure of the United States. Clay's nationalistic system included:

- Improving the financial sector of the economy. Under his leadership, Congress created the **Second Bank of the**

United States in 1816 to offer easy credit and stabilize the economy.

- Protecting struggling American manufacturers from the postwar influx of cheap British goods. He pushed the **Tariff of 1816** through Congress to place a 20 percent tax on all foreign goods. This also happened to be the first tariff Congress passed to protect industry rather than merely to increase revenue.

- Connecting the country via a system of roads and canals built with money raised from the new protective tariff. These **internal improvements** would help farmers ship their crops and goods to the East and manufacturers to ship their products to the West.

POSTWAR EXPANSION

The Era of Good Feelings at home affected foreign policy as well. Most significantly, the United States ended decades of hostility with Great Britain with the following agreements:

- **The Rush-Bagot Agreement** in 1817 to demilitarize the Great Lakes region

- **The Treaty of 1818** to establish a clear border between the United States and Canada from Minnesota to the Rocky Mountains at the forty-ninth parallel. The treaty also specified that the United States would jointly occupy the Oregon Territory in the Pacific Northwest (present-day Oregon, Idaho, Washington, British Columbia, and part of Montana) until 1828.

New States

Settlers carved out three new territories in the Deep South after the war:

- Louisiana became a state in 1812.

- Mississippi became a state in 1817.

- Alabama became a state in 1819.

Seizing Spanish Florida

General **Andrew Jackson**, meanwhile, illegally seized Spanish Florida on the pretext that Spain had plotted with the Seminole Indian tribe against the United States. Spain ultimately ceded Florida to the United States in 1819 in exchange for Washington's retraction on claims to Spanish Texas.

THE MONROE DOCTRINE

In 1823, John Quincy Adams devised the **Monroe Doctrine**. It represented the Monroe administration's most significant foreign policy achievement. The Monroe Doctrine stipulated that:

- European powers had to stay away from the New World.

- Old World powers could keep the colonies they currently had, but could not establish any new ones.

- America would support the growth of democracy throughout the western hemisphere.

British policy-makers had originally suggested the Monroe Doctrine to Monroe and Adams because they wanted to protect their West Indian colonies from the continental powers in Europe. Secretly, the British also feared American expansionism in the Caribbean and hoped that a joint declaration against intervention in the New World would both curb European aggression and stymie American plans. Adams realized that Britain wanted to bind the United States as much as it wanted to bind the rest of Europe, and so he encouraged Monroe to issue the doctrine on his own so as not to cripple American interests.

Even though the British failed to contain the United States, they still supported the Monroe Doctrine anyway and used Royal Navy warships to enforce it. The Monroe Doctrine allowed new Latin American democracies to flourish without fear of war with Spain, France, or Portugal.

JOHN MARSHALL AND THE SUPREME COURT

The Supreme Court issued a series of rulings during the Era of Good Feelings that also increased the power of the federal gov-

The Monroe Doctrine has since become a major tenet of American foreign policy, used and sometimes abused by U.S. presidents since Monroe to intervene and occasionally control developing South and Central American countries. Theodore Roosevelt famously added his "Roosevelt Corollary" to the Monroe Doctrine at the end of the nineteenth century to limit European nations' use of force to collect debts from Latin American countries.

ernment. The Court, still dominated by diehard Federalist Chief Justice **John Marshall**, upheld federal power more out of Hamiltonian beliefs in strong government than out of love for the new nationalism. The rulings included:

* *Dartmouth College v. Woodward* that states could not nullify or amend legal contracts (1819)

* *Cohens v. Virginia* that the Supreme Court had the authority to review decisions reached in the supreme courts of the individual states (1821)

* *McCulloch v. Maryland* that neither Hamiltonian "loose" interpretations of the elastic clause nor the Bank of the United States violated the Constitution (1819)

* *Gibbons v. Ogden* that Congress had the authority to regulate interstate commerce (1824)

Marshall's rulings during these early years played a huge role in consolidating the power of the federal government over the individual states and ensured that Federalist ideals would live on despite the party's early death.

THE PANIC OF 1819

A string of crises beginning at the end of Monroe's first term quickly dampened the "good feelings" of the era. The first crisis hit in the **Panic of 1819** and was caused at least in part by a change in credit policies of the Second Bank of the United States (SBUS) toward a more conservative lending policy. The bank was concerned about the practices of the rough-and-tumble **wildcat banks** in the West that were lending money quickly and without as much concern for regulations as other banks. The SBUS called in loans made to these banks, forcing the banks to call in loans they had made to thousands of pioneers along the frontier, mainly farmers. The new policies, combined with price declines in many agricultural areas, forced thousands of farmers off their land. The number of Americans in poverty and debtor prisons swelled for almost a decade until the economy rebounded.

INCREASING SECTIONALISM

Sectional tensions also arose in 1819 when the Missouri Territory applied for admission to the Union as a new slave state. Even though Missouri had met all of the qualifications, the northern-dominated House of Representatives denied the territory statehood because they didn't want to tip the sectional balance in the Senate in favor of the South with twelve slave states to only eleven free. The House then passed the **Tallmadge Amendment** in 1819 to gradually free slave children and declare that settlers couldn't take any more slaves into the territory.

THE MISSOURI COMPROMISE

Southern elites were outraged at what they acutely believed to be northern attempts to eliminate slavery. By 1819, they had become almost completely dependent on slave labor to produce cotton and reasoned that if slavery couldn't expand westward, then the southern way of life would certainly die. In other words, they feared that northerners in the free states would hem them in geographically and suffocate them economically. People in the South also feared that banning slavery in Missouri would set a precedent for all other new states. As a result, they rejected the Tallmadge Amendment in the Senate and then deadlocked Congress for several more months until House Speaker Henry Clay proposed the **Missouri Compromise**. Both southerners and northerners agreed to the following:

- Missouri would be admitted as a slave state.

- Maine would simultaneously be admitted as a free state to maintain the sectional balance.

- Slavery was declared illegal north of the 36° 30' parallel west of Missouri.

Impact of the Compromise

The Missouri Compromise of 1819 saved the Union from a potentially divisive issue. Most southerners liked the compromise because the slave South could expand westward. Northerners, on the other hand, also liked the compromise because slavery South of the 36° 30' parallel kept slavery contained in the South and out of most lands acquired in the vast Louisiana Purchase, which was a free territory. With the slavery issue at least temporarily settled, Americans could now focus on other matters.

*An elderly **Thomas Jefferson** wrote that the Missouri Compromise, "like a fire bell in the night awakened and filled me with terror. I considered it at once as the knell of the Union." The conflict over the expansion of slavery in new territories ultimately tore the Union apart in the Civil War.*

Timeline

1800	The Convention of 1800 ends the war with France.
	Thomas Jefferson is elected president of the United States.
1801	Congress passes the Judiciary Act of 1801.
1802	Congress repeals the Judiciary Act of 1801.
1803	Jefferson purchases Louisiana Territory.
	Supreme Court hears *Marbury v. Madison*.
1804	Jefferson is reelected.
	Lewis and Clark explore Louisiana Territory.
1807	The Chesapeake Affair incites war fever.
	Congress passes the Embargo Act.
1808	James Madison is elected president of the United States.
1809	Congress repeals the Embargo Act.
	Congress passes the Non-Intercourse Act.
1811	The Battle of Tippecanoe.
1812	United States declares war on Great Britain.
	Madison is reelected.
1814	New Englanders discuss secession at Hartford Convention.
	Treaty of Ghent ends War of 1812.
1816	Congress passes the Tariff of 1816.
	James Monroe is elected president.
1818	General Andrew Jackson invades Florida.
1819	The Panic of 1819 ends the Era of Good Feelings.
	Spain cedes Florida to the United States.
	The House passes the Tallmadge Amendment.
	The *McCulloch v. Maryland* ruling increases the power of federal government.
	Dartmouth College v. Woodward rules that states cannot amend legal contracts.

1820	The Missouri Compromise is proposed by Henry Clay.
	Monroe is reelected.
1823	John Quincy Adams devises the Monroe Doctrine.
1824	The *Gibbons v. Ogden* ruling gives Congress authority to regulate interstate commerce.

CHAPTER 6

Jacksonian Democracy: 1824–1848

||||||||||||||||||||||||||||||||||||||||||||||||||||||||||||

National pride surged after the War of 1812 with Great Britain, and Americans began defining their purpose and position in the world more ambitiously than before. Fueled by zeal and optimism, the United States expanded politically, geographically, and culturally. Believing that God had given America a Manifest Destiny to expand from the Atlantic to the Pacific coast, Americans crossed the Appalachians, forded the Mississippi River, and walked or rode in covered wagons westward all the way to California and Oregon by mid-century.

The geographic expansion of the American population coincided with an increase in social and political equality among America's citizens. Americans believed they could change their station in life and that hard work and determination could take them anywhere. This social and political equality, however, did not extend to all Americans, and the escalating issues of sectionalism and slavery would grow increasingly more divisive as mid-century approached. Finally, 1848 saw the rise to prominence of a Whig congressman from Illinois named Abraham Lincoln, whose influence on the country over the next fifteen years was impossible to foresee at the time.

The Election of 1824

Four major candidates contended for the presidency in the election of 1824:

- **John Quincy Adams**, the son of former president John Adams, represented New England.

- **Andrew Jackson**, the champion of the common man, drew widespread support from the West and South.

- **William Crawford**, a southern planter, advocated states' rights.

- **Henry Clay,** who championed the American System, appealed to wealthier Americans.

The fact that four candidates had decided to run for the presidency was proof that the Missouri Compromise of 1820, which allowed slavery in the South and prohibited it north of the 36° 30' parallel, had replaced the Era of Good Feelings with sectionalism and divisiveness. Americans held many differing views regarding the direction in which the country should move.

THE AMERICAN SYSTEM

Henry Clay ran on the "**American System**" platform, which sought to improve the fledgling United States by:

- Promoting internal improvements such as building canals and national roads

- Raising **protective tariffs** on foreign goods to help domestic manufacturers

- Establishing a **Bank of the United States** to stabilize the economy

The American System dominated the election of 1824. Candidates Clay and Adams both endorsed the system, but Jackson opposed it.

ADAMS'S CORRUPT BARGAIN

After a vicious campaign, Jackson emerged as the most popular candidate, garnering 99 electoral votes to Adams's 84, Crawford's 41, and Clay's 37. But since no single candidate received the necessary clear majority in the Electoral College, it fell to the House of Representatives to decide which of the top three candidates would become the next president. As speaker of the House, Clay threw his support to Adams in exchange for becoming the next secretary of state. Clay's support brought Adams to the presidency, but many Americans joined Jackson in denouncing Clay and Adams's **"corrupt bargain."** His reputation ruined, Adams had very little influence during his four years as president.

The Rise of Mass Democracy

By the 1830s, most states had eliminated voting qualifications such as literacy tests and property ownership, so that all white males could vote. As a result of this trend toward **universal manhood suffrage**, the number of voters increased dramatically, from 350,000 in 1824 to more than 2.5 million by 1840.

THE ELECTION OF 1828

By 1828, political leaders such as Adams and Clay, who promoted policies focused on internal improvements to the country, had split from Jackson's Democratic-Republicans (eventually to become known simply as Democrats) and formed their own National Republican Party. Adams and Jackson faced off once again in the presidential election of 1828. Not surprisingly, the tainted Adams lost, winning only New England.

POLITICS OF PERSONALITY

Jackson believed that his landslide victory in 1828 had given him a mandate from the people to do whatever he deemed right. As a result, he greatly expanded the powers of the presidency. For example, Jackson vetoed bills he personally disliked, unlike previous presidents who had only vetoed bills they thought unconstitutional. Jackson also strengthened the federal government at the expense of individual state governments.

THE SPOILS SYSTEM

Jackson believed that political power should rest with the people in a democracy. He used this belief as a justification for replacing many career civil servants in the capital with his own political allies. This action marked the rise of the Spoils System in nineteenth-century American politics, a system in which presidents award the best appointments in government to their friends and supporters. While previous presidents had practiced this system to a lesser degree, Jackson was the first to publicly attempt to justify and defend it.

> Unlike his predecessors, Jackson relied less on his cabinet secretaries than he did on a set of close friends and allies that critics dubbed his "Kitchen Cabinet." Jackson rarely sought advice outside of this inner circle. In fact, midway through his first administration, Jackson completely reorganized his cabinet and removed most of the secretaries he had originally appointed.

The Nullification Crisis

The tariff issue once again shot to the political foreground in 1828, when Congress unexpectedly passed the Tariff of 1828, setting duties on imported goods at nearly 50 percent, a great increase from the current duties. Jackson actually disliked the tariff and knew it would be unpopular but had pushed for its passage before his election to the presidency to further discredit Adams. As soon as he entered the White House, however, the so-called **Tariff of Abominations** (the Tariff of 1828) became his problem.

A tariff is a duty or tax on goods imported from abroad.
Northerners generally wanted tariffs in order to protect their
manufactured goods from imports. Southerners did not want high
tariffs because they relied heavily on trade with Britain. As a result,
tariffs became one of the major sectional issues in the years before
the Civil War.

CALHOUN'S SOUTH CAROLINA EXPOSITION

As a westerner, Jackson had no love for the new tariff, which hurt
the agricultural South and West, but he didn't seek its repeal
either. Jackson's vice president, **John C. Calhoun**, hated the Tariff of Abominations so much that he anonymously encouraged
his home state to nullify the law in a pamphlet published in 1828
called *The South Carolina Exposition and Protest*. Calhoun argued
that states could nullify any act of Congress they deemed unconstitutional because the states had created the central government
and therefore had greater power. Calhoun believed the South
Carolina legislature should nullify the new tariff because the tariff protected textile manufacturers in northern states and hurt
southern cotton-producing states when the price of cotton
abroad rose.

Calhoun expanded upon Thomas Jefferson and James Madison's
1798 **Virginia and Kentucky Resolutions** *when writing* The
South Carolina Exposition. *Like his democratic predecessors,*
Calhoun also drew on the Compact Theory of Government, which
states that there must be agreement between those who govern
and those who are governed, to defend the supremacy of states'
rights over the power of the federal government. Southerners
would use this same argument to justify secession in 1860 and
1861.

THE TARIFF OF 1832

Though the southern states protested vehemently against the Tariff of 1828, the tariff generated large revenues that helped the government pay many of its debts. With federal finances in better shape, Jackson signed the lower **Tariff of 1832**. Calhoun and South Carolinians, however, continued to protest. Although they despised the tax itself, they resented federal supremacy over the states even more. Consequently, legislators in South Carolina declared the new tariff null and void in the state and even threatened to secede if Jackson tried to enforce tax collection.

The Nullification Proclamation

Jackson was outraged at South Carolina's challenge to the authority of the federal government, and he issued his own **Nullification Proclamation** denying any state's right to nullify federal laws. Moreover, he declared nullification treasonous and threatened to hang the nullifiers himself. He organized a corps of army troops loyal to the Union and then railroaded the **Force Bill** through Congress in 1833, justifying the use of military force to collect tariff duties in South Carolina.

The Compromise Tariff of 1833

Just as violence seemed imminent, the "Great Compromiser," **Henry Clay**, proposed and passed the **Compromise Tariff of 1833**, which reduced tariff rates over the next ten years. Since no other state supported South Carolina, state legislators reluctantly decided to accept the new tariff. They did, however, nullify the Force Bill out of spite.

Jackson's Bank War

By 1832, the **Second Bank of the United States** had become the most important financial institution in the nation. Many Americans, however, hated the bank, especially farmers and land speculators who could not repay their loans after the agricultural market crashed during the Panic of 1819. Jackson himself had lost most of his money in 1819 and blamed the country's financial problems on the bank.

Henry Clay, afraid that Jackson and the Democrats might not renew the bank's charter in 1836, when it would otherwise expire, attempted to renew the charter several years early, in 1832. Clay also hoped to make the bank a key issue in the presidential election later that year. Congress passed a bill renewing the bank's charter, but Jackson vetoed it. Jackson believed that the strong national bank:

- Unfairly stifled competition from smaller state banks and private banks

- Violated the Constitution, which states that only the federal government could regulate currency

- Encouraged speculation that eventually caused panics and depressions

- Oppressed the poor while making rich financiers even wealthier

THE ELECTION OF 1832

Clay succeeded in making the bank one of the most important issues in the election of 1832. Three candidates contended for the presidency that year:

- Andrew Jackson ran on the Democratic ticket against the bank and lower tariffs.

- Henry Clay, representing the National Republicans, pressed for the bank, higher tariffs, and internal improvements.

- William Wirt, running for the **Anti-Masonic Party**, opposed the Order of the Masons.

Clay's plan to win the presidency by supporting the bank back-fired. Jackson won the election easily with the votes of millions of recently enfranchised voters in the poorer areas of the West and South who hated the bank.

> *Although never a major party, the Anti-Masonic Party was the first third party to run a candidate in a presidential election and the first to specify its aims in a detailed party platform. The Anti-Masonic Party's primary objective was to end the Freemasonry movement, a secret society with religious overtones found throughout the United States. The party tried to capitalize on the public's fear of conspiracies and secret societies at the time.*

Jackson Kills the Bank

Jackson interpreted his sweeping victory as a mandate from the people to destroy the Bank of the United States, and he did so by withdrawing all federal money and depositing it into smaller state banks instead. Afraid that the bank's death would encourage inves-tors to over-speculate in western lands, valuing them more than they were worth, Jackson also issued a **Specie Circular** in 1836 that required all land to be purchased with hard currency.

Indian Removal

Jackson, bowing to pressure from western settlers, convinced Congress to pass the **Indian Removal Act** in 1830, which authorized the forced relocation of tens of thousands of Native Americans to the "Great American Desert" west of the Missis-sippi, a land so inhospitable that most believed no white settlers would ever want to settle there.

NATIVE AMERICAN RESISTANCE

The Native American tribes affected by the Indian Removal Act did not move quietly. The U.S. army encountered some of the heaviest resistance from the Fox and Sauk in the Old Northwest region near the Great Lakes. Chief Black Hawk and his warriors resisted resettlement for two years until American troops ended the **Black Hawk War** in 1832. The Seminoles in Florida resisted relocation for seven years in the **Seminole War**.

Cherokees Fight the Law

The Cherokee tribe in Georgia also refused to comply with the new law. As one of the so-called Five Civilized Tribes, the Cherokee had actually taken great strides to assimilate into white southern culture. Most worked as farmers and some even owned large slave plantations. Instead of fighting for their homes, however, they challenged the law in court. Chief Justice John Marshall ruled in:

- *Cherokee Nation v. Georgia* in 1831 that the United States could not remove the Cherokee because they legally owned their lands as a separate nation independent from the United States

- *Worcester v. Georgia* in 1832 that Georgia could not force its laws on the independent Cherokee

The Trail of Tears

Jackson blatantly ignored the Court's rulings and forced the Cherokee to cede their lands and relocate to the Arkansas Territory. More than 12,000 Cherokee walked the **"Trail of Tears"** with the Choctaws, Chickasaws, Creeks, and conquered Seminoles. Thousands died from hunger, cold, and disease during this humiliating journey.

Van Buren, Harrison, and Tyler

Jackson, who had become old and weak, declined to run for a third term in 1836. His bold policies against nullification and the central bank had prompted his political opponents to form the new **Whig Party**, led by former National Republican leader Henry Clay. Like the National Republicans, the Whigs supported the American System, promoting internal improvements, creating protective tariffs, and supporting the bank.

ELECTION OF 1836

Four major candidates competed for the White House in 1836:

- **Martin Van Buren**, a Democrat and Jackson's hand-picked successor

- **Daniel Webster**, a prominent statesman from New England and Whig leader

- Hugh Lawson White, a Whig from Tennessee

- **William Henry Harrison**, yet another Whig and a famous war hero

The Whigs ran three candidates against Van Buren in the hopes that one of them could garner enough votes to oust the Jacksonian Democrats from the White House. The three candidates competing against each other, however, merely scattered Whig votes so that none of them had enough to defeat the popular Van Buren. As a result, Van Buren easily defeated his opponents to become the eighth president.

THE PANIC OF 1837

Van Buren's presidency was blighted by the Panic of 1837 and the ensuing depression. Jackson's Specie Circular, issued just before he left office, required the payment of public land to be in gold or silver rather than paper money. This caused a run on banks, especially those in the West, as thousands tried to withdraw their money in gold and silver coins. Commodity prices fell, hundreds of banks shut down, and millions of Americans found themselves out of work or too poor to farm.

In response, Van Buren forced Congressional Democrats to pass a **Divorce Bill** to separate federal money from unstable banks and redeposit it in a new and independent treasury. Van Buren hoped that such a move would restore Americans' faith in the economic stability of the government. But the depression only worsened and contributed to Van Buren's growing unpopularity.

THE HARD CIDER ELECTION OF 1840

The Depression ruined Van Buren's chances of reelection in 1840. Nevertheless, the Democrats nominated him again for lack of a better candidate. The Whigs, meanwhile, had grown wiser in the last four years and decided to focus their efforts on a single candidate instead of three. In the 1840 election, Democrats nominated Martin Van Buren, and Whigs nominated war hero William Henry Harrison. The Whigs appealed to common voters in the West and South by touting Harrison as a log-cabin-born, hard-cider-guzzling frontiersman. This strategy worked, and Harrison easily defeated Van Buren, much to the jubilation of Henry Clay and Daniel Webster. Yet, fewer than thirty days after taking the oath of office, Harrison died.

It was believed that Harrison died from pneumonia contracted while delivering a two-hour speech in the cold on his inauguration day. He had refused to wear a jacket to give his speech, despite the temperatures, and was the first president to die in office.

JOHN TYLER'S PRESIDENCY

Harrison's relatively unknown running mate, **John Tyler**, became president and proceeded to pursue his own agenda. Tyler, a former Democrat who'd only joined the Whig Party to oppose Jackson, had no love for federally funded internal improvements, higher protective tariffs, or a national bank. Instead, the new president tried to reduce tariffs, give more power to the individual states, and even vetoed a Whig bill to revive the Bank of the United States. Furious at Tyler's betrayal, Whig leaders officially expelled him from the party in 1842.

Manifest Destiny and Polk

In 1845, a New York newspaper editor wrote, "Our manifest destiny is to overspread the continent allotted by Providence for the free development of our yearly multiplying millions." The American public quickly latched on to **Manifest Destiny** and the belief that Americans had a mandate from God to spread democracy throughout North America. Thousands of settlers poured from the growing urban regions in the East to California, Oregon, and Texas. This belief in Manifest Destiny spread all the way to the highest levels of government, where congressmen and presidents traded, bought, annexed, and even went to war for new lands.

THE WEBSTER-ASHBURTON TREATY

The **Webster-Ashburton Treaty** of 1842 marked the government's first step toward fulfilling America's perceived destiny. The treaty, between the United States and Great Britain, settled the boundary disputes between the United States and Canada over the ore-rich Great Lakes region. It also stipulated that both countries would jointly occupy the Oregon Territory.

TEXAS

Texas declared independence from Mexico in 1836 and immediately requested annexation by the United States. Northern Whigs and others opposed to the expansion of slavery protested the creation of another slave state and blocked the southerners' move to annex Texas. Moreover, Congress had promised noninterference to Mexican officials during the war and thus couldn't legally annex Texas. Mexico, meanwhile, tried several times to retake its rebellious state over the next decade, with no success.

Britain's Plans for Texas

Forced to protect themselves without any assistance from the United States, Texans negotiated trade and security treaties with several European powers. Britain in particular became very interested in Texas because an independent Texas would help them by:

- Halting American expansion

- Weakening the Monroe Doctrine, which might eventually allow Britain to found new colonies in North America

- Providing another source of cotton for British textile manufacturers

ELECTION OF 1844

Texas became the hottest issue in the election of 1844 after American policymakers discovered Britain's plans. The election also focused on Oregon, tariffs, and the increasingly heated slavery issue. The major candidates of the election included:

- Henry Clay, a veteran Whig statesman, who ran on a platform against the annexation of Texas

- **James K. Polk**, a Democratic lawyer and Tennessee planter, who ran on a platform in favor of annexation

- James G. Birney, the new **Liberty Party** candidate, who was an abolitionist and ran on an antislavery platform

Historians often refer to the election of 1844 as the Manifest Destiny Election because candidates focused primarily on westward expansion. The issue of Texas loomed large, and the election also featured the first candidate to run on a platform advocating the abolition of slavery.

Texas Joins the Union

Polk barely won the election, with only 40,000 more popular votes than Clay. Sitting president John Tyler interpreted the victory as a mandate from the people to annex Texas. Before leaving office, Tyler asked Congress in 1845 for a joint resolution to annex Texas. Unlike the usual two-thirds vote of the Senate that was needed to ratify a treaty, the resolution required only a simple majority of each house. The resolution passed, and Texas was added to the Union as a slave state later that year.

Outraged, Mexico immediately withdrew its ambassador to the United States. More trouble arose when the two countries became embroiled in a border dispute. Americans claimed that the Rio Grande River divided Texas from Mexico, whereas Mexicans marked the border at the Nueces River farther north in Texas. Both sent troops to the region, the Americans camping north of the Nueces and the Mexicans to the south of the Rio Grande. War would soon erupt.

THE POLK PRESIDENCY

James K. Polk entered the White House with a three-pronged agenda. He wanted to reduce tariffs, acquire Oregon, and acquire California. Amazingly, he achieved all three goals in only four years' time.

Tariff Reduction. Polk successfully pushed the **Walker Tariff** through Congress in 1846 to reduce general tariff rates from 32 percent to 25 percent.

Oregon. Although the United States had jointly occupied the Oregon Territory with Great Britain for several decades, Polk wanted sole ownership of Oregon for the United States, all the way to the southern border of Alaska at the 54° 40' parallel. Most Americans supported the move for all of Oregon, particularly considering that nearly 5,000 Americans had settled there after crossing the continent on the perilous **Oregon Trail**.

Polk pressured Britain to relinquish Oregon to the point of threatening war, but eventually signed the compromise **Oregon Treaty** in 1846 to split Oregon at the forty-ninth parallel. Britain took all of present-day British Columbia while the United States took all the territory that eventually became Washington State, Oregon, Idaho, and parts of Montana.

California. Polk's greatest ambition of all was to add California to the United States. Polk particularly desired the glittering San Francisco Bay, which could open the United States to lucrative trade deals with Asia. Unfortunately for the president, Mexico had strong territorial claims to California. Polk's designs on California, as well as the U.S. troops stationed in Texas, led to conflict with Mexico once again.

The Mexican–American War

President Polk sent envoy John Slidell to Mexico in 1845, hoping to smooth relations with Mexico, resolve the Texas issue, and buy California. The president authorized Slidell to purchase California and New Mexico for a total of $25 million. Mexico, of course, refused the low offer and sent Slidell back to Washington. Undoubtedly knowing full well that Mexico would refuse the offer, Polk had simultaneously sent adventurer **John C. Frémont** to California, ostensibly on a scientific survey mission. At the same time, Polk sent several U.S. Navy ships to the California coast. General **Zachary Taylor** and 2,000 troops moved from their position north of the Nueces River and encamped along the northern shores of the Rio Grande River in disputed territory.

POLK ASKS FOR WAR

In April of 1846, Mexican troops crossed the Rio Grande and attacked Taylor's men camped in disputed territory. Immediately after receiving news of the Mexican attack, Polk "reluctantly" requested that Congress declare war. After much debate, Congress eventually acquiesced. As soon as Congress formally declared war the following month, U.S. forces defeated the Mexicans quickly and easily. In a little over a year and a half:

- Frémont and the navy seized California.

- American troops seized most of present day New Mexico and Arizona.

- Taylor seized all of northern Mexico after defeating an overwhelming Mexican force at the Battle of Buena Vista.

- General Winfield Scott seized Mexico City in September 1847 to end the war.

THE TREATY OF GUADALUPE–HIDALGO

American and Mexican diplomats signed the **Treaty of Guadalupe–Hidalgo** in 1848 to end the war. In the treaty:

- Mexico ceded California and most of present-day New Mexico, Arizona, Nevada, Colorado, and Wyoming to the United States.

- Mexico abandoned its claims to Texas.

- The Rio Grande River was established as the border between Texas and Mexico.

- The United States generously agreed to pay Mexico 15 million dollars for all lands acquired.

LINCOLN'S "SPOT RESOLUTIONS"

Despite the American victory and the enormous territorial gains that came with it, Polk faced severe criticism for the war in Washington. Whig congressman **Abraham Lincoln** continually badgered Polk about the exact spot where the Mexicans had engaged Taylor. These **"spot" resolutions** damaged Polk's reputation and led many to believe that the president had intentionally provoked the Mexicans in order to seize California.

> The Mexican War gave future Civil War commanders such as Robert E. Lee, Ulysses S. Grant, Stonewall Jackson, and William Tecumseh Sherman valuable experience on the battlefield. In fact, many of them served side by side in campaigns in Mexico and the West.

THE LEGACY OF THE MEXICAN–AMERICAN WAR

The vast majority of Americans had supported the war despite the $98 million price tag and the loss of approximately 12,000 men. However, the war was never perceived as a moral crusade based on the defense of democratic principles, because the United States hadn't fought for independence, freedom for oppressed peoples, or to save democracy. Rather, Americans had gone to war primarily in the name of Manifest Destiny, to expand and acquire more land. At war's end, most Americans felt jubilant that the United States finally spread from coast to coast. The ever-present issue of the expansion of slavery into the new territories, however, would quickly sour the spoils of victory.

Timeline

1824	The disputed presidential election of 1824 is dominated by the American System.
1825	House of Representatives chooses Adams for the presidency.
1828	Congress passes the "Tariff of Abominations."
	Andrew Jackson is elected president.
	John C. Calhoun publishes *The South Carolina Exposition*.
1830	Congress passes the Indian Removal Act.
1832	Jackson thwarts attempts to recharter the Bank of the United States.
	Congress passes the Tariff of 1832.
	Jackson is reelected.
	Jackson issues the Nullification Proclamation.
	The Black Hawk War ends one of the most destructive conflicts between pioneers and Native Americans.
1833	Congress passes Tariff of 1833.
	Jackson withdraws federal money from the Bank of the United States.
	Congress passes the Force Bill.
1834	The Whig Party forms.
1836	The Bank of the United States' charter expires.
	Texas declares independence from Mexico.
	185 Texans fight a 4,000-man Mexican army in the Battle of the Alamo.
	Jackson issues Specie Circular.
	Martin Van Buren is elected president.
1837	Thousands withdraw money from banks in the Panic of 1837.
	Congress refuses to annex Texas.
1838	The army forcibly removes the Cherokee on the "Trail of Tears."
1840	William Henry Harrison is elected president.
	The Liberty Party forms.

1841	William Henry Harrison dies a month after becoming president.
	Vice President John Tyler becomes president.
1842	The United States and Britain sign the Webster–Ashburton Treaty.
1844	James K. Polk is elected president.
1845	The United States annexes Texas.
1846	Congress passes the Walker Tariff.
	The United States resolves the dispute over Oregon with Great Britain.
	The Mexican War erupts.
	John Frémont seizes California.
1847	Gen. Winfield Scott captures Mexico City.
1848	The United States and Mexico sign the Treaty of Guadalupe–Hidalgo.

CHAPTER 7

A Growing Nation: 1820–1860

||||||||||||||||||||||||||||||||||||||||||||||||||||||||

Between 1820 and 1860, the United States developed at a staggering pace, transforming from an underdeveloped nation of mostly backwoods farmers and frontiersmen into an urbanized economic powerhouse. Americans were spreading west during this time, especially to California through the Oregon Trail, and south into Texas. The period was marked by a cultural renaissance, and new American artists and writers were creating major Romantic and Transcendental works. Americans voted in greater numbers than ever before and took an intense interest in national politics, especially in regard to Manifest Destiny and the issue of slavery.

These transformations, rather than foster national unity, helped drive the North and South further and further apart. The market revolution, wage labor, improved transportation, social reforms, and a growing middle class in the North contrasted sharply with the unchanging semifeudalistic social hierarchy in the South. In addition, each of the major debates on slavery and westward expansion shed greater light on the differences between the two parts of the country. As time passed, Americans in the North and South ultimately began viewing themselves as two very different peoples.

The Market Revolution

Between the 1820s and 1860, the **Industrial Revolution** transformed the national economy into a **market-based economy** that was heavily reliant on exportation of goods, especially cotton in the South, and the manufacturing of goods in the North. Internal improvements in transportation as well as new inventions spurred industrial and agricultural production and made transporting goods from one part of the country to another much easier.

THE SOUTHERN AGRICULTURAL REVOLUTION

Although textile manufacturing flourished in Great Britain, it lagged far behind in the United States, primarily because Americans lacked a source of cheap cotton. Southern planters had attempted to grow cotton in the eighteenth century but had almost completely switched to rice and tobacco by the dawn of the nineteenth century-because growing cotton required too much labor.

The Cotton Gin

Inventor **Eli Whitney** made growing cotton more profitable with the automatic **cotton gin**, which he invented in 1793. Whitney's cotton gin vastly reduced the amount of labor required to harvest cotton and transformed the southern economy virtually overnight. Planters quickly abandoned tobacco and rice for the suddenly profitable cotton. Cotton production in turn spurred the construction of textile factories in the North.

> *Before Whitney invented the cotton gin, it took one slave an entire day to separate a pound of cotton fibers from the seed. The gin, however, allowed one slave to produce as much as fifty pounds of cotton in a single day. This increase transformed the economic possibilities of the North and the South.*

Interchangeable Parts

Several years after inventing the cotton gin, Whitney perfected a system to produce a musket with **interchangeable parts.** Before Whitney, craftsmen had made each individual musket by hand,

and the parts from one musket would not necessarily work in another musket. With interchangeable parts, however, all triggers fit the same model musket, as did all ramrods, all flash pans, all hammers, and all bullets. Manufacturers swiftly applied the concept of interchangeable parts to mass-produce other identical goods.

THE WESTERN AGRICULTURAL REVOLUTION

Many of those new products in turn revolutionized agriculture in the West. John Deere, for example, invented a horse-pulled **steel plow** to replace the difficult oxen-driven wooden plows farmers had used for centuries. The steel plow allowed farmers to till more soil, in less time, for less money, without having to make repairs as often.

McCormick's Mechanical Mower-Reaper

In the 1830s, another inventor, Cyrus McCormick, invented a **mechanical mower-reaper** that quintupled the efficiency of wheat farmers. Often credited as the cotton gin of the West, the mower-reaper allowed farmers to grow large quantities of wheat instead of less profitable corn. As in the South, western farmers raked in huge profits as they acquired more land to plant greater quantities of wheat. More important, farmers for the first time began producing more wheat than the western markets could handle. Rather than letting it go to waste, they sold crop surpluses to the wageworkers in Northeast cities, which in turn helped those cities grow.

Over time, regional specialization emerged: the West farmed to feed the Northeast, the South grew cotton to ship to the Northeast, and the Northeast produced manufactured goods to sell in the West and South. This specialization would play a very large role in causing the Civil War and determining the victor.

THE TRANSPORTATION REVOLUTION

Western farmers, southern cotton growers, and northern manufacturers all relied on new forms of transportation to move their goods north and south, east and west across the country. Henry Clay's American System inspired state legislatures to construct a number of roads, canals, and other internal improvements to connect the Union.

Roads. Many northern states built turnpikes and toll roads during these years, the most famous being the **Cumberland Road**, or National Road, stretching from Maryland to St. Louis, Missouri, by the time construction finished in 1852. Other well-known roads include the Wilderness Road and the Lancaster Turnpike.

Canals. The **Erie Canal** that spanned the length of New York also helped northerners transport goods from the Great Lakes region to the Hudson River and ultimately the Atlantic. The canal also helped give birth to cities like Chicago, Cleveland, and Detroit, as ships from the Atlantic could now reach far inland. Other northern states built similar canals, usually to link the agricultural West with the industrial East.

Steamboats. The newly invented steamboat permitted fast, two-way traffic on all of these new waterways as well. For the first time in history, mariners didn't have to rely on winds and currents and could travel directly to any port at any time. Within a couple decades of their invention in 1807, steamboats chugged along all the major rivers and canals, and eventually on the high seas.

Railroads. Railroads were another conduit for moving people and goods quickly and cheaply. At first, developers laid tracks primarily along the Eastern seaboard from Virginia to Boston, and in the West from Chicago to Pittsburgh. In the decade prior to the Civil War, however, Americans laid tens of thousands of miles of track, almost all in the North.

In general, only northerners capitalized on the transportation revolution. Although southerners did use steamboats extensively to ship cotton, tobacco, and rice down the Mississippi River, the South boasted very few canals, railroads, or roads. This left the region relatively isolated, a fact of considerable import in the years prior to the Civil War. As a result, although the standard of living improved in all regions during these years, it improved the most in the West and North. Northern manufacturers shipped the bulk of their finished products to the West, while the West grew rich on northern grain purchases.

Northern Society

The market revolution and surge in manufacturing had a tremendous impact on northern society. New York, Boston, Philadelphia, Baltimore, Pittsburgh, and other major cities sometimes tripled or even quadrupled in size between 1820 and 1860 as people left their farms to find work in urban areas. Smaller towns also experienced population growth during these years.

THE WAGE LABOR SYSTEM

As northerners continued building factories, they needed more and more workers to tend the machinery. Rather than learning a trade skill as most workers had in the past, these day laborers worked alongside scores of others, feeding or regulating a machine for hourly pay under harsh conditions. Workers toiled in textile factories for as many as sixteen hours a day, six or seven days a week. Although wealthy business owners loved the cheap labor, wage laborers suffered from poor working conditions.

> *Some factories such as the* **Lowell Mills** *in Massachusetts employed only girls and young women. These factories, which provided room and board, attempted to "moralize" the women with heavy doses of religious preaching and strict discipline. Factory owners tended to employ young children, or "grease monkeys," because the children could easily maneuver through the large machines.*

Strikes and Reforms

Some workers chose to unite and strike in the 1830s and 1840s to protest the inhumane conditions and hours they were forced to work. The strikes caused such a stir in the national press that the government eventually took action. In 1840, for example, President Martin Van Buren established a ten-hour working day for all federal employees. Two years later, the Massachusetts Supreme Court legalized trade unions in the landmark 1842 decision *Commonwealth v. Hunt.* Ultimately, despite the exploitation of early wage laborers, the shift away from craftsmanship toward wage labor helped give rise to a substantial and powerful middle class.

GERMAN AND IRISH IMMIGRATION

Mass immigration from Ireland and Germany was another factor in the urbanization phenomenon. More than 100,000 Irish came to the United States every year in the late 1840s and 1850s to escape the Potato Famine in Ireland, which ultimately killed more than a million people. Most of these immigrants settled in New York, Boston, and later Chicago, but Irish districts emerged in every major northern city. Germans also came en masse to the United States during the same period to escape political persecution in central Europe. These German immigrants generally had more money than the Irish and therefore mostly settled outside the congested cities.

Nativism and the Know-Nothings

A significant number of native-born Americans resented the influx of Germans and Irish. These **"nativists"** considered the Irish and Germans ignorant and inferior human beings, incapable of understanding democracy or assimilating into mainstream American culture. Many Protestants also hated the Germans and the Irish for their Catholic beliefs. The anti-immigration American Party, or **Know-Nothing Party**, was popular among nativists in the 1850s.

> People in the secretive American Party became known as the "Know-Nothings" because they usually claimed not to know anything when questioned about the group. The party grew in the 1840s, reaching its peak in 1855 with forty-three congressional representatives, but soon declined and ceased to be a major political force after 1860.

Southern Society

Although the North and West experienced dramatic social changes, the South for the most part did not. Rather, the southern social fabric remained relatively unchanged between 1820 and 1860 because of the region's reliance on cotton production. Cotton production proved so profitable after the invention of the cotton gin that by 1860, the South produced 75 percent of Britain's cotton supply.

SOUTHERN SOCIAL HIERARCHY

Instead of evolving socially as the North had, the South continued to adhere to an archaic semi-feudalistic social order, which consisted of wealthy planter elites, slave-owning farmers, poor landless whites, and slaves.

Wealthy white plantation owners controlled the southern legislatures, represented the South in Congress, and had some of the largest fortunes in the country. Next came the white landowning subsistence farmers assisted by their one or two family slaves, followed by poor landless whites, who composed the vast majority of the southern population. Black slaves, of course, formed the base of the social hierarchy.

> Contrary to popular belief, only one out of every four southern males owned slaves in the 1850s. Moreover, these few slave owners usually owned only one or two slaves. The contemporary conception of large southern plantations with hundreds of slaves was in actuality very rare. However, it was undeniable that the southern economy would collapse without this workforce.

JUSTIFYING SLAVERY

Even though few southerners actually owned slaves, all whites firmly believed in the superiority of their social system. Even the poorest whites supported slavery because they dreamed of becoming wealthy slave owners. Whites justified slavery in many ways. Some championed the "paternal" nature of slavery by arguing that slave owners took care of the inferior race as fathers would small children. Others believed that slavery Christianized blacks and saved them from brutal lives as savages in Africa. All southerners, however, preferred their more "humane" southern slavery to the impersonal "wage slavery" in the North.

Revivalism and Utopianism

A new wave or spiritual revivalism spread across America in the early to mid-nineteenth century. A variety of new denominations and utopian sects emerged during these years, including the Methodists, the Baptists, the Shakers, the Mormons, and Millerites, among others.

THE SECOND GREAT AWAKENING

A newfound sense of spirituality deeply affected Americans in the **antebellum period**. This renewed interest in religion, which began with the **Second Great Awakening** around the turn of the nineteenth century, swept across the country primarily as a reactionary response to the Enlightenment and the so-called "Age of Reason" that had inspired thinkers such as Benjamin Franklin, Thomas Jefferson, and Thomas Paine.

Hundreds of preachers, including **Charles Grandison Finney** and Timothy Dwight, set up revivalist camps in rural areas and attracted thousands of converts throughout the country. The converted often became so frenzied that they would roll, jerk, shake, shout, and even bark in excitement.

Revivalism had the greatest impact on women. Shut out from politics and most facets of the new economy, women poured their energy into religion and reform. Many believed they could have a positive impact on society by converting their family, friends, and neighbors.

The Burned-Over District

Named for its abundance of hellfire-and-damnation preaching, the **Burned-Over District** in western New York produced dozens of new denominations, communal societies, and reform movements. This region was also burned-over (or, perhaps more appropriately, burned-*out*) from the economic changes it had undergone since the completion of the Erie Canal and the rapid development of the new market economy. Influenced by so many new ideas, visionaries, and forces, Americans in the Burned-Over District became some of the nation's greatest reform leaders.

Northern Denominations

Not all of the new Christian denominations were so "spirited." Although hellfire-and-damnation sermons appealed mostly to southerners and westerners, many northern denominations came to be highly regarded for their appeal to reason. Unitarians, Presbyterians, and Episcopalians, for example, attracted a huge following because of their belief in a loving God, free will, and denial of original sin.

UTOPIAN MOVEMENTS

In the spirit of the reform movement, more than 100,000 American men, women, and children between 1820 and 1860 searched for alternative lifestyles. Disenchanted with the world around them, utopian seekers aspired to a perfect society.

Mormons

Another new denomination from the Burned-Over District was the Church of Latter Day Saints, or **Mormon** Church. Founded by Ohioan **Joseph Smith** in 1830, Mormons believed God had entrusted them with a new set of scriptures called the Book of Mormon. Because Smith also advocated polygamy, Mormons faced intense hostility and persecution from Protestants throughout the Midwest.

When an angry Illinois mob murdered Smith in 1844, his disciple Brigham Young took charge of the church and led a mass migration to the desert around the Great Salt Lake (then claimed by Mexico). There the Mormons converted the barren lands into an oasis suitable for growing crops. Utah, the territory settled by the Mormons, eventually became a U.S. territory after the Mexican War, but did not become a state until 1896, when Mormons agreed to abandon the practice of polygamy.

Other Utopian Communities

A variety of other utopian communities appeared and disappeared throughout the mid-nineteenth century. These communities included:

- **New Harmony**, a community of roughly 1,000 Americans in Indiana who believed socialistic communities could end poverty. The community collapsed in just a few short years.

- **Brook Farm**, a community in Massachusetts closely affiliated with the Transcendentalist movement, preached harmony with nature and modest living. This community also collapsed within a few years.

- **Oneida Community**, in upstate New York, practiced free love, birth control, and eugenics.

- **The Millerites**, who eventually disbanded after Jesus failed to appear on October 22, 1843, as promised.

- **The Shaker Movement**, located in several states and boasted more than half a million members at its height, ultimately dissolved because believers were forbidden to marry or have sex.

The Reform Movement

Fueled by the Great Awakening, many progressive northerners, women in particular, strived to improve society. They launched a variety of reform movements against prostitution, the consumption of alcohol, and the mistreatment of prisoners and the insane. Other reformers tried to expand women's rights and improve education. Many of these movements actually succeeded in convincing northern state legislatures to enact new laws. Southern states, however, generally lagged behind, remaining socially conservative.

ABOLITIONISM

The abolitionist movement sought to eradicate slavery and quickly became the most visible reform movement during the antebellum period. Prominent northern abolitionists included Theodore Weld, Sojourner Truth, Frederick Douglass, Elijah P. Lovejoy, and **William Lloyd Garrison**, among many others.

Garrison and The Liberator

Garrison attained infamy after first publishing his antislavery newspaper *The Liberator* in 1831 and then cofounding the American Anti-Slavery Society two years later. A radical abolitionist who called for immediate emancipation, Garrison criticized the South so severely that many southern state legislatures issued warrants and bounties for his arrest or capture. Southerners feared Garrison because they incorrectly assumed he'd helped the black preacher **Nat Turner** lead a bloody slave uprising in Virginia the same year *The Liberator* debuted.

Anti-Abolitionism in the North

Not all northerners supported the abolition movement. In fact, many people actually felt ambivalent about emancipation or even opposed it outright. The blossoming trade unions and wageworkers, for example, hated abolitionists because they feared competition for jobs from free blacks. Most public figures and politicians, even Abraham Lincoln, shunned abolitionists for their radicalism and unwillingness to compromise. As a result, abolitionists at first had few friends and many enemies.

> The abolitionist movement became so raucous that the House of Representatives actually passed a *"gag resolution"* in 1836 to squelch all further discussion of slavery. It was this mentality and willingness to ignore a pressing issue that moved the nation toward civil war.

THE TEMPERANCE MOVEMENT

The **temperance movement** sought to ban the manufacture, sale, and consumption of alcohol. By the 1830s, Americans had earned a reputation for hard drinking, especially in the West and South, where settlers endured extreme hardship. Factory owners in the cities also lamented that alcoholism reduced worker output and caused too many on-the-job accidents. Women, moreover, charged that drinking ruined family life and only led to spousal and child abuse. As the new sense of morality spread throughout the country, more and more people campaigned against drinking.

Early Prohibition

The first chapter of the **American Temperance Society** formed in 1826 and blossomed into thousands of nationwide chapters within the following ten years. The society distributed fliers, pamphlets, and illustrations and paraded victims of abuse and reformed alcoholics through towns to preach against consumption.

The movement gained even more fame when T. S. Arthur published his novel *Ten Nights in a Barroom and What I Saw There* about the horrible effects of hard liquor on a previously quaint village. Several cities and states passed laws prohibiting the sale and consumption of alcohol, such as the so-called **Maine Law** in the northeastern state. However, no federal law or proclamation would make the sale or consumption of alcohol illegal until the 1920s.

PROHIBITING PROSTITUTION

Antebellum reformers struck out against prostitution in the rapidly growing industrial cities. Spearheaded almost entirely by upper- and middle-class women, antiprostitution societies fought not only to reduce the number of working girls on the streets but also to reform them. New York women founded the Female Moral Reform Society in 1834, which branched off to hundreds of other cities and towns by 1840. These societies also strove to end prostitution by decreasing demand. Many newspapers, for example, published the names of prostitutes' patrons, while many states enacted laws to punish clients as well as the prostitutes themselves. However, the world's oldest profession continued unabated.

PRISON REFORM

Reformers also launched a campaign to improve prisons. Early- to mid-nineteenth-century prisons often resembled medieval dungeons and usually only held Americans who couldn't repay their debts. Over time, reformers managed to change the system. Debtor prisons gradually began to disappear as Americans realized the barbarity of locking people away for bad luck or circumstances beyond their control. More and more states also prohibited the use of cruel and inhumane punishments. Reformers also succeeded in convincing several state legislatures that governments should use prisons to help reform criminals, not just incarcerate them.

REFORM FOR THE MENTALLY ILL

Insane-asylum reform went hand in hand with prison reform, as most Americans at the time believed that the mentally ill were no better than animals. As a result, prisons contained thousands of mentally ill prisoners. Prison reformer **Dorothea Dix** spearheaded asylum reform by compiling a comprehensive report on the state of the mentally ill in Massachusetts. The report claimed that jailers had chained hundreds of insane women in stalls and cages. Her findings convinced state legislators to establish one of the first asylums devoted entirely to caring for the mentally ill. By the outbreak of the Civil War, nearly thirty states had built similar institutions.

EDUCATION REFORM

Reformers sought to expand public education too. Most nineteenth-century Americans considered public education only fit for the poor. Wealthier Americans could, of course, pay for their children to attend private primary schools and secondary academies, but they loathed the idea of paying higher taxes to educate the poor.

Over the course of the antebellum period, more and more cities and states acknowledged that public education would expand democracy, improve productivity, and make better citizens. For example, **Horace Mann**, the secretary of the Board of Education in Massachusetts, fought for higher teacher qualifications, better pay, newer school buildings, and an improved curriculum.

For the first time, women also gained access to higher learning during the antebellum period. Feminist Mary Lyon, for example, established the all-women's Mount Holyoke Seminary in 1837, while progressive Oberlin College began admitting women the same year.

1820–1860

THE WOMEN'S SUFFRAGE MOVEMENT

Women reformers also fought for gender equality. In the years before the Civil War, many Americans continued to believe that men and women worked in separate spheres: men outside the home, and women inside. Sometimes referred to as the "cult of domesticity," this social norm encouraged "good" women to make the home a happy and nurturing environment for their wage-laborer husbands, on top of maintaining day-to-day housekeeping.

The Seneca Falls Convention

As the American economy changed and more women left the sphere of the home for the workforce, many women began demanding more social, political, and economic rights. Prominent leaders of the women's rights movement included Lucretia Mott and **Elizabeth Cady Stanton**. These women astounded Americans and Europeans alike when they met at the **Seneca Falls Convention** in Seneca Falls, New York, in 1848. There, women leaders drafted a **Declaration of Sentiments** in the spirit of the Declaration of Independence to declare that women were equal to men in every way. Of the many sentiments declared, the call for full political suffrage shocked the world the most.

The American Renaissance

The early nineteenth century gave rise to **Romanticism**, a cultural movement in Europe and America that revolted against the certainty and rationalism of the Enlightenment. In America, Romanticism manifested itself as a literary and artistic awakening in thought, literature, and the arts. Americans took great interest in the movement, idealizing its emphasis on the individual and the common man. Romanticism underscored feeling and emotion, in contrast with the balance, harmony, and form of eighteenth-century Classicism.

THE ROMANTICS

Romantics, such as John Greenleaf Whittier, Louisa May Alcott, and Henry Wadsworth Longfellow, tried to capture their thoughts and emotions as well as the spirit of the new America. Other social commentators included the so-called **Dark Romantics**, such as Edgar Allan Poe, Herman Melville, and Nathaniel Hawthorne, who took a more critical view of American society in the years before the Civil War.

THE TRANSCENDENTALISTS

The New England **Transcendentalists** argued that not all knowledge comes from the senses and that ultimate truth "transcends" the physical world. Transcendentalists believed in the divinity of man's inner consciousness and thought that nature revealed the whole of God's moral law. Between 1830 and 1850, Transcendentalists like **Ralph Waldo Emerson**, Henry David Thoreau, and Walt Whitman championed self-reliance and a rugged individuality that matched the character of the developing nation.

AMERICAN ART

For the first time, American painting was reaching a level comparable to that of contemporary European artists. American artists worked within the Romantic Movement and sought to create unique aesthetic forms. Folk art attained popularity as did landscape paintings by the **Luminists** and **Hudson River School**. Americans also liked **Currier and Ives** lithographs, which portrayed rural and domestic scenes.

The blossoming artistic scene, however, belied a growing unease throughout the country. The slavery issue in particular began to occupy center stage in American politics, especially as new western states petitioned to join the Union. The disputes escalated into sporadic violence in the 1850s, pushing the North and South closer and closer to civil war.

Timeline

1793	Eli Whitney invents the cotton gin.
1798	Whitney invents interchangeable parts for firearms.
1800	The Second Great Awakening begins.
1807	Robert Fulton invents the steamboat.
1823	Lowell Mills opens in Waltham, Massachusetts.
1825	The Erie Canal is completed.
	The New Harmony commune is founded.
1826	The American Temperance Society is founded.
1828	The first American railroad is completed.
1830	The Transcendentalist movement begins.
	Joseph Smith establishes the Mormon Church.
	Charles Grandison Finney begins conducting Christian revivals.
1831	Nat Turner leads a slave rebellion in Virginia.
	William Lloyd Garrison begins publishing *The Liberator*.
1833	The National Trades Union forms.
	Garrison and Theodore Weld found the American Anti-Slavery Society.
1834	Cyrus McCormick invents the mechanical mower-reaper.
1836	The House of Representatives passes the "Gag Resolution."
1837	John Deere invents the steel plow.
	Oberlin College begins admitting women.
	Mary Lyon establishes Mount Holyoke Seminary.
1840	Van Buren establishes a ten-hour working day for federal employees.
1841	The Brook Farm commune is founded.
1843	Dorothea Dix crusades for prison and insane asylum reform.
	Millerites prepare for the end of the world.
1846	Mormons begin migration to Utah.

1848	The Seneca Falls Women's Rights Convention is held.
	The Oneida Community is founded.
1850	Nathaniel Hawthorne publishes *The Scarlet Letter*.
1851	Herman Melville publishes *Moby-Dick*.
1852	The Cumberland Road is completed.
1854	Henry David Thoreau writes *Walden*.
	T. S. Arthur publishes the novel *Ten Nights in a Barroom and What I Saw There*.
1855	Walt Whitman publishes *Leaves of Grass*.

CHAPTER 8

Prelude to War: 1848–1859

||||||||||||||||||||||||||||||||||||||||||||||||||||||

Some historians call the Mexican War the first battle of the Civil War, because it ignited an intense debate within America over the westward expansion of slavery. Most northerners generally opposed slavery in the Mexican Cession (the territory comprising present-day California, Arizona, New Mexico, Nevada, Colorado, Utah, and Wyoming), while southerners thought the expansion of slavery necessary in order to maintain their social and economic way of life.

By 1857, disputes over slavery had become so bitter and violent that peaceful resolution seemed impossible. The Compromise of 1850 had only served to preserve the peace for a few short years, and historians now view it as proof of the inability of the statesmen involved to forcefully address an issue that threatened to destroy their way of life. The events in Kansas during the 1850s, in which pro- and antislavery forces fought bloody battles to determine whether Kansas would become a free or a slave state, as well as the caning of Charles Sumner, an antislavery senator from Massachusetts, show the extent to which the debate had unraveled. As a result, it only took a little nudging to bring the North and South to the brink of war. The Lincoln–Douglas debates in 1858 captured the nation's attention, and while by all accounts Lincoln lost the debates, he was thrust into the public spotlight. Lincoln would return to the debate floor in 1860 as the presidential candidate for the Republican party.

Slavery and Expansion

The new lands west of Texas that had been yielded to the United States at the end of the Mexican War rekindled the debate over the westward expansion of slavery. Southern politicians and slave owners wanted to permit slavery in the West out of fear that a ban would spell doom for the institution, as the South would lose the newly created seats in Congress. Whig northerners, however, viewed slavery as a moral evil and wanted it banned. Tensions mounted when Pennsylvanian congressman David Wilmot proposed banning slavery in the territory in the **Wilmot Proviso** in 1846, even before the Mexican War had ended. Outraged, southerners immediately killed the proposition in the Senate.

THE ELECTION OF 1848

The debate over the westward expansion of slavery dominated the election of 1848 despite the death of the Wilmot Proviso, which would prohibit slavery in the western territories. Three major candidates contended for the presidency that year:

- **Lewis Cass**, on the Democratic ticket. Cass championed **popular sovereignty**, which would allow people in the western territories to decide for themselves whether to legalize slavery in their state

- **Zachary Taylor**, the Whig candidate, a Mexican–American War hero who chose not to address the slavery issue

- **Martin Van Buren**, the **Free Soil Party** candidate, who ran on an abolitionist platform

Van Buren's entry into the race split the Democrats and allowed Zachary Taylor to win easily. Although Taylor's silence on the slavery question quelled further discussion for a time, the issue resurfaced less than a year later when California applied for statehood. As a result, a great debate quickly divided northerners and southerners in Congress over the future of slavery beyond the Mississippi.

THE COMPROMISE OF 1850

In 1850, the North and South once again agreed to compromise on the issue of slavery and California's acceptance into the

California's population exploded in 1849 when tens of thousands of Americans dashed out West in the Gold Rush hoping to strike it rich. These fortune hunters were called "'49ers" for the year they left home. While thousands moved west, few struck it as rich as they had dreamed.

Union. Although **Henry Clay** deserves most of the credit for engineering the compromise, a younger generation of politicians, like Illinois senator **Stephen Douglas**, hammered out most of the details of the **Compromise of 1850**:

- California entered the Union as a free state.

- Northerners and southerners agreed that popular sovereignty would determine the fate of slavery in all other western territories.

- Texas gave up territorial claims west of the Rio Grande (in New Mexico) in return for $10 million.

- Washington, D.C., abolished the slave trade but not slavery itself.

- Congress passed a new and stronger **Fugitive Slave Law**, which required northerners to return runaway slaves to southern plantation owners.

Although President Taylor opposed the compromise, he unexpectedly died most likely from cholera in 1850 before he could veto it. Instead, Vice President **Millard Fillmore** became president and signed the compromise into law in September 1850.

Significance of the Compromise

The Compromise of 1850 benefited the North far more than the South:

- California's admission tipped the precious sectional balance in the Senate in favor of the North with sixteen free states to fifteen slave states.

- California's admission to the Union as a free state set a precedent in the West against the expansion of slavery.

- Southerners conceded to end the slave trade in Washington, D.C.

- The compromise averted civil war for ten more years, allowing the North to develop industrially.

Though the compromise granted Californians popular sovereignty, meaning they were allowed to decide for themselves whether to allow slavery, northerners knew that slavery would never take root in the West. Cotton couldn't grow in the arid western climate, and therefore the need for slaves would not be as great as it was in the South.

> *Even though the agreement clearly favored northerners, southerners were willing to make so many concessions because they truly believed the Compromise of 1850 would end the debate over slavery. This belief turned out to be very far from the truth.*

Northern Reaction to the Fugitive Slave Law

The new Fugitive Slave Law only fanned the abolitionist flame instead of relieving sectional tensions. Even though most white Americans in the North harbored no love for blacks, they didn't want to re-enslave those who had escaped to freedom. Consequently, armed mobs of northerners sometimes attacked slave catchers to free captured slaves. On one occasion, it took several hundred troops and a naval ship to escort a single captured slave through the streets of Boston and back to the South to prevent mobs from freeing him. The law helped transform abolitionism from a radical philosophy into a mainstream movement in the North.

The Underground Railroad

Even though very few slaves actually escaped to the North, the mere fact that northern abolitionists encouraged slaves to run away infuriated southern plantation owners. Despite this fury, there were those in the South who helped slaves escape to freedom. The **Underground Railroad** successfully ferried as many as several thousand fugitive slaves into the North and into Canada during these years. "Conductor" **Harriet Tubman** supposedly delivered several hundred slaves to freedom herself.

Harriet Beecher Stowe's 1852 novel *Uncle Tom's Cabin* also had a profound effect on northerners. Stowe sold hundreds of thousands of copies within just a few months and turned many northerners against slavery.

> *Harriet Beecher Stowe's* Uncle Tom's Cabin *turned northern public opinion against slavery and the South so much that when Abraham Lincoln met Stowe in 1863, he commented, "So you're the little woman who wrote the book that made this great war!"*

PIERCE AND EXPANSION IN 1852

After the Compromise of 1850, southerners quickly sought out new territories to expand the cotton kingdom. The election of **Franklin Pierce** to the presidency in 1852 only helped their cause. Pierce was a pro-South Democrat from New England and a firm believer in Manifest Destiny who also hoped to expand the United States.

Walker in Nicaragua

Pierce became particularly interested in acquiring new territories in Latin America during his presidency. He even went so far as to quietly support a coup in Nicaragua led by southern adventurer **William Walker**, who hoped that Pierce would annex Nicaragua as Polk had annexed Texas in 1844. The plan failed, however, when several other Latin American countries sent troops to remove Walker from power.

Cuba, Japan, and the Gadsden Purchase

Pierce also threatened to steal Cuba from Spain in a letter called the **Ostend Manifesto**. His plans failed when northern journalists received a leaked copy of the letter and published it in 1854. Despite these failures, Pierce did acquire 30,000 square miles of New Mexican territory from Mexico in the **Gadsden Purchase** in 1853 and successfully opened Japan to American trade later that year.

The Kansas–Nebraska Crisis

To prevent railroad developers from building a transcontinental railroad through the South and Southwest, which would aid the spread of slavery, Illinois senator **Stephen Douglas** proposed instead to build the line farther north through the vast unorganized territory west of the Mississippi River. Douglas proposed the **Kansas–Nebraska Act** in 1854 to create two new territories, Kansas and Nebraska, North of the 36° 30' parallel, as the law stipulated that developers could only lay railroad tracks in states or in federal territories. Because Douglas knew that southerners would never approve two new free territories, he instead declared that **popular sovereignty** would determine whether Kansas and Nebraska would enter the Union as free or slave states.

Kansas-Nebraska Act

Slave state or territory
Free state or territory
Territory open to slavery

Douglas made an enormous error in proposing the Kansas–Nebraska Act. Southern Democrats and Whigs alike jumped at the opportunity to open northern territories to slavery and quickly passed the act. Northerners, however, felt outraged that Douglas and the southerners had effectively revoked the sacred Missouri Compromise of 1820, which banned slavery north of the 36° 30' parallel. Hundreds of riots and protests consequently erupted in northern cities, and many people began to feel that differences between the North and South had become irreconcilable.

The Kansas–Nebraska Act split both the Whig and Democratic parties into sectional factions as southern Whigs voted with the southern Democrats against their northern counterparts to pass the act through Congress. The Whig party never recovered from the split.

BLEEDING KANSAS

As soon as Congress passed the Kansas–Nebraska Act, thousands of proslavery Missourians crossed the state line into Kansas and claimed as much land as they could. Hoping to make Kansas another slave territory, these **"Border Ruffians"** also rigged elections and recruited friends and family in Missouri to cast illegal ballots. Others voted multiple times or threatened indifferent settlers to vote in favor of slavery. Shocked, northern abolitionists flocked to the state to establish their own free-soil towns.

The Pottawatomie Massacre

Violence eventually erupted when a group of Border Ruffians burned the free-soil (antislavery) town of Lawrence. In retaliation, a deranged abolitionist named **John Brown**, along with his own band of men, butchered five proslavery settlers in the **Pottawatomie Massacre**. No court ever punished Brown or his followers. Within a few months, Border Ruffians and free-soilers in **"Bleeding Kansas"** had become embroiled in a bloody civil war that foreshadowed the looming greater Civil War.

1848–1859

The Caning of Charles Sumner

The crisis in Kansas deeply shocked and divided Americans, as evidenced by the caning of Massachusetts senator **Charles Sumner** on the Senate floor. Incensed over an antislavery speech Sumner had delivered after violence erupted in Kansas, Congressman Preston Brooks from South Carolina mercilessly beat Sumner with his cane on the floor of the Senate. The beating nearly killed the Massachusetts senator, who ultimately left the Senate for several years to receive medical treatment. Southerners hailed Brooks as a hero, while northerners called him a barbarian. Violence on the floor of the Senate, and the vastly differing reactions to the violence, were more indicators that pro- and antislavery factions had moved beyond debate.

THE ELECTION OF 1856

Bleeding Kansas dominated the election of 1856, and parties nominated Kansas-neutral candidates in the hope of avoiding sectionalism. The Whig Party had by this time completely dissolved over the slavery and popular sovereignty question, and former Whigs in the North chose to unite with the Free-Soil Party and unionist Democrats to form the new **Republican Party**. There were three candidates for president in 1856:

- **John C. Frémont**, the new Republican-nominated adventurer, on a platform against the westward expansion of slavery.

- **James Buchanan**, the Democrat-nominated and relatively unknown who championed popular sovereignty (allowing states to decide for themselves whether to enter the Union as slave or free).

- **Millard Fillmore**, ex-president of the nativist **Know-Nothing Party**, on an anti-immigration platform.

Because most southern state legislatures threatened to secede from the Union if Frémont became president, Buchanan won easily. Many northerners, shocked by the violence in Kansas and unprepared for a larger civil war, ultimately voted for the Democrat in order to keep the Union intact, whether they agreed with popular sovereignty or not.

The South's political victory with Buchanan in 1856 actually helped ensure the North's military victory in the Civil War, as it gave the North more time to develop its manufacturing capabilities. The North's ability to manufacture guns, cannons, and other supplies proved vital to the Union victory and also highlighted the economic differences with the South, which had abundant resources but no way to manufacture the items that it needed.

1848–1859

THE LECOMPTON CONSTITUTION

Because abolitionist settlers and Border Ruffians couldn't agree on a territorial government in Kansas, they each established their own. The free-soil legislature resided in Topeka, and the proslavery government in Lecompton. After free-soilers boycotted a rigged election to choose delegates to draft a state constitution in 1857, proslavery settlers decided to write their own. After drafting the **Lecompton Constitution**, which permitted slavery and placed no restrictions on the importation of slaves into the territory, they then applied for statehood as a slave state.

President Buchanan immediately accepted the constitution and welcomed Kansas into the Union. The Republican-dominated Congress, however, refused to admit Kansas. Senator Douglas declared that Congress would only admit Kansas after honest elections had determined whether the state would be free or slave. The following year, an overwhelming number of Kansas voters flatly rejected the Lecompton Constitution in a referendum, and Kansas entered the Union as a free state in 1861.

Bleeding Kansas and the Lecompton Constitution revealed the inherent weakness of the idea of Popular Sovereignty, in which a popular vote would decide the slavery issue. The issue of slavery had become so charged with emotion that certifiable elections were almost impossible, as both sides seem willing to intimidate voters and illegally affect the outcome of elections.

Prelude to War

North-South relations worsened throughout Buchanan's four years in office. By 1859, civil war appeared inevitable.

THE DRED SCOTT CASE

In the 1840s, a Missouri slave named **Dred Scott** sued his master for his family's freedom on the grounds that they had lived with his master for several years in the free states north of the 36° 30' parallel. In fact, his wife and daughter had been born in the North but had become slaves as soon as they accompanied Scott back into the South. In 1857, the case landed in the Supreme Court, where Chief Justice Roger Taney and other conservative justices ruled that only citizens, not slaves, could file lawsuits in federal courts. Moreover, Taney declared the Missouri Compromise of 1820 unconstitutional because the government could not restrict the movement of private property.

Essentially, Taney and the Court argued that slaves had no legal rights because they were property. Taney hoped that the **Dred Scott Decision** in *Dred Scott v. Sanford* would permanently end the sectional debate over slavery.

Northern Backlash to Dred Scott

Instead, the Dred Scott ruling only exacerbated sectional tensions. Southerners praised the ruling while northerners recoiled in horror. Thousands took to the streets in the North to protest the decision, and many questioned the impartiality of the southern-dominated Supreme Court. Several state legislatures even nullified the decision and declared that their states would never permit slavery, no matter who ordered them to do so. Many also accused James Buchanan of bias when journalists uncovered that the president had pressured a northern Supreme Court justice into siding with Taney and the southerners.

THE LINCOLN-DOUGLAS DEBATES

In this atmosphere of national confusion, a relatively unknown former congressman named **Abraham Lincoln** challenged Stephen Douglas to a series of public debates in their home state of Illinois. Lincoln hoped to steal Douglas's seat in the Senate in the 1858 elections and to be the first to put the question of slavery to the voters. Douglas accepted Lincoln's offer and engaged Lincoln in a total of seven public debates in front of several thousand people. Lincoln denounced slavery as a moral wrong and voiced his desire to see the "peculiar institution" banned entirely in the West. At the same time, however, he also expressed his deep desire to preserve the Union.

Douglas, meanwhile, called Lincoln a radical abolitionist and argued in the **Freeport Doctrine** that only popular sovereignty would provide a democratic solution to resolving the slavery debate in the West. Even though Lincoln lost the Senate seat, the **Lincoln–Douglas Debates** made Lincoln a national figure.

JOHN BROWN'S RAID

On October 16, 1859, John Brown of Pottawatomie, Kansas, stormed an arsenal at **Harpers Ferry**, Virginia, with twenty other men hoping to spark a slave rebellion in Virginia and throughout the South. Strangely, the insane Brown had forgotten to inform any slaves of his intentions, and therefore no slaves rose up against their masters. Instead, Brown and his men found themselves trapped inside the arsenal and surrounded by federal troops. Brown eventually surrendered after a long and bloody standoff that killed more than half his men, including his own son.

After a speedy trial, a federal court convicted and hanged Brown. Before his death, the unwavering Brown dramatically announced that he'd gladly die if his death brought the nation closer to justice.

Reactions North and South

Southerners applauded Brown's execution, because his raid on Harpers Ferry had touched on the southerners' deepest fear: that the slaves would one day rise up against them. To them, Brown had been a criminal and a traitor of the worst kind. Northerners, however, mourned his death because they considered him an abolitionist martyr, especially after so boldly denouncing slavery with his final words. He instantly became a national hero and patriot, despite the fact that he'd clearly broken the law. The northerners' reaction shocked southerners, driving the two groups further apart.

1848–1859

Timeline

1846	David Wilmot proposes the Wilmot Proviso.
1848	The Mexican War ends.
	The Free Soil Party forms.
	Zachary Taylor is elected president.
1849	California petitions for admission to the Union.
1850	The Compromise of 1850 includes the passage of the Fugitive Slave Law.
	Taylor dies from cholera.
	Millard Fillmore becomes president.
1852	Franklin Pierce is elected president.
	Harriet Beecher Stowe publishes *Uncle Tom's Cabin*.
1854	Pierce threatens to acquire Cuba in the Ostend Manifesto.
	Stephen Douglas proposes the Kansas–Nebraska Act.
	The Republican Party forms.
1855	William Walker takes Nicaragua.
1856	The Bleeding Kansas crisis shocks northern abolitionists.
	The Pottawatomie Massacre foreshadows the Civil War.
	Charles Sumner is attacked in the Senate.
	James Buchanan is elected president.
1857	Buchanan accepts the Lecompton Constitution.
	The Supreme Court issues its Dred Scott decision.
	The Panic of 1857 hits.
1858	Congress rejects the Lecompton Constitution.
	Abraham Lincoln and Stephen Douglas debate slavery in Illinois.
1859	John Brown raids Harpers Ferry.

CHAPTER 9

The Civil War: 1860–1865

||||||||||||||||||||||||||||||||||||||||||||||||||||||||||

The Civil War was the most catastrophic event in American history. More than 600,000 Americans died in the war, more than all those who died in every other American war combined. Though the war was bloody and horrendous, sometimes pitting father against son, it ultimately brought the North and South closer together.

Since the signing of the Constitution, the North and the South had developed into two distinct regions with two distinct economies and social structures. They had grown apart and were especially divided over the institution of slavery and individual states' rights versus the federal government. The war ended both debates, ensuring that slavery would perish and that federal power would dominate over states' rights, settling the sectional debate once and for all.

The Civil War proved to the world that democracy worked. Lincoln recognized the historical significance of the war even before he had won. In his Gettysburg Address, he argued that the outcome of the Civil War would determine the fate of representative government for the entire world. In his own words, ". . . we here highly resolve . . . that government of the people, by the people, for the people, shall not perish from the earth."

Lincoln and Secession

Very little held the United States together in 1860: the political parties had dissolved into sectional parties, and even churches had split over the slavery issue. People in the North simply couldn't understand the South's insistence on expanding the "slavocracy" westward, while southerners thought that northerners wanted to completely destroy their way of life. As a result, Americans on both sides of the Mason-Dixon Line wondered and worried about who would become the next president in 1860.

ELECTION OF 1860

Four candidates contended for the presidency in the election of 1860:

- **Abraham Lincoln** ran on the Republican ticket in favor of higher protective tariffs and more internal improvements, with promises to maintain the Union at all costs.

- **Stephen A. Douglas** ran for the northern Democratic Party, also on a pro-Union platform.

- **John C. Breckinridge** ran as a southern Democrat in strong support of slavery.

- **John Bell** ran with a breakaway group of compromising Republicans on the Constitutional Union Party ticket.

Because none of the slave states even put Lincoln's name on the ballot, the election eventually became two sectional elections, with Lincoln versus Douglas in the North and Breckinridge and Bell in the South. In the end, Lincoln won the presidency with approximately 39 percent of the popular vote, all eighteen free states, and a clear majority of 180 votes in the Electoral College.

SECESSION

Immediately after the election, South Carolina's legislature convened a special convention and voted unanimously to secede from the Union. South Carolina then issued **"A Declaration of the Causes of Secession,"** which reviewed the threats against slavery and asserted that a sectional party had elected a president hostile to slavery. By February 1861, six other slave states had followed suit, including Mississippi, Florida, Alabama, Georgia, Louisiana, and Texas.

The Crittenden Compromise

Hoping to prevent war, Senator John Crittenden from Kentucky proposed another compromise. He suggested adding an amendment to the Constitution to protect slavery in all territories South of 36° 30'. Popular sovereignty would determine whether the southwestern territories would enter the Union as free or slave states. Conversely, all territories north of 36° 30' would be free. Many southerners contemplated this **Crittenden Compromise**, but Lincoln rejected it out of the belief that the people had elected him to prevent the westward expansion of slavery.

Lincoln's First Inaugural Address

In his **First Inaugural Address**, Lincoln reaffirmed the North's friendship with the South, stressed national unity, and asked southerners to abandon secession. Moreover, he declared secession illegal and vowed to maintain the Union at all costs.

Fort Sumter

After declaring their independence, South Carolina authorities demanded the immediate withdrawal of all U.S. troops from **Fort Sumter**, a small island in Charleston Harbor. When Lincoln didn't comply, South Carolina militiamen shelled the fort on April 12, 1861, until the garrison's commander surrendered. Not a single soldier died during the fight, leading many southerners to conclude that northerners lacked the will to fight. The fall of Fort Sumter also convinced Arkansas, North Carolina, Tennessee, and Virginia to secede. The war had begun.

NORTHERN AND SOUTHERN ADVANTAGES

In retrospect, Union victory seems to have been inevitable. The Confederate struggle was doomed, lost in the romantic imagery of a lost cause, a small southern band fighting against a larger northern force. Large-scale industrialization, an enormous population, more resources, more weaponry, and a better transportation network gave the North a huge advantage. The Union also featured an efficient Navy and had the ability to build more ships. The Union quickly used its Navy to its advantage and blockaded southern ports.

At the time, however, these northern advantages seemed negligible because the South had superior military leaders, a captive labor force, hope for help from Europe, and the benefit of fighting a defensive war on familiar soil. As a result, both the North and the South naively believed they could defeat the other quickly and easily.

> The Civil War brutally tore families apart. One of Senator Crittenden's sons, for example, served as a general in the Union army, while another served as a general in the Confederacy. Even Abraham Lincoln himself had a brother-in-law fighting for the South.

The North

The Fall of Fort Sumter prompted Lincoln to prepare for war. He called for volunteers to enlist in the army and navy, ordered a naval blockade of southern ports, and moved troops to protect Washington, D.C. Congress later passed a number of sweeping measures to help industrialists and bolster the national economy.

THE BORDER STATES

Only ten of the fourteen slave states followed South Carolina and seceded from the Union. The other four—Maryland, Delaware, Kentucky, and Missouri—remained loyal to the United States. West Virginia eventually seceded from Virginia in 1863 and joined the Union as a free state. These five **border states** were crucial to the North because they geographically split the North from the South. Additionally, if the North were able to keep control of the border states, then they would discredit the Confederacy's claim that the Union would emancipate all slaves. Maryland and Delaware also had many factories that could have doubled the South's industrial capabilities, and Maryland's secession would have isolated Washington, D.C., from the rest of the North.

To ensure these states' loyalty, Lincoln sometimes had to resort to force to prevent them from joining the Confederacy. He suspended the **writ of habeas corpus** in Maryland, allowing the government to arrest suspected Confederate sympathizers and hold them without trial, and declared martial law in 1861 after pro-Confederacy protestors attacked U.S. soldiers marching to Washington, D.C.

BENDING THE CONSTITUTION

Lincoln also faced opposition from people in the North. On one side, **Peace Democrats** accused him of starting an unjust war, while **Radical Republicans** in his own party accused him of being too soft on the Confederacy. Many on both sides also criticized him for usurping unconstitutional powers to achieve his goals. Among other actions, Lincoln had suspended the writ of habeas corpus, ordered a naval blockade of all southern ports without Congress's permission, increased the size of the army without Congress's consent, and authorized illegal voting methods in the border states to ensure they wouldn't secede.

Chief Justice Roger Taney of the Supreme Court deemed these actions unconstitutional, but Lincoln ignored him, believing that desperate times called for drastic measures. Congress and most northerners generally approved of his decisions anyway.

THE 1862 CONGRESS

Congress, for its part, legislated a flurry of progressive new laws as soon as the South seceded from the Union. Without any states-rights advocates, northern Republicans easily passed the following acts:

- **The Morrill Tariff Act** to help northern manufacturers by doubling the prewar tariff on imported goods

- **The Legal Tender Act** to create a stable national currency

1860–1865

- **The National Banking Act** to strengthen banks and enforce the Legal Tender Act

These acts gave the federal government unprecedented power over the economy and provided stability to the robust industrial economy in the North, both of which ultimately helped the North defeat the South.

THE DRAFT AND DRAFT RIOTS

In 1863, Congress also passed a conscription law to draft young men into the Union Army. The law demanded that men either join the army or make a $300 contribution to the war effort. Although designed to promote support for the war among the rich and poor alike, this "$300 rule" effectively condemned the poorer classes to military service. Thousands of urban poor people staged protests against the law in dozens of northern cities. Protests in New York escalated into a full-scale riot in mid-1863, when racist whites from the poorest neighborhoods burned and looted parts of the city. Protestors also murdered nearly 100 people in the **New York City Draft Riot** before federal troops arrived.

THE NORTHERN ECONOMY

Throughout the war, northern factories continued to pump out weapons, clothing, and supplies for Union soldiers. Manufacturers increased production of agricultural equipment to help the farmers in the West produce more wheat and corn to feed the troops. The fields in the West benefited from good weather throughout the war, while the South suffered from extreme drought.

Oil production and coal mining became big industries in the North during these years as well. Alternatively, because the South had only a limited number of factories, Confederate troops often fought with antiquated weapons in tattered homespun uniforms and had little to eat.

Northern Women

In the North, women organized the United States Sanitary Commission to provide medical relief and other services to soldiers.

Other northern women worked to help starving and homeless freed slaves. Several thousand northern women also worked as nurses.

Almost 400 women disguised themselves as men and fought in the war as soldiers. Dozens also worked as spies. Women in the North and in the South played an increasing role in society and in the economy with men and sons away at war.

The South

Delegates from the first seven secessionist states (South Carolina, Mississippi, Alabama, Georgia, Florida, Texas, and Louisiana) met in Montgomery, Alabama, in February 1861 to form the government of the new **Confederate States of America**. Using the U.S. Constitution as a template, they drafted a new constitution, chose Richmond, Virginia, to be the new capital, and selected Mississippi planter **Jefferson Davis** as the Confederacy's first president.

PRESIDENT DAVIS

Although Davis had more political experience than Lincoln (he'd served as secretary of war and as a U.S. senator), he proved to be a poor commander in chief. Unlike Lincoln, he didn't understand the importance of public opinion and as a result didn't connect well with voters. Moreover, his nervousness and refusal to delegate authority alienated many cabinet members, congressmen, and state governors. He often had difficulty controlling his own government.

FEDERATION VS. CONFEDERATION

Although the South used the U.S. Constitution as a model, the Confederate government differed radically from that of the United States, primarily because the drafters of the Confederate constitution wanted to protect the rights of the member states. To ensure that individual state governments would remain strong, southerners refused to give their federal government any real authority. In other words, the Richmond government more

1860–1865

closely resembled a loose organization of strongly independent states rather than the tightly knit federation of the United States.

Keeping the Confederacy Together

Because the individual state governments in the South had more power than the central government, Davis had trouble controlling the states and coordinating the war. Lack of control proved to be the South's greatest weakness in the war for all of the following reasons:

- State governors refused to send their troops across state lines, even to assist in battle.

- State legislatures generally refused to support the Richmond government financially.

- A nation founded on secession couldn't logically withhold the right of member states to secede.

As a result, the central government in Richmond never had any money, lacked control over the national economy, couldn't maintain a strong national army, and couldn't even prevent states from seceding from the Confederacy during the final weeks of the war.

THE CONSCRIPTION ACT

The Richmond government passed the **Conscription Act of 1862** to force young men in all secessionist states into the national army. Like the draft in the North, the Confederate conscription law hurt poor people the most because it exempted wealthy planters and landowners.

Conscription Breeds Class Conflict

Although conscription eventually worked for the North despite the draft riots, it failed miserably in the South. Confederate regiments often suffered extremely heavy losses—and the poor southerners knew it. Poor soldiers resented the fact that they fought and bled in the war to support the rich whites who had started the war in the first place. They didn't see why they had to fight, and their own families had to starve, while the elites in Richmond ate well every night and slept safely and warmly in their beds. Not surprisingly, desertion unfolded as the southern military's greatest problem during the war.

COURTING GREAT BRITAIN

Davis hoped to end the war quickly by securing international recognition from Europe and possibly even a military alliance with Great Britain. He and most southerners realized that international recognition would legitimize the Confederacy and justify their cause. Moreover, an alliance with Britain would allow them to break the Union blockade that surrounded southern ports so that they could supply soldiers with weapons and food.

The Alabama and the Laird Rams

Because southern planters provided 75 percent of the cotton purchased by British textile manufacturers, Confederate policymakers thought Britain would certainly support them. For a time, Britain did harbor southern ships and even built Confederate warships, such as the **CSS Alabama**, which eventually captured or sank more than sixty Union ships on the high seas. British shipbuilders also agreed to build two ironclad warships with **Laird rams** that the Confederate navy could use to pierce the hulls of enemy ships. Despite this assistance from Britain, Davis never managed to secure either official recognition or the alliance he so badly needed. This failure was due mainly to the following:

- British manufacturers had warehouses full of excess cotton shipments and didn't need southern cotton so urgently.

- British manufacturers had found other sources of cotton in India and Egypt.

- The poorer classes in England opposed slavery and thus opposed helping the South.

- Lincoln threatened to declare war on Britain if Britain helped the Confederacy.

As a result, the Laird rams were eventually scrapped, and Richmond lost all hope for help from Europe.

1860–1865

COLLAPSE OF THE SOUTHERN ECONOMY

Unable to break through the Union blockade around the southern ports, and thus unable to buy goods or sell cotton, the South witnessed its economy slide into a deep depression in 1862. Worse, inflation skyrocketed when the individual states and private banks printed more cheap paper money to counter the depression. The depression was so bad that many desperate women looted the Confederate capital in the **Richmond Bread Riots** of 1863 in search of food and out of anger at the inept central government.

> The value of a single Confederate dollar hyperinflated so much that its value dropped by the minute. People standing in line to buy food quite often found themselves without enough money by the time they made it to the front of the line, because prices had changed. Tens of thousands of southerners consequently starved to death.

Southern Women

As the southern economy collapsed, so too did southern society. The war's drastic effect on southern lives tore into the very fabric of society. Women, for example, took on traditionally masculine jobs while the men fought on the battlefield. Some women ran farms and plantations, some ran businesses, and some had to supervise slaves. Wealthier women, in particular, were jarred by the harsh reality of physical labor and rationing. Southern women had to be incredibly innovative and resourceful to feed, clothe, and shelter their families every day.

The Early Years of the War

Both the North and South hurried to create an army and navy after the fall of Fort Sumter, while thousands of men quickly enlisted out of fear they'd miss the fight. The initial enthusiasm and optimism, however, faded as soon as the "ninety-day war" turned into the bloodiest conflict in American history.

THE FIRST BATTLE OF BULL RUN

The first significant battle of the Civil War occurred at Manassas Junction, thirty miles southwest of Washington, D.C., in 1861. Civilians from both sides attended to watch the show, some even with picnic lunches. The battle proved far bloodier than anyone had expected when the Union soldiers fled and left several thousand dead and wounded behind. Dismayed, northerners buckled down for a long and bitter war, while southerners emerged with a false sense of strength.

THE BATTLE OF SHILOH

Just as the First Battle of Bull Run had shocked northerners, the Battle of Shiloh in April 1862 shattered southerners' hope for a quick and easy victory. Union General **Ulysses S. Grant** engaged Confederate forces at Shiloh, Tennessee, in a battle that killed tens of thousands of men. The eventual victory demonstrated Lincoln's unbending resolve to preserve the Union.

NAVAL BATTLES

The Confederate navy tried to break through the U.S. Navy's blockade with their new ironclad ship, the *Virginia*. Formerly an old Union warship named the *Merrimack*, southerners had salvaged the ship and refitted it with iron armor to make it impervious to cannonballs. The Union eventually developed its own ironclad, the *Monitor,* to destroy the *Virginia*. The two warships engaged in a battle in the Chesapeake Bay in 1862, and though neither ship achieved a clear victory, the so-called **Battle of the Ironclads** marked the beginning of a new era in naval warfare.

The Union Navy continued to tighten its grip on the South and eventually freed the lower Mississippi by seizing New Orleans from the Confederates. The Navy then began working its way up the Mississippi River to tear the Confederacy in two.

THE BATTLE OF ANTIETAM

In September 1862, Union and Confederate forces engaged each other in the **Battle of Antietam**. **Robert E. Lee**, the

1860–1865

Confederate General, trying to move the war into the North, had crossed the Potomac with 40,000 men. Union General **George McClellan** moved his troops to meet Lee in western Maryland. Tens of thousands of soldiers died during the single bloodiest day of the entire war. An aide to Union General George McClellan had actually found Lee's battle plan prior to the engagement, but McClellan chose not to make full use of the information. Despite this missed opportunity, Lee was eventually forced to move his tattered army back across the Potomac to Virginia.

Lincoln Fires McClellan

As commander of the Army of the Potomac in Washington, D.C., George McClellan was the highest-ranking general in the Union army even though he had not yet reached forty. Despite his popularity with the troops, the civilian leaders in Washington disliked him because he seemed to avoid fighting battles. Lincoln needed military victories and wanted to end the war as quickly as possible—he knew voters wouldn't support a long and drawn-out war.

To make matters worse, as the war entered its second year, McClellan grew increasingly critical of Lincoln and the Republicans. He made personal jabs against the president in public and privately speculated that only he, personally, could end the war and save the Union. Lincoln eventually fired the disobedient and overly cautious McClellan and filled his post with several other incompetent generals before finally naming Ulysses S. Grant commander of all Union forces.

Antietam's Significance

Lee's failure at Antietam proved incredibly costly for the South because it convinced Britain and France not to support the Confederacy in the Civil War. Without international recognition or military assistance, Davis had little hope of breaking the Union blockade or defeating the Union army. The North's victory at Antietam also gave Lincoln the opportunity to issue the Emancipation Proclamation.

EMANCIPATION

Lincoln decided in 1862 to emancipate the slaves held in areas under Confederate control for three reasons:

- Slave labor helped sustain the Confederacy economically.

- Turning the war into a moral cause would boost support for the war in the North.

- Emancipation would ensure that Britain and France would not enter the war.

> *Although Lincoln did view slavery as a moral evil, he issued the Emancipation Proclamation not out of love for blacks, but because he thought it would help the Union defeat the Confederacy. In fact, he once remarked, "If I could save the Union without freeing any slave, I would do it; and if I could save it by freeing all the slaves, I would do it; and if I could do it by freeing some and leaving others alone, I would also do that. What I do about Slavery and the colored race, I do because I believe it helps to save this Union."*

Emancipation Proclamation

Although first issued in September 1862, the **Emancipation Proclamation** actually took effect on January 1, 1863. The proclamation:

- Freed all slaves behind Confederate lines

- Did not free any slaves in the border states

- Allowed free blacks to join the U.S. army and navy

Slavery had been at the root of every sectional conflict since delegates had made the Three-Fifths Compromise at the Constitutional Convention in 1787. Lincoln needed to cure the disease that had caused the war, not just treat the symptoms. Even though the proclamation didn't emancipate slaves in the border states—Lincoln didn't want any of them to secede in anger—it did mark the beginning of the end for the "peculiar institution" for every state in the Union. Democrats, meanwhile, criticized Lincoln for wedding the goals of emancipation and reunification.

1860–1865

About 180,000 African Americans served in the United States Colored Troops division, or roughly 10 percent of the army. Around 30,000 more blacks served in the U.S. Navy, making one out of every four sailors African American.

The Turning Point

The year 1863 marked a turning point in the war and the beginning of the end for the Confederacy. Not coincidentally, it was also the year that Lincoln's search for a capable general ended with the selection of Ulysses S. Grant.

SIEGE OF VICKSBURG

Ulysses S. Grant was a General in the Union Army at the beginning of 1863, in charge of troops trying to gain control of the Mississippi River. Grant turned the tide of the war in the West after laying siege to the port city of Vicksburg, Mississippi, on the Mississippi River. Having been unable to conquer Confederate forces protecting the city, Grant chose instead to merely surround the city and wait until starvation forced the Confederates to surrender, which they did on July 4, 1863, Independence Day.

Many historians agree that the surrender of Vicksburg was the most important Union victory of the war. The surrender gave the Union control of the Mississippi River and split the Confederacy in half. Subsequently, Lincoln promoted the victorious Grant to commander of all Union forces.

BATTLE OF GETTYSBURG

As fate would have it, the Union achieved not one, but two major victories on Independence Day in 1863. While Grant was accepting Vicksburg's surrender in Mississippi, Union forces were repelling Robert E. Lee's invasion into Pennsylvania at the **Battle of Gettysburg**. After three days of some of the bloodiest fighting in the war, Lee retreated back to Confederate territory, leaving a

Unlike his southern counterpart Robert E. Lee, Ulysses S. Grant lacked a distinguished pedigree and had been only an average student at West Point. In fact, he'd even been court-martialed and discharged from the army for being drunk while on duty. He later volunteered in a local militia when the Civil War broke out, where he eventually caught Lincoln's eye. Grant achieved so many victories on the battlefield that when critics accused him of alcoholism, President Lincoln merely retorted, "Find out what he is drinking and send a case of it to my other generals."

third of his entire army among the 50,000 soldiers that lay dead or wounded on the battlefield.

*Lincoln commemorated the Union victory at Gettysburg with a short speech simply known as the **Gettysburg Address**. In the speech, Lincoln argued that the outcome of the Civil War would be of the utmost importance for the entire world because it would prove whether democracy could work.*

Death Knell for the South

Lee's defeat at Gettysburg crushed the South: twice the South had invaded the North, and twice it had failed (at Antietam and Gettysburg). The loss of the Mississippi at the Battle of Vicksburg proved even more damaging in the long run because it deprived southerners of their primary mode of transportation in the West.

The Union victories also boosted morale and support for the war in the North and increased Lincoln's popularity. In addition, the Union blockade's chokehold on the South had finally begun to take its toll on the southern economy. By 1863, the Confederacy couldn't trade cotton for war supplies or food. Still, Davis continued to wage war for two more years hoping that chance, providence, or Great Britain would help him.

Davis continued to fight in the hope that a long and protracted war would eventually turn northern public opinion against Lincoln and the war itself. He particularly hoped Lincoln would lose his bid for reelection in 1864 to the Peace Democrats, who would end the war and leave the South alone.

1860–1865

The Final Year

As the fighting dragged on into its fourth year, Lincoln felt increasing pressure to end the war. He knew that even the fieriest abolitionists couldn't tolerate much more bloodshed. As a result, Lincoln put more pressure on his generals to bear down on the Confederacy with as much military might as possible and end the war quickly.

SHERMAN'S MARCH TO THE SEA

Abraham Lincoln and Ulysses S. Grant knew the South had to be defeated soon if they ever hoped to restore the Union. In 1864, Grant ordered his close friend and fellow general **William Tecumseh Sherman** to take a small force through the heart of the Deep South and destroy everything in his path. Grant hoped that this destruction would bring the South to its knees. Sherman embarked on his famous **March to the Sea** that summer, burning the city of Atlanta and then marching toward Savannah, Georgia. Along the way, he destroyed railroads, burned homes, razed crops, and looted, plundered, and pillaged the entire countryside. Sherman eventually seized Savannah and then marched northward to South Carolina.

> Sherman fought a **total war** against the South, waging war directly on civilians by plundering, marauding, and destroying the landscape. He hoped that extreme hardship would eventually break the southerners' will to continue fighting and force them to surrender.

GROWING OPPOSITION IN THE NORTH

A growing number of **Peace Democrats** had meanwhile begun to call for an immediate end to the war. More commonly known as **Copperheads**, after the poisonous snake, these Democrats believed that Lincoln and his generals had adequately demonstrated the futility of the war. Many Copperheads in the pro-southern **"Butternut region"** in Ohio, Indiana, and Illinois felt outraged that Lincoln had turned the conflict into a war over slavery. **Radical Republicans** in his own party criticized Lincoln because they thought the Emancipation Proclamation should have freed all slaves South *and* North.

THE ELECTION OF 1864

As a result, bitterness and uncertainty clouded the crucial election of 1864. Democrats who supported the war joined Republicans in giving Lincoln a lukewarm nomination for a second term, despite opposition from the radicals. Lincoln chose War Democrat Andrew Johnson from the conquered state of Tennessee as his running mate in the hope that Johnson would win more votes from Democrats in the North.

Together, Lincoln and Johnson campaigned on a simple platform for continuation of the war until the South surrendered unconditionally. Peace Democrats, on the other hand, nominated former general George McClellan on an equally simple platform calling for immediate peace. In the end, Lincoln won with 55 percent of the popular vote.

A Mandate for Unconditional Surrender

The election of 1864 was in many ways the most crucial event during the entire conflict. The election determined the outcome of the war; if McClellan and the Peace Democrats had won, the war would have ended immediately. The election ruined the Confederacy's last hope for survival. Lincoln's reelection provided a clear mandate from northern voters for unconditional surrender. Surprisingly, many of the soldiers themselves—Democrat as well as Republican—had voted for Lincoln because they wanted to finish what they had begun.

1860–1865

THE SOUTH COLLAPSES

The South, meanwhile, was on the brink of collapse. The naval blockade, refusals for assistance from Britain, Sherman's March, internal class conflicts, and the complete meltdown of southern society and the economy had taken their toll. Thousands of men deserted the army daily as thousands more southern women and children starved at home. Jefferson Davis tried desperately to hold his government together, but none of the states would cooperate. In the final month of the war, the South grew so desperate that they even began offering slaves their freedom if they would enlist in the Confederate army.

The Hampton Roads Conference

In one final attempt to save the Confederacy, Davis requested a ceasefire to discuss peace. Lincoln agreed and sent a delegation to the **Hampton Roads Conference** in February 1865. Negotiations quickly ended, however, because Lincoln refused to settle for anything less than unconditional surrender, which Davis refused to give.

APPOMATTOX

In April 1865, Grant's forces broke through Robert E. Lee's defenses and burned the Confederate capital at Richmond. With his men half starved and heavily outgunned, Lee chose to surrender rather than send his remaining troops to their death. Grant accepted Lee's unconditional surrender at Appomattox Courthouse on April 9, 1865 and provided the southerners with food for their march home. Union troops captured Jefferson Davis and other ranking Confederates as they tried to flee Virginia. The Civil War had ended.

THE ASSASSINATION OF LINCOLN

Lincoln lived just long enough to see the war's end. **John Wilkes Booth**, a southern sympathizer, assassinated the president on April 14, 1865, as he sat with his wife in a box at Ford's Theater in Washington, D.C., mere days after Grant accepted Lee's surrender at Appomattox. Booth shot Lincoln and then jumped down to the stage below, shouting, "*Sic semper tyrannis*," a Latin phrase meaning "thus always to tyrants."

Timeline

1860	Abraham Lincoln is elected president.
	South Carolina secedes from the Union.
1861	Alabama, Arkansas, Florida, Georgia, Louisiana, Mississippi, North Carolina, Tennessee, Texas, and Virginia secede.
	North Carolina, Tennessee, Texas, and Virginia secede.
	South Carolina attacks Ft. Sumter.
	The first significant battle of the Civil War occurs at the Battle of Bull Run.
1862	Congress passes the Legal Tender Act.
	Confederacy passes the Conscription Act.
	Congress passes the Confiscation Act.
	The Union defeats the Confederacy at the Battle of Antietam.
1863	Lincoln's *Emancipation Proclamation* takes effect.
	Congress passes the National Bank Act.
	Drafts are initiated in the North.
	Southern women loot the Confederate capital in the Richmond Bread Riots in Richmond, Virginia.
	Nearly 100 people are murdered in the Draft Riots in New York City.
	The Battle of Gettysburg crushes the South.
	The Siege of Vicksburg gives the Union control of the Mississippi River.
1864	Grant takes command of Union troops.
	Lincoln is reelected.
	Sherman begins his March to the Sea.
1865	Davis proposes Hampton Roads peace conference.
	Robert E. Lee surrenders to Grant at Appomattox Courthouse.
	Abraham Lincoln is assassinated.

CHAPTER 10

Reconstruction: 1862–1877

||||||||||||||||||||||||||||||||||||||||||||||||||||||

Despite the Union's victory on the battlefield, sectional differences between North and South still seethed, and the prospect of rebuilding and healing the United States amid such chaos and destruction was daunting. The competing needs of southern blacks and whites—as well as those of northern emigrants to the region— made the challenges of reestablishing the United States as a cohesive and functional country largely insurmountable. This process, which came to be known as Reconstruction, proved virtually endless for those involved. Local, state, and national leaders wrestled with complex questions, such as how to mend the broken South and how a new society would embrace both Confederate elites and former slaves.

Modern historians regard Reconstruction as a failure. Although Radical Republicans restored the Union politically, they failed to protect African Americans from abuse by white southern elites. By the end of the 1870s, former Confederates had reclaimed power in the southern states and virtually reinstated slavery.

Wartime Reconstruction

Historians refer to efforts to reunite and reform the nation during the Civil War as a dress rehearsal for Reconstruction. During this phase, President **Abraham Lincoln**, Congress, and military leaders issued a number of proclamations, acts, and field orders related to the ongoing war. Such actions fueled ongoing conflicts over issues including:

* Emancipation and the rights of African Americans

* The fate of the Confederacy

* Landownership in the South

* The transformation of the southern labor system and economy

LINCOLN'S PROCLAMATIONS

President Lincoln wanted to win the war without annihilating the Old South, whereas Congress wanted to dramatically transform southern society. Still, Lincoln's ultimate goal was to reunite the nation. He wanted to abolish slavery because he knew that this would cripple the southern economy; on the other hand, Lincoln believed emancipation should unfold gradually so as not to alienate the proslavery border states in the Union. Lincoln issued two proclamations during the war addressing reunification and emancipation: the **Emancipation Proclamation** and the **Proclamation of Amnesty and Reconstruction**.

Emancipation Proclamation

Lincoln earned the moniker "the Great Emancipator" for the **Emancipation Proclamation** he issued on January 1, 1863. Despite the nickname, Lincoln's proclamation only liberated slaves in the states at war with the Union. Not surprisingly, months passed before many of those slaves found out they were free. The proclamation did *not* free any slaves in the border states or in areas of the Confederacy occupied by the Union. Nonetheless, Lincoln's proclamation made slavery a central issue of the war.

The proclamation deprived the Confederacy of its labor force and thus crippled the region's economy. It also legalized the enlistment of freedmen, who wanted to fight to keep their freedom.

This influx of men reinvigorated the Union military and greatly contributed to the defeat of the Confederate forces.

SECEDED STATES

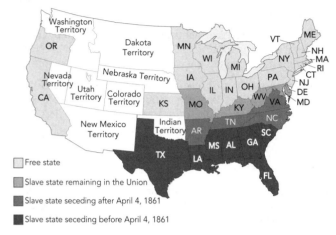

Free state

Slave state remaining in the Union

Slave state seceding after April 4, 1861

Slave state seceding before April 4, 1861

> In September 1862, Lincoln issued an ultimatum to the Confederacy after a major Union victory at Antietam. After only one day of fighting, a cumulative total of 23,000 soldiers lay dead or wounded. Lincoln told the Confederacy to either return to the Union by January 1, 1863, or all women, men, and children enslaved in rebellious states would be "forever free."

Proclamation of Amnesty

Lincoln outlined his postwar vision for reunification when he issued the **Proclamation of Amnesty and Reconstruction** in December 1863. More commonly known as **Lincoln's Ten-Percent Plan**, the proclamation promised the following:

- The pardoning of all Confederates who signed an oath of allegiance to the United States, excluding government and military leaders.

- The recognition of any southern state government, provided that 10 percent of the state's voters in the election of 1860 pledged their allegiance to the United States. Arkansas, Louisiana, and Tennessee reorganized under these terms in 1864 but were not recognized by Congress.

- The protection of lower-ranking Confederate officers from trial and execution for treason

- The return of political rights and land confiscated by the federal government to the Confederates after they received pardons and accepted the emancipation of black people

- The prosecution of Confederate military and civilian officials and others who left federal positions to join the Confederacy. Ex-Confederates who killed or tortured Union soldiers, both black and white, would also be denied amnesty.

CONGRESS'S ACTS

Congress favored a more aggressive approach to freeing the slaves than President Lincoln. Even though Republicans in Congress never completely agreed on any issue during Reconstruction, almost all of them wanted to punish the South.

Freeing Slaves in the District of Columbia

In April 1862, Congress passed legislation to free enslaved African Americans in Washington, D.C. Lincoln consented, but only reluctantly, as the **First Confiscation Act** of 1861, guaranteed compensation to the District's slave owners. In July 1862, Congress also passed the **Second Confiscation Act**, which freed all blacks enslaved by government officials in Confederate states. The Confiscation Act of 1862 also freed all southern slaves who sought refuge behind Union lines.

The Wade-Davis Bill

Republicans in Congress led by **Thaddeus Stevens** and **Benjamin Wade** opposed Lincoln's Ten-Percent Plan because they wanted to punish the southerners who had caused the war. Furthermore, they sought to pass additional legislation to protect free blacks. In response to Lincoln's Proclamation of Amnesty and Reconstruction, Wade and Congressman **Henry Winter Davis** of Maryland sponsored the **Wade-Davis Bill** to appoint provisional military

Some 180,000 African Americans served in the Union forces during the Civil War. Perhaps the most famous of these was **Harriet "the Moses of Her People" Tubman**, who personally led as many as 300 slaves to freedom via the Underground Railroad. Recruited by military officials in 1862, she taught survival skills to black refugees in the South Carolina Sea Islands. Tubman also nursed wounded soldiers, served as a spy, and even led troops into battle. Despite her commitment, Tubman never received pay for her services.

governors in the former Confederate states. The bill also required that more than 50 percent of white men in each state take an oath of allegiance to the Union before a new constitution could be drafted. Additionally, this new constitution would have to renounce both slavery and secession and disenfranchise all former Confederate leaders.

Although Congress passed the Wade-Davis Bill in July 1864, Lincoln thought it too radical and refused to sign it. Hoping to avoid the controversy of an outright veto, he simply **"pocket vetoed"** the bill by withholding his signature until Congress adjourned for the year. Without Lincoln's signature, the Wade-Davis Bill died.

UNION MILITARY LEADERS' ACTIONS

At the beginning of the Civil War, many Union commanders supported slavery. Some even returned escaped slaves to their Confederate owners, reasoning that they were fighting to preserve the Union, not to free black people. But over time, a number of northern military officers began to advocate emancipation. Many petitioned for emancipation in order to rid themselves of the responsibility for the thousands of black refugees, or **"contraband of war,"** that flooded Union camps. Consequently, commanders often issued special field orders to help them defeat the Confederacy by depriving the South of its slaves. After the war and the end of slavery, these generals led the way in redefining the status of blacks in the South. Military leaders also made decisions regarding southern landownership and helped establish a free labor system.

The Port Royal Experiment

In January 1862, **Brigadier General William Sherman** asked the federal government to send teachers to instruct the former slaves on the Sea Islands of South Carolina. This request eventually evolved into the **Port Royal Experiment**, which became a model for educating black people and organizing black communities. Later that year, Lincoln officially emancipated black Sea Islanders, and the U.S. Army began redistributing abandoned plantation lands to the freedmen. In exchange, many blacks on the Sea Islands produced cotton for Union factories and enlisted in the military.

Black and white missionaries from the North also established a string of schools on the islands. These schools educated thousands of former slaves and inspired others to found schools for freed people throughout the South. Unfortunately, federal support for the schools waned after Lincoln's assassination.

General David Hunter and General Order 11

The Union's **General David Hunter** twice defied Lincoln's decree regarding the status of blacks during the war. In March 1862, he ignored the ban on blacks in the military and recruited black men for a special combat unit. In May 1862, he issued **General Order 11** to emancipate slaves in Georgia, Florida, and South Carolina. Lincoln disbanded the combat unit and nullified the order.

General William Sherman and Special Field Order 15

In January 1865, after his infamous **March to the Sea** through Georgia, **General William Sherman** met with twenty black leaders in Savannah to determine the needs of former slaves. The freedmen told Sherman and Secretary of War **Edwin M. Stanton** that black people wanted land. A few days later, Sherman issued **Field Order 15** to redistribute confiscated land in forty-acre parcels to blacks in Florida and on the Sea Islands off Georgia and South Carolina. Only blacks were allowed to settle these lands.

1862–1877

In less than a month, more than 40,000 freed people received land from the government. The new landowners also received surplus government mules. After the war ended, President Andrew Johnson allowed white planters to reclaim these lands. As a result, thousands of blacks became destitute.

> Sherman's generosity led freed blacks throughout the South to believe that they would all receive "forty acres and a mule" as repayment for centuries of servitude. However, most freed blacks never received this. Consequently, this phrase has come to signify an empty promise.

The Freedmen's Bureau

General Oliver O. Howard ran the **Bureau of Freedmen, Refugees, and Abandoned Lands**. More commonly known as the **Freedmen's Bureau**, this agency was created a month before the war ended to provide food, clothing, and medicine to freed people and poor whites. The Bureau also founded the **Freedmen's Bank** and established more schools. Although the Bureau provided freed people some protection against aggressive whites who tried to take their land and exploit their labor, the organization ultimately undermined blacks.

Essentially, the agency steered freed people into the abusive free-labor systems that replaced slavery. southern state and local governments supported these systems in order to meet the region's demand for food and jumpstart the agrarian economy. The Freedmen's Bureau was perpetually underfunded by Congress and thus never had the manpower or resources equal to the huge task facing it.

Presidential Reconstruction

When the Civil War ended in April 1865, President Lincoln asserted that the former Confederate states merely had been "out of their proper practical relation with the Union." In fact, Lincoln firmly believed that these states "had never really left the Union." A few days after Lincoln made this statement, on April 14, 1865, Confederate sympathizer **John Wilkes Booth** assassinated Lincoln. Lincoln's vice president, **Andrew Johnson**, immediately became president. Surprisingly, Johnson pardoned thousands of Confederate leaders and championed the restoration of white supremacy in the South.

An outraged Congress quickly established the **Committee of Fifteen** to devise progressive new plans for Reconstruction. Republicans fought Johnson's repeated attempts to block constitutional amendments and congressional acts meant to protect freed people and punish ex-Confederates. In the end, Republicans' triumph over the president paved the way for Radical Reconstruction.

JOHNSON'S PLAN

A former Tennessee slaveholder, President Johnson did everything in his power to reinstate southern elites. He implemented a three-pronged strategy to stymie congressional attempts to reform the South:

1. **The Amnesty Proclamation** to pardon former Confederate leaders. This proclamation allowed these elites to reclaim land given to freed people and returned white supremacists to power in the state governments.
2. The vetoing of all legislation designed to grant and protect African Americans' civil liberties.
3. The rallying of conservatives and reactionaries to halt all attempts to change the social order of the South.

Johnson's Amnesty Proclamation

Johnson shrewdly issued and implemented his Amnesty Proclamation during the congressional recess from May to early December 1865. The proclamation resembled Lincoln's Ten-Percent Plan. For example, it required that southern states approve the **Thirteenth Amendment** to abolish slavery before they could rejoin the Union. But Johnson added a couple of stipulations of his own. He denied amnesty to rich Confederates (i.e., those worth more than $20,000) and required the repudiation of all debts that were owed by the Union to Confederates.

Most important, he firmly believed that he should reconstruct the Union without the help of Congress.

President Johnson also accepted Reconstruction governments in Arkansas, Louisiana, and Tennessee created in 1862 during Lincoln's presidency. Moreover, he made governors out of **native Unionists** who had remained loyal during the war. Despite his professed hatred for Confederate leaders, Johnson pardoned 13,000 people, including former Confederate military and civilian officials and allowed the secessionist states to write new constitutions, even if 10 percent of voters had not taken the loyalty oath. As a result, Johnson readmitted all eleven Confederate states into the Union by December 1865 and prematurely declared Reconstruction over.

Johnson's Presidential Vetoes

Johnson repeatedly exercised his right to veto legislation of the Republican Congress. Most of this legislation was passed to elevate the social and political status of black people. Congress overrode the following of Johnson's vetoes:

- **The Civil Rights Act of 1866**, which granted citizenship to blacks and safeguarded their civil liberties

- **The Fourteenth Amendment**, which safeguarded blacks' citizenship rights and reduced congressional representation of states that denied black males voting rights

- **The Freedmen's Bureau Bill**, which extended the life of the agency and increased its authority to help freed people and poor whites

Race Riots and "Swing Around the Circle"

Many whites in the South responded furiously to the Civil Rights Act of 1866 and the Fourteenth Amendment. Riots erupted in Memphis, Tennessee, and New Orleans, and hundreds of blacks were murdered. The rampant racism and violence shocked Americans in the North who turned an accusing eye toward Johnson for his leniency.

The president in turn blamed the radicals in Congress in his infamous **"Swing Around the Circle"** speeches. Traveling throughout the country, he often got carried away lambasting Republicans, prowar Democrats, blacks, and anyone else who challenged him. As a result, he blackened the Democratic Party's already tarnished reputation and inadvertently persuaded many northerners to vote Republican in the 1866 Congressional elections.

"Swing Around the Circle" refers to the pattern in which Johnson toured the country in 1866 in a mostly futile attempt to gain support among northern voters. He visited Philadelphia, New York City, upstate New York, and Ohio, then finally returned to Washington, D.C. This tour was incredibly unsuccessful.

Radical Reconstruction

The race riots and murders combined with Johnson's "Swing Around the Circle" campaign convinced northerners that the president could no longer be trusted to reconstruct the Union. Instead, they turned to Republicans, who consequently swept the 1866 congressional elections. **Radical Republicans** and their moderate allies dominated both the House of Representatives and the Senate and therefore had the ability to override any presidential vetoes. As a result, their ascension to office in early 1867 marked the beginning of **Congressional Reconstruction**, sometimes known as **Radical Reconstruction**.

MILITARY RECONSTRUCTION

Congress began the task of reorganizing the South with the **First Reconstruction Act** in March 1867. Also known as the **Military Reconstruction Act** or simply the **Reconstruction Act**, this bill reduced the secessionist states' claim to conquered territories. Congress carved the South into five military districts, which were each governed by a Union general in charge of the Reconstruction process.

Congress also declared martial law and dispatched troops to keep the peace and protect persecuted blacks. All former secessionist states had to once again draft a new constitution, ratify the **Fourteenth Amendment**, and provide suffrage to blacks. To safeguard black voting rights, Republicans passed the **Second Reconstruction Act,** placing Union troops in charge of voter registration. Congress overrode two presidential vetoes to pass these bills.

THE FIFTEENTH AMENDMENT

Radicals believed that giving blacks the right to vote was the only way to prevent southern elites from seizing power again. Even though Congress demanded that the southern states enfranchise blacks, Republicans still feared that whites might one day revoke this right. To prevent this, they decided to incorporate black suffrage into the Constitution itself: in 1869 they passed the **Fifteenth Amendment** to guarantee that all black males had the right to vote. Furthermore, Republicans made ratification a prerequisite for all southern states still awaiting readmission. Three-fourths of the states finally ratified the amendment in 1870.

Enfranchising Blacks in the South and North

The Fifteenth Amendment enfranchised not only blacks but also poor southern white males. Prior to the Civil War, all southern states had restricted the vote to landowners. This restriction excluded most white males—as well as blacks and women—from political participation. The amendment also forced reluctant northern states to enfranchise blacks. Even when most state constitutions in the South gave blacks the right to vote, most northern states still refused to do so. The Fifteenth Amendment changed the political status of blacks throughout the entire United States.

The Quest for Women's Suffrage

The passage of the Fifteenth Amendment in 1869 had an enormous effect on the women's suffrage movement as well. Prior to the Civil War, the quest for women's suffrage and abolition had been closely united, as both groups strove to achieve political and

1862–1877

civil rights for those not represented in politics. After the Union victory, many women like **Elizabeth Cady Stanton** and **Susan B. Anthony** thought they had won suffrage for both blacks and women. But radicals in Congress feared that if they granted the right to vote to all men *and* women, they would lose support in both the South and North. Consequently, many women felt betrayed by their exclusion from the Fifteenth Amendment.

REPUBLICANISM TAKES ROOT IN THE SOUTH

With their right to vote safeguarded, southern blacks flocked to register, and by the beginning of 1868, more than 700,000 freedmen had signed up. Not surprisingly, all declared themselves Republicans, as they identified the Democrats with secession and slavery. Almost the same number of landless white males registered.

Black Political Power

African-American civic societies and grassroots political organizations sprouted up everywhere. Most of them were led by prominent blacks who had been freedmen before the war. Black voters quickly dominated the electorate in South Carolina, Alabama, Louisiana, Florida, and Mississippi, giving the Republican Party control over the Reconstruction process in those states. The new voters also elected many black politicians to state legislatures throughout the South. Fourteen black politicians served in the House of Representatives, and Mississippians elected two blacks to the Senate.

JOHNSON TRIED AND ACQUITTED

Congress passed several bills in 1867 to limit President Johnson's power. The **Tenure of Office Act** sought to protect prominent Republicans within the Johnson administration by forbidding their dismissal without congressional authorization. Although the act applied to all office holders approved by Congress, radicals specifically wanted to keep Secretary of War Edwin M. Stanton in office to check Johnson's control over the military. In defiance, Johnson ignored the act, fired Stanton in the summer of 1867 during a congressional recess, and replaced him with Union General **Ulysses S. Grant**. Afraid that Johnson could effectively end military reconstruction in the South, Congress ordered the president to reinstate Stanton when it reconvened in 1868. Johnson refused, Grant subsequently resigned, and Congress put Stanton back in office over the president's objections.

Tired of presidential vetoes and obstruction to Congressional Reconstruction, House Republicans impeached Johnson by a vote of 126 to 47 for violating the Tenure of Office Act and slandering Congress. The Senate tried Johnson in May 1868 in front of a gallery of spectators. Radical Representatives **Thaddeus Stevens** and Benjamin Butler served as prosecutors but couldn't convince a majority of senators to convict the president. The final tally was one vote shy of a conviction.

Even though President Johnson had stubbornly opposed Congress, he had not violated the Constitution. Several Republican senators realized that radicals wanted to remove Johnson simply because he had disagreed with them over Reconstruction, not because of a technical violation of the Tenure of Office Act. No other president was impeached until Bill Clinton in 1998.

Reconstruction in the South

As the Union Army advanced deeper into southern territory during the war's end, more and more slaves enjoyed the fruits of freedom. The army did free some slaves, but most freed themselves by refusing to work and walking away. Tens of thousands of blacks, for example, followed Sherman's troops on his **March to the Sea** in 1864. The end of the war brought jubila- tion and celebrations. Thousands of blacks left their homes in search of lost family members, while many black couples took the opportunity to marry, knowing no one could ever forcibly separate them again.

Most former slaves faced considerable challenges with their newly acquired freedom. Despite the Radical Republicans' best efforts to protect their civil liberties and voting rights, the freed men and women still faced persecution from racist whites. By the end of Reconstruction blacks had freedom—but not equality.

> Sherman's **March to the Sea** was a sign that the Union victory was imminent. On November 12, 1864, he led his troops out of Atlanta toward the Atlantic coast, and the Confederacy could present no obstacle great enough to stop him.

CARPETBAGGERS AND SCALAWAGS

Many northerners jumped at opportunities in the South in the wake of Confederate General Lee's surrender in early April of 1865. These "**carpetbaggers**" (nicknamed for the large carpet bags many of them brought with them) came for a variety of reasons: to promote education, to modernize the South, and to seek their fortunes. White southern Unionists, or "**scalawags**," also played roles in achieving the same aims. Both carpetbaggers and scalawags served in legislatures in every reconstructed state.

THE BLACK CODES

White elitist regimes in the southern states did everything in their power to prevent blacks from gaining too much power. After Republicans in Congress passed the Civil Rights Act of 1866, every southern legislature passed laws to exert more control on African Americans. These **Black Codes** ranged in severity and outlawed everything from interracial marriage to loitering in public areas.

Southern whites passed these laws partly because they feared a free black population, especially in states where blacks outnumbered whites. Many also worried that freed slaves would terrorize their masters, rape white women, and ruin the economy. Most planter elites passed the codes simply to ensure that they would have a stable and reliable work force.

Black Codes often dictated that former slaves sign labor contracts for meager wages. Although Congress forced state legislatures to repeal the codes once the radicals took control of Reconstruction, whites still managed to subtly enforce them for years after Reconstruction had ended.

Black Codes differed from state to state but were all similar in the following ways:

- All blacks had to sign labor contracts.

- Blacks could not own land.

- Individuals accused of vagrancy who were unable to pay fines could be sentenced to hard labor on chain gangs.

- States could force orphaned children into apprenticeships that resembled slavery.

- Whites could physically abuse blacks without fear of punishment.

BLACK CHURCHES AND EDUCATION

Most freed men and women had a burning desire to educate their children. They recognized that knowledge (especially the previously forbidden ability to read and write) was power and that their futures depended upon it. The Freedmen's Bureau and former abolitionist groups from the North succeeded in founding schools for thousands of blacks. Because white clergymen had often upheld slavery in their sermons prior to the Civil War, many blacks went on to establish their own congregations.

THE SHARECROPPING SYSTEM

Blacks craved economic independence and resisted white efforts to consign them to chain gangs or wage labor on large plantations. Instead, they preferred the **sharecropping system**, in which former plantation owners divided their lands and rented each plot—or share—to a single black family. The family farmed its own crops in exchange for giving a percentage of the yield to the landowner. In fact, many families sharecropped on their former masters' lands. Landless whites also became sharecroppers for the elites, so that by 1880, almost all farmers in the South sharecropped.

THE KU KLUX KLAN

Violence also posed a serious threat to African Americans in the South. A secret white-supremacist society called the **Ku Klux**

1862–1877

Ironically, the new sharecropping system kept blacks tied to their small plots and indebted to white landowners in ways that closely resembled slavery. Cotton prices steadily declined in the postwar years, from roughly fifty cents per pound in 1864 to a little over ten cents a pound at the end of Reconstruction. With very little money, most black farmers could only purchase items on credit at the local shops. Consequently, blacks generally experienced very little real freedom.

Klan formed in Tennessee in 1866 to terrorize blacks. White-robed Klansmen would harass, beat, and lynch both blacks and white Republicans. They ordered blacks to stay away from voting polls and punished those who didn't obey; in one extreme case, Klansmen butchered several hundred black voters in Louisiana in 1868. Congress eventually passed the **Ku Klux Klan Act** of 1871, which allowed it to act against terrorist organizations. Still, racist violence continued to be a serious problem.

Grant's Presidency

As the presidential election of 1868 drew near, Republicans nominated Civil War hero **Ulysses S. Grant**. Grant had proven himself an effective leader in the army and served as a reminder that Republicans had won the war. Democrats nominated former governor of New York **Horatio Seymour**. Seymour hated emancipation, supported states' rights, and wanted to wrest control of Reconstruction out of Congress's hands. In the end, Grant received 214 electoral votes to Seymour's 80, but only 300,000 more popular votes. Republicans also maintained control of Congress. During the Grant years, Congress funded more projects and distributed more money than ever before in U.S. history.

A MULTITUDE OF SCANDALS

Scandal and corruption characterized Grant's two terms in office. Although the president himself was never involved, his lack of political experience hampered his ability to control other politicians.

The Fisk-Gould Gold Scandal

Scandal rocked Washington before Grant had even completed his first year in office. In 1869 the financial tycoons **Jim Fisk** and **Jay Gould** bribed many cabinet officials, including Grant's own brother-in-law, to overlook their attempt to corner the gold market. They even conned Grant himself into agreeing not to release any more of the precious metal into the economy. On September 24, 1869, they succeeded in inflating gold prices. The U.S. Treasury managed to prevent an economic catastrophe by releasing more gold into the economy, in spite of Grant's earlier promise.

The Crédit Moblier Scandal

Corruption also infected the railroads. In 1872, Union Pacific Railroad executives created a dummy construction company called **Crédit Moblier**. They then hired Crédit Moblier at outrageous prices to lay track. To protect their huge profits, the executives bribed several congressmen and even Vice-President **Schuyler Colfax** to keep quiet. Colfax ultimately resigned after an exposé revealed his shady dealings. Even though Grant had no involvement in the scandal, it nevertheless damaged his reputation.

The Whiskey Ring Scandal

Yet another scandal broke two years later in 1874, when investigators discovered that several Grant-appointed federal employees had skimmed millions of dollars from excise tax revenue. The president vowed to hunt down and punish all those involved in the **Whiskey Ring** but swallowed his harsh words upon discovering his own secretary's involvement.

THE ELECTION OF 1872

Fed up with scandals in Grant's administration, a significant number of Republicans broke from the radicals and moderates in Congress just before the 1872 elections. Known as **Liberal Republicans**, these men wanted to end corruption, restore the Union as quickly as possible, and downsize the federal government. They nominated *New York Tribune* editor **Horace Greeley** for the presidency.

1862–1877

Strangely enough, Democrats also nominated Greeley, because he opposed the army's presence in the South and wanted to end Reconstruction. Despite the scandals, radicals and moderates again nominated their war hero Grant. On Election Day, Grant easily won with 286 electoral votes to Greeley's 66, and received more than 700,000 more popular votes.

The Liberal Republicans

Led by businessmen, professionals, reformers, and intellectuals, Liberal Republicans helped shape politics in the postwar years. They disliked big government and preferred limited government involvement in the economy. Some historians have argued that the Liberal Republicans even opposed democracy because they detested universal manhood suffrage and didn't want to enfranchise blacks.

THE DEPRESSION OF 1873

Although Grant faced as many problems in his second administration as he had during his first, none were so catastrophic as the **Depression of 1873**. Bad loans and overspeculation in railroads and factories burst the postwar economic boom and forced millions of Americans onto the streets over the next five years. The poor clamored for cheap paper and silver money for relief, but Republicans refused to give in to their demands out of fear that cheap money would exacerbate inflation. Instead, they passed the **Resumption Act of 1875** to remove all paper money from the economy. The act helped end the depression in the long run, but it made the interim years more difficult to bear.

THE END OF RADICAL RECONSTRUCTION

The Resumption Act proved politically damaging for the Radical and moderate Republicans in Congress. Because they insisted on passing hard-money policies during a time when up to 15 percent of Americans had no work, many Republicans in the North voted with the Democrats in the 1874 congressional elections. Their votes, combined with white votes in the South, ousted many Republicans from Congress and gave the Democrats control of the House of Representatives for the first time since 1856. The remaining radicals in Congress suddenly found themselves commanding the weak minority party. In short, the elections of 1874 marked the end of Radical Reconstruction.

The End of Reconstruction

As the economy plummeted, so too did northerners' willingness to pursue Radical Reconstruction. Americans had neither the time nor the energy to worry about helping former slaves, punishing Ku Klux Klan terrorism, or readmitting states when so many of them didn't even have jobs. In fact, many in the North had grown tired of Radical Republican zeal altogether.

THE CIVIL RIGHTS ACT OF 1875

Despite their weakness, Republicans managed to pass one final piece of radical legislation through Congress. The **Civil Rights Act of 1875** aimed to eliminate social discrimination and facilitate true equality for black Americans by stipulating the following:

- Racial discrimination would be outlawed in all public places such as theaters, hotels, and restaurants.

- Blacks would have the same legal rights as whites.

- Blacks could sue violators in federal courts.

Toothless Legislation

The Civil Rights Act of 1875 proved highly ineffective, because Democrats in the House of Representatives made it virtually unenforceable. The law required individual blacks to file their own claims to defend their rights; the federal government wouldn't do it for them. Because lawsuits required money, time, and considerable effort, House Democrats knew that the law would have very little practical impact.

REDEMPTION

The weak Republican foothold in the South had only gotten weaker as northerners lost interest in Reconstruction. By the mid-1870s, the depression and the Klan had driven off most white Unionists, carpetbaggers, and scalawags, which left African Americans to fend for themselves. Without any support from southern whites or Congress, Democrats easily seized power once again and "redeemed" the southern state legislatures one by one. Some Democrats even employed violence to secure power by killing Republicans or terrorizing blacks away from the polls. By 1877, Democrats once again controlled every southern state.

COURT RULINGS AGAINST RADICAL RECONSTRUCTION

Several Supreme Court rulings in the 1870s and 1880s also heralded the death of Reconstruction. For example:

- The *Slaughterhouse* cases of 1873: the Fourteenth Amendment did not protect citizens from state infringements on their rights.

- *United States v. Cruikshank* in 1876: only states, not the federal government, could prosecute individuals in violation of the 1871 Ku Klux Klan Act.

- The *Civil Rights* cases of 1883: the Fourteenth Amendment only applied to discrimination by the government (not from individuals).

THE ELECTION OF 1876

Democrats poured a lot of energy into the 1876 presidential election in order to oust Grant and redeem the White House. The party nominated New York prosecutor **Samuel J. Tilden**, who railed against the corrupt Grant administration. After briefly toying with the idea of choosing Grant again for an unprecedented third term, Republicans finally selected Ohio governor **Rutherford B. Hayes**.

Hayes had served in the war as a Union general, had no overly controversial opinions, and came from the politically important state of Ohio. On Election Day 1876, Hayes won only 165 electoral votes and lost the popular election by roughly 250,000 votes. Tilden, on the other hand, had won the popular vote and had 184 electoral votes, but he lacked the extra electoral vote necessary to become president.

The Compromise of 1877

The election results in South Carolina, Louisiana, and Florida were still in dispute because of confusing ballots. Normally, the president of the Senate would recount the ballots in front of Congress. Because the president of the Senate was a Republican and the Speaker of the House was a Democrat, neither man could trust the other to count the votes honestly.

Instead, Congress passed the **Electoral Count Act** in 1877 to establish a special committee to recount the votes fairly. The committee consisted of fifteen men from the House, the Senate, and the Supreme Court—eight Republicans and seven Democrats. Not surprisingly, the committee concluded by a margin of one vote that Hayes had won the disputed states. Deadlock ensued once again, until both sides agreed to compromise.

In the **Compromise of 1877**, Democrats and Republicans agreed to let Hayes become president in exchange for the complete withdrawal of federal soldiers from the South. Shortly after Hayes took office, he ordered the last remaining troops out of South Carolina and Louisiana. Reconstruction had finally ended.

Timeline

1862	First and Second Confiscation Acts passed.
1863	Abraham Lincoln issues the Proclamation on Amnesty and Reconstruction.
	Lincoln issues the Emancipation Proclamation.
1864	Lincoln is reelected.
1865	Sherman issues Special Field Order #15.
	Congress establishes the Freedmen's Bureau.
	Robert E. Lee surrenders to Grant.
	John Wilkes Booth assassinates Lincoln.
	Andrew Johnson becomes president.
	Johnson begins Presidential Reconstruction.
	The Thirteenth Amendment is ratified.
1866	Congress passes the Civil Rights Act of 1866.
	The Ku Klux Klan is founded in Tennessee.
	Race Riots erupt in Memphis and New Orleans.
	Johnson "Swings Around the Circle" in an attempt to gain support from northern voters.
1867	Radical Reconstruction begins.
	Congress passes the First and Second Reconstruction Acts.
	Congress passes the Tenure of Office Act.
1868	Johnson is impeached by the House of Representatives.
	The Senate acquits Johnson.
	The Fourteenth Amendment is ratified.
	Ulysses S. Grant is elected president.
1869	Jim Fisk and Jay Gould attempt to corner the gold market.
1870	The Fifteenth Amendment is ratified.
1871	Congress passes the Ku Klux Klan Act.

1872	The Republican Party splits.
	The Crédit Moblier scandal erupts.
	Samuel J. Tilden prosecutes Boss William Tweed.
	Grant is reelected president.
1873	Depression of 1873 begins.
	Supreme Court hears Slaughterhouse cases.
1874	Democrats retake control of the House.
	The Whiskey Ring scandal erupts, futher tarnishing President Grant's record.
1875	Congress passes the Civil Rights Act of 1875.
	Congress passes the Resumption Act.
1876	Democrats and Republicans dispute presidential-election results.
1877	Congress passes the Electoral Count Act.
	Democrats and Republicans strike the Compromise of 1877.
	Rutherford B. Hayes becomes president.
	Hayes withdraws all federal troops from the South.

CHAPTER 11

The Growing Nation: 1877–1901

IIIIIIIIIIIIIIIIIIIIIIIIIIIIIIIIIIIIIIIIIIIIIIIIIIIIIIIIII

As Reconstruction ended and Americans approached a new century, dramatic contradictions emerged in the United States. Though North and South had reunited, sharp divisions and stark contrasts emerged in the North, South, and West. Although America beckoned to people from all over the world, immigrants often found hardship and prejudice in both growing cities and the frontier.

While pioneers staked their claims in the West, the government displaced and destroyed Native American populations. African Americans claimed their citizenship but suffered indignities and physical intimidation when they tried to exercise their rights. Booming industries and technological innovations spawned great cities and economic security for a new middle class. Yet ruthless entrepreneurs and corrupt politicians exploited a growing underclass of women, children, and men who became the working poor.

Gilded Age Politics

The corruption and scandals that plagued President Ulysses S. Grant's administration worsened during the course of the **Gilded Age**, an era of tremendous growth in business and industry. Networks of powerful men and loyal underlings composed political machines in which bribes and pay-offs fueled politicians' quests for power. **Political bosses** embroiled in this **spoils system** (the process by which these bosses paid money to control votes, candidates, and other aspects of the voting system) obtained and maintained control over the political system for many years.

> Powerful political "bosses" in different cities coerced residents to vote for their candidate of choice. Those candidates would then turn over kickbacks and bribes to the boss in appreciation for getting them elected. The most notorious party boss of his time was Boss **William Tweed**, who ran the Tammany Hall Democratic machine in New York City. Most politicians elected in the post–Civil War era were the products of machine party politics.

THE STALWARTS, HALF BREEDS, AND MUGWUMPS

Rutherford B. Hayes squeaked into the White House by only one electoral vote after the **Compromise of 1877** (see page 187), and he remained virtually powerless during his four years in office. The real winners in the election were Republican spoils-seekers who flooded Washington, D.C., in search of civil service jobs. Unfortunately, disputes over the spoils split the Republican party (also known as the Grand Old Party) into three factions:

- **The Stalwarts**—led by New York Senator **Roscoe Conkling**—composed the conservative faction of the Republican party.

- **The Half-Breeds**—led by Maine Senator **James G. Blaine**—the moderate faction of the Republican party. The Stalwarts gave them their disparaging name.

- **The Mugwumps**, a group of liberal Republicans who opposed the spoils system.

None of these groups trusted any of the others, and so the Republican party had trouble passing any significant legislation while in office.

THE "FORGOTTEN PRESIDENTS"

Many historians have dubbed the Gilded Age presidents—Grant, Hayes, Garfield, Arthur, Cleveland, and Harrison—the **"Forgotten Presidents."** Some historians have even suggested that Gilded Age presidents lacked personality precisely because Americans didn't want any bold politicians who might ruin the peace established after the Civil War. Essentially, Americans wanted to focus on other matters like their own prosperity rather than face any more potentially divisive issues.

Garfield and Arthur

Hayes had fallen out of favor with Republicans by the election of 1880, and he only planned to seek one term as president. They nominated the relatively unknown **James A. Garfield** and his Stalwart running mate, **Chester A. Arthur**. Democrats nominated Civil War veteran Winfield Scott Hancock, and the pro-labor **Greenback Party** nominated **James. B. Weaver**. Garfield received a sizeable majority of electoral votes on Election Day but won only slightly more popular votes than Hancock. Bickering for the spoils dominated Garfield's brief stay in the White House, which ended unexpectedly in 1881 when an insane Stalwart named Charles Guiteau shot and killed him. Guiteau hoped Arthur would become president and give more federal jobs to his loyal Stalwarts.

Although Arthur did replace Garfield, the assassination only convinced policymakers to reform the spoils system by passing the **Pendleton Act** in 1883. The act created the **Civil Service Commission** to hire federal employees based on examinations and merit rather than political patronage. Over time, these examinations gradually reformed the system.

Grover Cleveland

Despite the Pendleton Act, political spoils continued to dominate politics and the next presidential election in 1884. Republicans nominated the Half-Breed James Blaine while Democrats nominated New York governor **Grover Cleveland**. Democrats accused Blaine of conspiring with wealthy plutocrats to win the White House, and Republicans attacked Cleveland for having fathered an illegitimate son. In the end, Cleveland barely defeated Blaine with forty more electoral votes and 29,685 more popular votes. Cleveland's four years in office between 1885 and 1889 were uneventful.

Benjamin Harrison

Afraid that Democrats would succeed in lowering their precious protective tariffs, Republicans rallied big business in the North and nominated **Benjamin Harrison** for the presidency in 1888. A grandson of former president William Henry Harrison, Benjamin Harrison campaigned for an even higher tariff. Democrats nominated Cleveland again but couldn't garner enough electoral votes to keep the presidency. Harrison slid into office. He worked the Republican majority in Congress and passed the following acts:

* **The Sherman Silver Purchase Act** to purchase more silver for currency

* **The Dependent Pension Act** to distribute more money to aging Civil War veterans and their families

* **The McKinley Tariff**, a controversial tariff that set duties on foreign goods to about 50 percent

Industrialization

The North emerged from the Civil War as an industrial powerhouse ready to take on the world. Rich with seemingly unlimited natural resources and millions of immigrants ready to work, the United States experienced a flurry of unprecedented growth and industrialization during the Gilded Age. As a result, some historians have referred to this era as America's **second industrial revolution** because it completely transformed American society, politics, and the economy. Mechanization and marketing were the keys to success in this age: companies that could mass-produce goods and convince people to buy them amassed enormous riches, while those that could not ultimately collapsed.

TRANSCONTINENTAL RAILROADS

The mass industrialization of the economy during the Gilded Age had its roots in the Civil War. Besides creating a huge demand for a variety of manufactured goods, the war also spurred Congress and the northern states to build more railroads. The rather progressive Congress of 1862 also authorized construction of the first railroad to run from the Pacific to the Atlantic. Because laying track cost so much money, the federal government initially provided subsidies by the mile to the railroad companies in exchange for discounted rates.

Congress also provided federal grants for land on which companies could lay the track. With free land and tens of thousands of free dollars per mile, railroading quickly became a highly profitable business venture. The **Union Pacific Railroad** began construction on the transcontinental line in Nebraska during the Civil War and pushed westward while Leland Stanford's **Central Pacific Railroad** pushed eastward from Sacramento. Tens of thousands of Irish and Chinese laborers laid most of the track. The two lines met near Ogden, Utah, in 1869.

Railroads formed the cornerstone of the new industrialized economy. They ferried raw materials, finished products, food, and people across the entire country in a matter of days instead of the months or years it had taken before the Civil War. By the end of the war, the United States had 35,000 miles of track, mostly in the industrialized North. By the end of the century, that number had jumped to almost 200,000 miles of track connecting the North, South, and West.

Vanderbilt: Railroad Tycoon

Soon, other railroads—including the Southern Pacific Railroad, the Santa Fe Railroad, and James J. Hill's Great Northern Railway—spanned the Western expanse. Federal subsidies and land grants made railroading such a huge business that it bred a new class of "new money" millionaires like Stanford and Hill. **Cornelius Vanderbilt** and his son William H. Vanderbilt were perhaps the most infamous of these railroad tycoons during this era. They bought out and consolidated many of the rail companies in the East and streamlined operations to lower costs. The Vanderbilts also established a standard track gauge and replaced the iron rails with lighter but more durable steel. Their innovation and cutthroat business practices earned them over $100 million.

> Vanderbilt's use of the steel rail in the 1870s and 1880s helped give birth to the American steel industry. Prior to the mid-nineteenth century, railroaders had shied away from steel because of its high cost. But William Kelly's discovery of the **Bessemer process** for making steel revolutionized the industry: blowing cold air on hot iron would make high-quality steel for a fraction of the cost.

Railroad Corruption

Not all railroading profits were earned in a legitimate manner. The industry was filled with dozens of scams and embezzlement schemes to make insiders rich. Besides the infamous **Crédit Moblier scandal** (see page 183), railroads also inflated the prices of their own stocks and doled out uncompetitive rebates to favored companies. These practices hurt common people. Some of the states passed new laws to clamp down on the unruly railroads, but the Supreme Court shot all of them down when it ruled that only the federal government could regulate interstate commerce in the 1886 **Wabash Case.**

CAPTAINS OF INDUSTRY

Whereas past generations had sent their best men into public service, young men during the Gilded Age sought their fortunes in the private sector, where a little persistence and ruthlessness could reap enormous profits almost overnight. Unregulated by the government, these so-called **captains of industry** did whatever they pleased to make as much money as possible. In fact, their business practices were quite often so unscrupulous that the term *industrialist* soon became synonymous with the nickname *robber baron*.

Carnegie, Morgan, and U.S. Steel

By the end of the 1900s, **Andrew Carnegie** was the wealthiest and most famous steel magnate in the United States. Carnegie created a veritable steel empire through a business tactic called **"vertical integration."** Instead of relying on expensive middlemen, Carnegie bought out all of the companies needed to produce his steel. He made it, shipped it, and sold it himself. Eventually he sold his company to Wall Street banker **J. P. Morgan**, who in turn used the company as the foundation for the new **U.S. Steel Corporation** in 1901. By the end of his life, Carnegie had become one of the richest men in America with a fortune of nearly $500 million.

Rockefeller's Standard Oil

Oil also became big business during the Gilded Age. Although Americans needed very little oil before the Civil War, demand surged during the machine age in the 1880s, 1890s, and early 1900s. Everything required oil during this era, from factory machines to ships; this demand continued with cars in the 1920s. The oil industry also popularized the use of bright kerosene lamps.

John D. Rockefeller and his **Standard Oil Company** became the biggest names in the oil industry. Whereas Carnegie had employed vertical integration to create his empire, the ruthless Rockefeller used a method called **"horizontal integration"** to make sure he monopolized the industry. He bought out all the other oil companies to make sure he had no competition, and in doing so, created one of America's first monopolies, or **trusts**, to corner the market on a single commodity.

THE PLUTOCRACY

This period in American history witness a marked divide between the upper and lower classes. In time, the majority of plutocrats developed the belief that their riches had come not from their good fortune and circumstance but from their own superiority over the poorer classes.

Social Darwinism

In line with Charles Darwin's sensational new theory of natural selection, many of the new rich applied the mantra of "survival of the fittest" to society. In the words of one **Social Darwinist**, "The millionaires are the product of natural selection." Many of the wealthy believed they had become so fabulously rich because they were smarter and had worked harder than everyone else.

The Gospel of Wealth

On the other hand, more religious plutocrats preached the **"Gospel of Wealth,"** believing that God had given them riches for their genius and tenacity. The flip side to Social Darwinism and the Gospel of Wealth was that the poor were in turn considered ungodly and/or biologically inferior.

Philanthropists

Fortunately, not all of the new rich believed the poor should be left to fend for themselves. Many of the new rich demonstrated a keen interest in helping the less fortunate. Andrew Carnegie was by far the most generous of these Gilded Age philanthropists. Having come from a poor family himself, Carnegie firmly believed he would be disgraced if he died wealthy without having helped others. As a result, he donated more than $350 million to dozens of organizations by the time he died.

REGULATING BIG BUSINESS

To rein in the growing number of unwieldy trusts, Congress passed the **Interstate Commerce Act** in 1887, which outlawed railroad rebates and kickbacks. In addition, the act established the **Interstate Commerce Commission** to monitor the railroad companies' compliance with the new laws. To protect consumers by outlawing big trusts, Congress also passed the **Sherman Antitrust Act** in 1890.

Toothless Legislation

Although designed to regulate the corrupt railroad companies, the Interstate Commerce Commission had so many exploitable loopholes that it had almost no effect. Railroads still continued to issue rebates, demand outrageous fares, and charge different customers different prices for the same journey. The act did, however, establish an arena in which the competing railroad corporations could settle disputes without fighting disastrous rate wars. In this sense, the Interstate Commerce Commission helped stabilize the industry rather than control it. The similarly weak Sherman Anti-Trust Act also had very little effect at reining in the trusts.

The Labor Movement

The workforce changed drastically as the economy became more industrialized and mechanized. Competition for jobs grew stiffer as millions of women, immigrants, blacks, and farmers moved to the cities to find work. A mechanized economy also meant that companies required new and different sets of job skills. Unfortunately, organized labor generally floundered without any government regulation.

Many Americans regarded labor unions as socialists, anarchists, and rabble-rousers. The federal government even prosecuted a number of labor unions as trusts under the Sherman Antitrust Act of 1890. Nevertheless, so many skilled and unskilled workers joined labor unions between 1860 and 1900, that by the turn of the century, many Americans and the government had begun to reconsider employees' right to strike.

THE NATIONAL LABOR UNION

Founded in 1866, the first national labor union was simply called the **National Labor Union (NLU)**. The NLU sought to represent both skilled and unskilled laborers in one large organization. Though it had no ties to either political party, the union generally supported any candidate who would fight for shorter working days, higher wages, and better working conditions. The NLU only existed for six short years, thanks to the Depression of 1873. Union members found it difficult to bargain collectively when companies could easily hire thousands of new immigrant "scabs," or strike breakers, to replace them.

THE KNIGHTS OF LABOR

Another union called the **Knights of Labor** survived the depression. Originally begun as a secret society in 1869, the Knights picked up where the NLU had left off. It too united all skilled and unskilled laborers, but unlike the NLU, it allowed blacks and women to join. The Knights won a series of strikes in their fight against long hours and low wages. The Knights of Labor also died prematurely after Americans falsely associated them with the anarchists responsible for the **Haymarket Square Bombing** in Chicago in 1886. Additionally, the Knights found it difficult to successfully bargain collectively because they represented such a diverse group of workers.

LABOR STRIKES

Many of the fledgling unions that went on strike during the latter half of the nineteenth century did so to protest poor working conditions, long workdays, and inadequate pay. But most Americans at the time frowned on collective bargaining, which made it difficult for the unions to make any significant gains.

The Railroad Strike of 1877

In 1877, when the railroad companies announced a second 10 percent pay cut in four years, workers met to organize a National Trainmen's Union and plan a general strike. After the railroads fired union organizers, numerous strikes erupted on July 16 throughout the country. President Hayes eventually authorized state governors to use federal troops to suppress the ensuing riots.

The Coeur d'Alene Strike

The **Coeur d'Alene Strike** occurred in Coeur d'Alene, Idaho, in 1892, when several silver-mine owners collectively slashed miners' wages. The silver miners' union protested the wage cuts but had little effect, as eager immigrant scabs quickly replaced the organized laborers. Frustrated, a number of union protestors destroyed one of the mines in the city of Coeur d'Alene with dynamite. President Benjamin Harrison sent over 1,000 federal troops to end the violence.

The Homestead Strike

Meanwhile, employees of Andrew Carnegie's Homestead Steel Works near Pittsburgh, Pennsylvania, had launched a strike of their own to protest wage cuts. Pittsburgh police refused to end the strike, so Carnegie hired 300 detectives from the renowned Pinkerton Detective Agency to subdue the protestors. Still, the laborers won a surprising victory after a rather bloody standoff. Harrison once again sent troops to break the **Homestead Strike**.

The Pullman Strike

Grover Cleveland made a similar decision in 1894 to end the **Pullman Strike** at the Pullman Palace Car Company in Chicago. When the company cut employees' wages by 30 percent in the wake of the depression, labor organizer **Eugene V. Debs** organized a massive strike. Over 150,000 American Railroad Union Members refused to work. Some even destroyed Pullman's famed Palace cars and delayed trains as far away as California. Cleveland sent federal troops to break up the strike and had Debs arrested.

THE AMERICAN FEDERATION OF LABOR

A new labor union called the **American Federation of Labor (AFL)** grew to form an umbrella organization that coordinated the efforts of several dozen smaller, independent unions.

Founded by **Samuel Gompers** in 1886, the AFL sought better wages, shorter working days, better working conditions, and the creation of all-union workplaces. Unlike its predecessors, the National Labor Union and the Knights of Labor, the AFL only represented skilled white male craftsmen in the cities and exluded farmers, blacks, women, and unskilled immigrants. The AFL survived the rocky Gilded Age and eventually became one of the most powerful labor unions in the twentieth century.

Gilded Age Society

The Gilded Age also heralded the dawn of a new American society as the nation's base shifted from agriculture to industry. Millions of Americans flocked to the cities in the post–Civil War era. By 1900, nearly 40 percent of Americans lived in urbanized areas, as opposed to the 20 percent in 1860. Many young people left their farms in search of the new wonders cities had to offer: skyscrapers, electric trolleys, and department stores, among others. Industrialization and the population swell in urban areas also spawned consumerism and a middle class.

INCREASED IMMIGRATION

A new wave of immigration contributed to a population explosion. Coming mostly from war-torn regions of southern and eastern Europe like Italy, Greece, Poland, Russia, Croatia, and Czechoslovakia, the majority of these new immigrants had less money and education than the Irish and Germans who had preceded them. By the early twentieth century, a wave of immigrants over a million strong flooded eastern cities every year. Most barely managed to eke out a living in the New World through low-paying, undesirable, and unskilled jobs in factories or in packinghouses.

Nativist Resurgence

Nativist Americans often despised the new wave of immigrants, claiming they would never assimilate into American society because of their illiteracy, poverty, languages, and inexperience with democracy. Some Protestants also disliked the fact that new immigrants were primarily Catholic, Eastern Orthodox, or Jewish.

Moreover, there was a fear among some Anglo-Saxon Americans that the eastern and southern Europeans would either dilute the race or eventually "outbreed" American whites. In response, the **American Protection Association** formed and lobbied for immigration restriction. Congress eventually conceded and, in 1882, barred criminals and the extremely destitute from entry.

Interestingly, many Americans despised the Chinese, who had proven themselves in the West to be inexpensive yet excellent workers. Afraid that Chinese laborers would replace American laborers, workers' organizations pressed Congress to pass the **Chinese Exclusion Act** *in 1882 to ban Chinese immigration. The act remained in place until 1943.*

SLUMS

The sudden influx of nearly a million poor people a year gave rise to slums in the cities. Much of this population inhabited the new **dumbbell tenement** buildings, so named because they resembled giant dumbbells. Entire families usually lived together in tiny, one-room apartments, sharing a single bathroom with other families on the floor. As dumbbell tenements were filthy, poorly ventilated, and poorly lit, they were conducive to disease.

Jane Addams and Hull House

Several reformers tried to fight the increasing poverty and social injustices that were rampant in the cities, including the college-educated **Jane Addams**, who founded **Hull House** in Chicago. Located in one of the city's poorest neighborhoods, Hull House provided counseling, daycare services, and adult education classes to help local immigrants survive in the United States. The success of Hull House soon prompted **Lillian Wald** to open the **Henry Street Settlement House** in New York.

The successes of Jane Addams and Lillian Wald led other reformers to open similar settlement houses in other eastern cities with large immigrant populations. In time, women like Addams and

Wald used their positions to fight for temperance, women's suf-frage, civil rights, and improved labor laws.

FAITH-BASED REFORM

Religious communities were another antipoverty force in the slums. Catholic churches and Jewish synagogues led the fight by offering services to the newly arrived immigrants, helping them find their way in the cities. Protestant speeches and lectures became very popular events, as did faith-based social organiza-tions like the Young Men's Christian Association, or YMCA, and the Young Women's Christian Association, or YWCA.

Christian Science

The post–Civil War period witnessed the birth of several new religions, such as **Christian Science**, which was founded by **Mary Baker Eddy**, who believed that faith could cure all disease. Hundreds of thousands of people converted, as the church spread throughout America.

THE WOMEN'S MOVEMENT

Women achieved significant gains during the latter half of the nineteenth century. Many urban women found jobs, married later, had fewer children, and used various methods of birth con-trol. Feminist **Charlotte Perkins Gilman**'s 1898 book *Women and Economics* demanded that women shirk their traditional roles as homemakers to find independence in the new America. She and other feminists like **Elizabeth Cady Stanton** also demanded the right to vote. Another leading figure, **Victoria Woodhull**, shocked Americans by advocating the use of contraceptives in spite of the **Comstock Law** of 1873, which outlawed the use of the U.S. mail to distribute contraceptives and information about contraceptives.

PLESSY V. FERGUSON *AND CIVIL RIGHTS*

African Americans did not fare as well as women in the struggle for equality. In 1896, the Supreme Court even upheld the policy of segregation by legalizing "separate but equal" facilities for blacks and whites in the landmark decision *Plessy v. Ferguson*. In doing so, the court condemned African Americans to more than another half century of second-class citizenship.

Washington v. Du Bois

Black leaders continued to press for equal rights. For example, **Booker T. Washington**, president of the all-black **Tuskegee Institute** in Alabama, encouraged African Americans to become economically self-sufficient so that they could then challenge whites on social issues. The Harvard-educated black historian and sociologist, **W.E.B. Du Bois**, however, ridiculed Washington's beliefs and argued that African Americans should fight for social and economic equality at the same time. Their dispute highlighted the rupture in the Civil Rights movement during the end of the nineteenth century.

The West

Railroads not only transformed industrial cities in the East but also in the West. This transformation happened primarily because travel had become easier, cheaper, and safer. The transcontinental lines moved people, grain, cattle, ore, and equipment across the vast expanses of the Midwest, over the Rocky Mountains and Sierra Nevada and to the fertile valleys of California and Oregon.

THE HOMESTEAD ACT

Although Americans had continued to move in a steady stream westward, even during the Civil War, this phenomenon picked up steam once the war had ended. Several million Americans surged into the great unknown regions beyond eastern Kansas and Nebraska. Settlers particularly wanted cheap federal land offered by Congress in the **Homestead Act** of 1862. For a small fee, any settler could stake out a 160-acre western claim so long as he and his family improved the land by farming it and living on it.

THE NATIVE AMERICAN WARS

In 1881 author **Helen Hunt Jackson** published her book, *A Century of Dishonor*, a book that described the federal government's history of cruelty toward Native Americans over the previous hundred years. The book launched a new debate about whites' relationship with Native Americans and prompted many people to conclude that assimilation would be the only solution to the problem.

The Sioux Wars

As white settlers pushed farther and farther westward, they repeatedly shoved Native Americans off their lands. Not surprisingly, the two groups frequently clashed. In 1864, for example, Union troops slaughtered several hundred Native American women and children at the **Sand Creek Massacre** in Colorado.

The U.S. Army also fought the Sioux tribes in the Black Hills of Dakota Territory during the 1860s and 1870s. These battles were dubbed the **Sioux Wars**. Lieutenant Colonel **George Armstrong Custer** made his infamous Last Stand during this war at the **Battle of Little Bighorn**, when more than 250 of his troops fell under the hands of Chief **Sitting Bull** and his warriors. The Sioux's victory was short-lived, and they were defeated a year later.

Chief Joseph, Geronimo, and Wounded Knee

The army also fought the Nez Percé tribe in the Pacific Northwest. United under **Chief Joseph**, the Nez Percé refused to relinquish their lands to white settlers without a fight. They fled all across the Northwest before the army finally defeated them and relocated the tribe to Kansas.

The Apaches in New Mexico Territory led by **Geronimo** also fought bravely to protect their homes until their eventual defeat. Hundreds of Native Americans also died at the **Massacre at Wounded Knee** in 1890 during the army's attempt to stamp out the **Ghost Dance Movement**, which called for a return to traditional Native American ways of life and challenged white supremacy.

The Dawes Severalty Act

In order to make room for more whites, the federal government first tried to herd natives onto tribal-owned reservations on the poorest land in the Dakotas, New Mexico, and Oklahoma. Under pressure from reformers who wanted to "acclimatize" Native Americans to white culture, Congress eventually passed the **Dawes Severalty Act** in 1887. The Dawes Act outlawed tribal ownership of land and instead forced 160-acre homesteads into the hands of Indians and their families with the promise of future citizenship. The act tried to forcibly assimilate Native Americans into white culture as quickly as possible.

> In 1893, American historian **Frederick Jackson Turner** argued in his now famous essay, The Significance of the Frontier in American History, that the closure of the West presented the United States with a serious problem. He claimed that the western frontier had been one of the nation's defining characteristics, and he worried about what would happen to American culture, society, and government now that the West had been won. The West had always represented a sense of infinite possibility for Americans; for Turner, the settling of the West left a void in the American identity.

TRANSFORMATIONS IN AGRICULTURE

Investors and land speculators followed close behind the rugged homesteaders who had staked their claims in the great unknown and also had a share in transforming the West. Agricultural prices remained relatively high during the good times between the Depression of 1873 and the **Depression of 1893**, so many farmers with a little capital switched from subsistence farming to growing single cash crops. In the Midwest, growing only wheat or corn or raising cattle to maximize profits in the cities was common for farmers.

The Plight of Small Farmers

The incorporation of farming, high protective tariffs, and the Depression of 1893 ruined subsistence farmers in the Midwest and South. Many of the cash crop farmers found themselves deep in debt and couldn't afford the unregulated railroad fares to ship their products to cities. Over a million impoverished farmers eventually organized under a social organization called the **National Grange** to fight for their livelihood. They managed to win some key victories in several Midwestern legislatures, supported the Greenback Party in the 1870s, and eventually by the **Populist Party** in the 1890s.

The Rise and Fall of Populism

Benjamin Harrison's **McKinley Tariff** was one of the highest tariffs in U.S. history—even higher than the 1828 Tariff of Abominations that had nearly split the Union. The tariff particularly hurt farmers in the West and South, who sold their harvests on unprotected markets and bought expensive manufactured goods.

THE POPULISTS

In seeking revenge for the McKinley Tariff, the farmers voted Republicans out of the House of Representatives in the 1890 congressional elections. Some of them even formed a pseudo-political party in the late 1880s called the **Farmers' Alliance**. By the time the 1892 elections rolled around, the Alliance had merged with other liberal Democrats to form the **Populist Party**. Populists nominated former Greenback Party candidate **James B. Weaver** and campaigned for the following:

- Unlimited cheap silver money (they wanted a rate of sixteen ounces of silver to one ounce of gold)
- Government ownership of all railroads and telephone companies
- A graduated income tax
- Direct election of U.S. senators
- Single-term limits for presidents
- Immigration restriction
- Shorter workdays

GROVER CLEVELAND ELECTED AGAIN

The Republicans and Democrats again nominated Benjamin Harrison and Grover Cleveland, respectively, for the presidency in 1892. Weaver and the Populists also entered the race, as did John Bidwell on behalf of the fledgling Prohibition Party. The Populists did surprisingly well and managed to receive over a million popular votes and twenty-two electoral votes. The McKinley Tariff had ruined Harrison's chance for reelection, so the presidency reverted to Cleveland, who became the only president to serve two inconsecutive terms.

Cleveland's second round in the White House was a lot rockier than his first. The Depression of 1893—the worst depression the country had ever seen—hit just months after he took the oath of office. Additionally, Congress passed the **Wilson-Gorman Tariff** in 1894 in spite of Cleveland's promise to significantly reduce the tariff. This certainly affected his popularity.

Silver, Gold, and J. P. Morgan

Even worse, the federal government had nearly gone bankrupt. Wily investors had traded their silver for gold in a convoluted scheme that ultimately depleted the nation's gold reserves below the $100 million mark. Had this trend continued, the government would not have had enough gold to back the paper currency in circulation or prevent the economic collapse that would have resulted.

Cleveland addressed this situation by repealing the 1890 Sherman Silver Purchase Act to prevent the loss of any more gold. This had no effect, and by the following year, the government had only $41 million in the Treasury. Cleveland and Congress ultimately appealed to Wall Street financier J. P. Morgan to bail them out. For a hefty price, Morgan agreed to loan the government $62 million to put it back on its feet.

Coxey's Army

The Depression of 1893 and Cleveland's repeal of the Sherman Silver Purchase Act only made the Populist movement stronger. More and more disillusioned Democrats flocked to the Populist Party in the hopes of winning free silver and more power for the people. The Depression also encouraged other would-be reformers to cry out for change. The wealthy Ohioan Jacob S. Coxey petitioned the government for cheap money and debt-relief programs. When **"Coxey's Army"** reached the capital in 1894, however, city officials arrested them for marching on the grass.

ISLANDS IN THE PACIFIC

After the U.S. Census Bureau declared the continental frontier closed in 1890, Americans began looking overseas to expand. A number of islands in the Pacific Ocean became the first to fall under colonization and the American flag. Hawaii was the plum of the Pacific for its pleasant climate, which was perfect for growing sugar cane. Americans had actually been settling Hawaii and living with the native islanders for over a hundred years. The white American minority had repeatedly petitioned Congress for annexation and had even overthrown the peaceful Hawaiian **Queen Liliuokalani** to seize control of the government in 1893. Outraged, the anti-expansionist Grover Cleveland rejected annexation and condemned the revolt against the queen.

CLEVELAND UPHOLDS THE MONROE DOCTRINE

Cleveland also threatened war with Great Britain over a territorial dispute in South America—one that didn't even involve U.S. territory. Both Venezuela and the British colony of Guiana claimed a huge tract of land rich with gold ore along the border. Invoking the Monroe Doctrine (i.e., the principle that mandated that the Americas were no longer open for European colonization), Cleveland threatened the British with war if they didn't back off.

Eventually, Britain acquiesced. They sought arbitration to settle the dispute, not so much because they feared the United States (Britain still had the largest navy in the world) but because they didn't want to alienate a potential ally as European relations grew increasingly chillier. Cleveland's bold stance impressed many Latin American nations, who began to see the United States as a friendly protector.

THE ELECTION OF 1896

Cleveland had no chance for reelection to a third term. He had
failed to correct the Depression of 1893, barely managed to keep
the U.S. Treasury full, angered many middle-class constituents by
using federal troops to end the Pullman Strike, and neglected to
keep his promise to significantly reduce the Wilson-Gorman tariff. These problems proved insurmountable for him.

As the election of 1896 approached, Democrats instead nominated the so-called "Boy Orator" from Nebraska, **William
Jennings Bryan**, on a Populist-inspired platform for free silver
after he had delivered his rousing **"Cross of Gold Speech,"** con-
demning the gold standard. The Populists threw their support to
Bryan and the Democrats to keep the Republicans out of office.

> *Bryan's Cross of Gold Speech electrified Populists and Democrats.
> A passionate and dynamic speaker, Bryan compared Americans
> to the New Testament story of Jesus' final moments before
> crucifixion when proclaimed, "We will answer their [Republicans']
> demands for a gold standard by saying to them: 'You shall not
> press down upon the brow of labor this crown of thorns, you shall
> not crucify mankind upon a cross of gold!'"*

McKinley Kills Free Silver

The Republicans nominated Congressman **William McKinley**,
sponsor of the controversial McKinley Tariff, on a pro-business
platform. Wealthy Ohioan businessman **Marcus Hanna**
financed most of the campaign and convinced his colleagues in
the East to support McKinley. Despite Bryan's whirlwind speaking tour through the South and Midwest, it was Hanna's politick-
ing that won McKinley the presidency that year.

McKinley appealed to a wide range of Americans. Conservative
Americans feared cheap money and inflation so much that they
flocked to McKinley and the Republican camp. Wealthy businessmen in the East dumped about $6–12 million into McKinley's
campaign, making it the fattest campaign fund of any American
candidate ever. Some Democrats quite reasonably claimed that
McKinley had purchased the White House. McKinley ultimately

killed the Populists' dream of free silver in 1900 when he signed the **Gold Standard Act** to peg the value of the dollar to an ounce of gold. He also signed the **Dingley Tariff** in 1897 to set overall tariff rates at about 45 percent.

> *Free silver became an important issue in the late nineteenth century. The Depression of 1873 caused the market price of silver to drop dramatically. Inflationists turned to silver and hoped its free coinage would stabilize the economy. President McKinley killed this possibility in 1900.*

A Key Election

Historians regard the election of 1896 as one of the most important elections of the nineteenth century, and certainly the most significant election since the Civil War. First, it represented a victory of urban middle-class Americans over agrarian interests in the West and South. Populism had never really spread into the cities, and Bryan's appeal for free silver and inflation had alienated even the poorest Americans in the cities who depended on a stable dollar for survival. The Bryan campaign thus marked the last attempt to win the presidency through appeals to rural voters. It also marked the death of the Populist movement, which lost steam when it supported the Bryan campaign, essentially merging with the Democratic Party.

> *McKinley's victory also ushered in a new age in American politics that was dominated by conservatives and called the **Fourth Party System.** Republicans would control the White House for most of the next thirty-six years until the election of Franklin Delano Roosevelt in 1932. This period was marked by an enormous expansion of the middle class, continued migration to the cities, weaker political parties, the growth of industry, and more government concern for consumers and laborers.*

The Spanish-American War

William McKinley entered the White House just as the nation was gearing up to its biggest foreign flare-up yet: the Cuban crisis. Spain still controlled the island just ninety miles south of Florida despite repeated American attempts to wrest it away. Depressed sugar prices in the 1890s led Cuban farmers to rebel against their Spanish overlords in a bloody revolution. Spanish forces under General "Butcher" Weyler tried to crack down on the insurrection by herding all suspected revolutionaries—including children—into concentration camps. Americans learned about the situation from the lurid "**yellow press**" of the day as newspaper titans **William Randolph Hearst** and **Joseph Pulitzer** printed sensationalistic stories to outdo each other in a competition for readers.

> Hoping to boost sales with exclusive coverage on the war with Spain, Hearst sent the renowned painter Frederick Remington to Cuba to cover the war. To Remington's dismay, he allegedly issued the order, "You furnish the pictures and I'll furnish the war!"

REMEMBER THE MAINE!

The controversial **de Lôme letter** outraged Americans. Published in newspapers in 1898, the letter from Spanish minister to the United States Dupuy de Lôme derided McKinley as a dimwitted politician. Shortly thereafter, more than 250 American seamen serving aboard the **USS Maine** died when the ship mysteriously exploded while anchored in Havana Harbor. Although Spanish officials and historians have concluded that a boiler-room accident caused the explosion, Americans at home quickly concluded that Spanish agents had sabotaged the ship. Millions cried, "Remember the *Maine*!" and pressured Congress and McKinley for war.

WAR ERUPTS

McKinley didn't want war; however, he eventually requested a war declaration from Congress in April 1898 out of fear that William Jennings Bryan and "free silver" would win the election of 1900. Congress consented on the grounds that the Cuban people needed to be liberated. To justify the cause, Congress passed the

Teller Amendment, which promised Cuban independence once they had defeated the Spaniards. Americans won the war quickly and easily, thus causing the Spanish Empire to collapse.

Dewey in the Philippines

Acting outside his orders, assistant secretary of the Navy **Theodore Roosevelt** ordered Commodore **George Dewey** to seize the Spanish-controlled Philippine Islands in Asia. Dewey defeated the Spanish fleet in a surprise attack on Manila Bay without losing a single man. Congress then annexed Hawaii on the pretext that the Navy needed a refueling station between San Francisco and Asia. While Dewey fought the Spanish on the sea, insurgent **Louis Aguinaldo** led a Filipino revolt on land. Although Britain didn't participate in the fighting, it did help prevent other European powers from defending Spain.

The Rough Riders in Cuba

The U.S. Army, meanwhile, invaded Cuba with over 20,000 regular and volunteer troops. The most famous of the volunteers were the **Rough Riders**, commanded by the recently commissioned Lt. Colonel Roosevelt, who had left his civilian job to join the "splendid little war." As its name implied, this volunteer company consisted of a sordid lot of ex-convicts and cowboys mixed with some of Roosevelt's adventurous upper-class acquaintances. Roosevelt and the Rough Riders helped lead the charge to take the famous San Juan Hill outside the city of Santiago. Cuba eventually fell, and Spain retreated.

POSTWAR LEGISLATION

The United States honored the **Teller Amendment of 1898** (which declared that the United States did not have an interest in controlling Cuba after the war) and withdrew from Cuba in 1902, but not before including the **Platt Amendment** in the Cuban constitution to give the United States a permanent military base at Guantanamo Bay. The war gave McKinley more headaches than it cured. First, McKinley had to fight an insurrection led by Filipino rebel Louis Aguinaldo against American forces in the annexed Philippines. It took several years of bloody jungle warfare before U.S. forces defeated him, but even then, Filipinos resisted assimilation into white American culture.

The Supreme Court ruled in the 1901 **Insular Cases** that people in newly acquired foreign lands did not have the same constitutional rights as Americans at home. Congress still upheld the 1900 **Foraker Act** that granted Puerto Ricans limited self-government and eventually full U.S. citizenship in 1917. Finally, McKinley had to contend with the vocal new **Anti-Imperialist League** and its prominent membership, which challenged his expansionist policies and the incorporation of new "unassimilable" peoples into America.

Timeline

1862	Congress passes the Homestead Act.
1866	National Labor Union forms.
1867	The National Grange forms.
1869	The Transcontinental Railroad is completed.
	The Knights of Labor forms.
	Wyoming grants women the right to vote.
1870	Standard Oil Company forms.
1873	Congress passes the Comstock Law.
	Depression of 1873 begins.
1874	Woman's Christian Temperance Union forms.
1875	Sioux Wars occur in Black Hills, Dakota Territory.
1876	Alexander Graham Bell invents the telephone.
	Custer's Last Stand takes place at the Battle of Little Bighorn.
1877	Railroad workers strike across the United States.
	The Nez Percé War occurs.
	Rutherford B. Hayes is elected president.
1879	Thomas Edison invents the light bulb.
	Mary Baker Eddy founds Christian Science.
1880	James A. Garfield is elected president.
1881	Garfield is assassinated.
	Chester A. Arthur becomes president.
	Booker T. Washington becomes president of the Tuskegee Institute.
	Helen Hunt Jackson publishes *A Century of Dishonor*.
1882	Congress passes the Chinese Exclusion Act.
1883	Congress passes the Pendleton Act.
1884	Grover Cleveland is elected president.
	Mark Twain publishes *Huckleberry Finn*.
1885	The Farmers' Alliance forms.

1886	The Haymarket Square Bombing occurs in Chicago.
	The Supreme Court rules that only the federal government can regulate interstate commerce in the *Wabash* case.
	The American Federation of Labor (AFL) forms.
1887	Congress passes the Interstate Commerce Act.
	Congress passes the Dawes Severalty Act.
1888	Benjamin Harrison is elected president.
	Edward Bellamy publishes *Looking Backward*.
1889	Jane Addams founds Hull House in Chicago.
1890	Congress passes the Sherman Silver Purchase Act.
	Congress passes the Sherman Antitrust Act.
	Jacob Riis publishes *How the Other Half Lives*.
	Congress passes the McKinley Tariff.
	U.S. Census Bureau declares the continental frontier closed.
	The Sioux Ghost Dance Movement challenges white supremacy.
	The U.S. army challenges Native American ways of life in the Massacre at Wounded Knee.
	Alfred Thayer Mahan publishes *The Influence of Sea Power upon History*.
1891	The Populist Party forms.
1892	Miners strike in Coeur d'Alene, Idaho.
	Laborers win victory in the Homestead Steel Strike.
	Cleveland is reelected president.
1893	The Depression of 1893 ruins subsistence farming in the Midwest and South.
	Lillian Wald founds the Henry Street Settlement in New York.
	The Anti-Saloon League forms.
	Frederick Jackson Turner publishes *The Significance of the Frontier in American History*.

1894	"Coxey's Army" marches on Washington, D.C.
	Congress passes the Wilson-Gorman Tariff.
	The Pullman Strike occurs.
1895	J. P. Morgan bails out the U.S. government.
1896	The Supreme Court rules on *Plessy v. Ferguson*.
	William Jennings Bryan delivers his "Cross of Gold" speech.
	William McKinley is elected president.
1897	Congress passes the Dingley Tariff.
1898	Eugene V. Debs forms the Social Democratic Party.
	Charlotte Perkins Gilman publishes *Women and Economics*.
	The Anti-Imperialist League forms.
	The USS *Maine* explodes in Havana Harbor.
	The Spanish–American War begins.
	The United States annexes Hawaii.
	Congress passes the Teller Amendment.
	Admiral Dewey seizes the Philippines at Manila Bay.
1899	Aguinaldo leads the Filipino Insurrection against the United States.
1900	Congress passes the Gold Standard Act.
	Congress passes the Foraker Act.
	McKinley is reelected.
1901	U.S. Steel Corporation forms.
	The Supreme Court rules against equal constitutional rights for Americans on foreign soil in *Insular* Cases.
	Congress passes the Platt Amendment.

CHAPTER 12

The Progressive Era and World War I: 1901–1920

||||||||||||||||||||||||||||||||||||||||||||||||||||||||||||

As American society entered the twentieth century, it adapted to the ongoing processes of industrialization, as well as to demographic changes. Responding to these transformations, people interested in social welfare advocated reforms in business practices, government structure, and labor law, which formed the basis of a movement called progressivism. Progressivism was both a grassroots and an institutional phenomenon.

As the federal government sought to define the relationship between business and society, big business faced increasing legislation and regulation. Yet, a number of factors eventually pulled the United States away from progressivism and into World War I, the greatest war the world had ever known. Even though American forces only participated in the war during the final year, they gave Britain, France, and Italy a distinct advantage over their exhausted Austro–Hungarian, German, and Turkish enemies. Unfortunately, many conservatives at home would not allow Wilson to create the international governing body he desired to prevent future global conflicts. The United States and the rest of the world would regret this decision in the days leading up to the Second World War.

Big Stick Diplomacy

An ardent imperialist, Theodore Roosevelt carried out much of William McKinley's foreign policies, as well as some aggressive policies of his own. His comfort with forcefully coercing other nations to comply with America's will on a number of occasions prompted anti-imperialists and other critics to dub his foreign policy **"Big Stick" Diplomacy**.

CHINA AND THE FIRST OPEN DOOR NOTES

After losing the Sino–Japanese War of 1895, the Chinese could only watch as Japan, Russia, and the Europeans carved their ancient country into separate spheres of influence. Afraid that Americans would be unable to compete for lucrative Chinese markets, McKinley's policymakers scrambled to stop the feeding frenzy. In 1899 President **William McKinley**'s secretary of state, **John Hay**, boldly sent his **First Open Door "Notes"** to Japan and the European powers requesting that they respect Chinese rights and free trade. The British backed the agreement, but France, Germany, Russia, and Japan agreed only on the condition that other countries adhered to the note too.

The Boxer Rebellion

Naturally, many Chinese deeply resented Japanese and European conquest, and as a result a new nationalistic movement called the **Boxer Movement** spread across China like wildfire. Hoping to cast out all foreigners, a highly deluded Boxer army invaded Beijing in 1900. The Boxer Army believed they would be divinely protected from enemy bullets. They took a number of foreign diplomats hostage and then barricaded themselves in the city. Nearly 20,000 French, British, German, Russian, Japanese, and American soldiers joined forces to rescue the diplomats. After the coalition had quelled the short-lived **Boxer Rebellion**, Hay then issued his **Second Open Door Note** in 1900 to request the other powers respect China's territorial status in spite of the rebellion.

THE ELECTION OF 1900

Territorial gains overseas during the Spanish–American War and events unfolding in China made foreign policy and imperialism the dominant issue in the election of 1900.

Republicans nominated the popular McKinley for more prosperity and expansion and chose former Rough Rider Theodore Roosevelt to be his new running mate. Democrats once again selected the old favorite William Jennings Bryan on an anti-imperialism platform.

To most of the Democrats' dismay, Bryan also insisted on pushing for free silver again, even though his free silver platform had allowed McKinley to win in the previous election. Roosevelt and Bryan traveled throughout the country and played to the crowds on two whirlwind campaigns. In the end, free silver killed Bryan once more, and McKinley won with almost a million more popular votes and twice as many electoral votes. McKinley's tragic death by an anarchist's bullet, just months into his second term, pushed Theodore Roosevelt into the White House.

> President McKinley was assassinated by Leon Czolgosz on September 6, 1901. Czolgosz was quickly tried, found guilty, and executed. Some recent historians have speculated that he was clinically insane, but this was never proven.

THE PANAMA CANAL

Roosevelt was not one to shy from responsibility or action, and the boisterous new president immediately went to work, particularly on his pet project to build a canal across Central America. Territorial gains made during the war made it necessary to create a canal in order to ferry merchant and military ships from the American ports in the Atlantic to the Pacific.

The Hay-Pauncefote Treaty

In a display of amity, Britain graciously annulled the 1850 Clayton-Bulwer Treaty that had previously prevented the United States from building such a canal in the past. Instead, they signed the new **Hay-Pauncefote Treaty** in 1901, giving Americans full ownership of any future canal. After purchasing land in the Colombian province of Panama from a French construction company, Roosevelt and Congress then petitioned the Colombian government to sell permanent rights to the land. The Colombians disagreed and demanded more money.

Gunboat Diplomacy

Furious, Roosevelt struck a deal with Panamanian rebels, who were dissatisfied with Colombian rule. He offered independence and American protection in exchange for land to build a canal. The rebels quickly consented and captured the provincial capital in 1903 while U.S. Navy gunboats prevented Colombian troops from marching into Panama. Roosevelt immediately recognized Panama's independence and sent Hay to sign the **Hay–Bunau–Varilla Treaty**, which relinquished ownership of canal lands to the United States. Construction on the canal began the following year, despite Colombian protests. Contractors eventually completed the **Panama Canal** in 1914.

ROOSEVELT'S COROLLARY TO THE MONROE DOCTRINE

Roosevelt further angered Latin Americans when he twisted the Monroe Doctrine by making policy according to his own interpretation. When several South American and Caribbean countries defaulted on their loans, Germany and Britain sent warships to forcibly collect the debts. Afraid that aggressive Europeans would use the debts as an excuse to permanently reinsert their feet into Latin America's doorway, Roosevelt simply slammed the door shut in their faces. In 1904, he announced his own **Roosevelt Corollary to the Monroe Doctrine** by declaring that the United States would collect the debts owed and then pass them on to the European powers. In other words, only the United States could intervene in Latin American affairs. He then sent troops to the Dominican Republic to enforce debt repayment and to Cuba to suppress revolutionary forces in 1906.

TENSIONS WITH JAPAN

Relations between the United States and Japan during the Roosevelt years also soured. In 1905, Roosevelt mediated a dispute between Russia and Japan to end the Russo–Japanese War. Although Roosevelt's efforts won him the Nobel Peace Prize, both powers left the negotiating table unhappy and blamed the American president for their losses.

The Gentlemen's Agreement

Tensions mounted when the San Francisco Board of Education caved into popular anti-Japanese sentiment and banned Japanese students from enrolling in the city's public schools. Japanese diplomats in Washington, D.C., protested loudly and even threatened war. Roosevelt resolved the situation in the 1906 **"Gentlemen's Agreement,"** in which San Francisco promised to retract the racist ban in exchange for Japanese pledges to reduce the number of yearly emigrants to the United States.

The Great White Fleet

Roosevelt sent sixteen new battleships around the world, ostensibly on a good-will tour. In fact, they were sent to demonstrate American military might to the Japanese. When the **Great White Fleet** stopped in Tokyo in 1908, Japanese and American officials signed the **Root-Takahira Agreement**, in which both agreed to respect the Open Door policy in China and each other's territorial integrity in the Pacific.

Roosevelt and the Progressives

During his two terms as president, Roosevelt promoted his view of the federal government as an impartial force for the public good, rather than as an advocate for particular interests. For example, he used the power of the government to restrain corporations. In his second term, Roosevelt focused more on enacting social reforms. His progressive policies included engaging in anti-trust activities, supporting regulatory legislation, and championing environmental conservation. Roosevelt used his presidency as a **"bully pulpit,"** from which he gave speeches supporting his views on society and government.

THE MUCKRAKERS

The term **muckrakers** referred to the investigative journalists and crusading writers who sought to expose injustice and corruption and spark social change. During Roosevelt's presidency, these writers helped spur the passage of progressive legislation with their works, including:

- *Wealth Against Commonwealth* (1894) by Henry Demarest Lloyd, investigating monopolies like the Standard Oil Company

- *History of the Standard Oil Company* (1904) by Ida Tarbell, also targeting Standard Oil

- *How the Other Half Lives* (1890) by Danish immigrant Jacob Riis, relying on photographs as well as text to describe the living conditions of the urban poor

- *The Shame of the Cities* (1904) by Lincoln Steffens, exposing municipal corruption

- *The Jungle* (1906) by Upton Sinclair, describing unsanitary conditions in the meatpacking plants

Roosevelt labeled exposé writers "muckrakers" after a character in the book **Pilgrim's Progress** *who would search for stories about corruption (i.e., they would "rake" up "muck") where there was very little corruption in the first place. Roosevelt meant the name as an insult, but the muckrakers took up the name proudly.*

ROOSEVELT'S SQUARE DEAL

Roosevelt's domestic progressive agenda came to be collectively known as the "Square Deal" and sought to regulate big business, protect consumers, and conserve the nation's natural resources.

Trustbusting

As part of his strategy to regulate big business, Roosevelt revived the 1890 **Sherman Antitrust Act** and prosecuted the giant **Northern Securities Railroad Company** in 1902. The Supreme Court backed the president when it upheld the Sherman Antitrust Act and ordered Northern Securities to dissolve in 1904. Roosevelt then used the Sherman Antitrust Act to prosecute dozens of other trusts.

The Anthracite Coal Strike

In 1902, the **United Mine Workers** went on strike in West Virginia and Pennsylvania to demand shorter workdays and better pay. Months passed with no resolution as mine managers refused to meet the workers' demands. In order to prevent a national coal shortage, Roosevelt finally intervened by threatening to seize the coalmines and use federal troops to run them, forcing management to seek arbitration. The strike eventually ended in October 1902. Soon after, the arbitration awarded miners both shorter workdays and higher wages.

Regulatory Legislation

Roosevelt won the 1904 election with nearly 58 percent of the popular vote—the largest popular majority a presidential candidate had ever garnered. He therefore increased his push for progressive reforms in his second term with the following acts:

- **The Elkins Act** of 1903, which instituted penalties for giving and receiving railroad rebates. Railroads had given rebates to shippers in order to guarantee their continued business.

- **The Hepburn Railroad Regulation Act** of 1906, which gave the Interstate Commerce Commission the power to control railroad rates, inspect company books, and assign a uniform standard of bookkeeping.

- **The Meat Inspection Act** of 1906, which required federal inspectors to examine meat.

- **The Pure Food and Drug Act** of 1906, which allowed the federal government to regulate the sale of medicine and foods.

The Jungle by Upton Sinclair provides gruesome detail on the meatpacking industry and caused profound ripples in society at the time of its publication. People were shocked about the filthy conditions in which their meat was manufactured; the public outcry at The Jungle led to the creation of the FDA. This book is still widely taught today.

Conservation

Roosevelt supported environmental conservation policies as a major tenet of his domestic program. He added millions of acres to the national forest system to conserve forests for future use, and he also increased the size of the National Park System to protect some lands from development.

PROGRESSIVISM ON THE STATE LEVEL

Many reformers sought legislative and electoral changes that would give more power to the voters. These progressives succeeded in achieving the following:

- **The direct primary**, to elect nominees for office instead of party bosses
- **The legislative initiative**, which allowed the electorate to vote directly for specific legislation, rather than going through the state legislature
- **The referendum**, which allowed the electorate to vote on whether to accept or reject government legislation
- **The recall**, which allowed the electorate to vote government officials out of office in special elections

Robert M. La Follette

Governor Robert La Follette of Wisconsin incorporated many progressive policies into his government. Under his leadership, progressives in Wisconsin implemented a wide variety of measures, including:

- Workers' compensation and workplace regulation

- Environmental conservation legislation
- Higher taxes on railroads and other corporations
- The first modern state income tax in the nation

La Follette continued his push for progressive reform as a U.S. senator, representing Wisconsin from 1906 to 1925.

AMERICAN SOCIALISM

The socialist movement in the United States also reached its height during the Progressive Era. The Socialist party contained diverse constituents, with its members extending beyond core urban immigrant areas to the rural Midwest and South. Different groups of socialists envisioned different solutions to society's problems, with some advocating radical action, such as the over-throw of capitalism. Other socialists advocated more moderate measures, which would include small private businesses as an alternative to large corporations.

> Founded in 1905, the **Industrial Workers of the World (IWW)** was considered one of the most radical socialist factions. Led by **William Dudley Haywood**, the IWW (also known as the Wobblies) advocated militant action such as sabotage to overthrow the government in favor of an all-inclusive union. The organization still exists today, though with considerably less influence.

The Taft Years

With the support of Theodore Roosevelt, **William Howard Taft** ran as the Republican candidate for president in the election of 1908. The Democrats again nominated **William Jennings Bryan.** Taft appealed to members of both parties and thus won the election with 321 electoral votes to Bryan's 162. However, Taft's popularity did not last long, and his presidency conse-quently lasted only one term. By the end of his presidency, he had alienated progressives and had fallen out of favor with his former friend and ally Roosevelt.

TAFT'S DOLLAR DIPLOMACY

Whereas Roosevelt had employed big stick diplomacy to bend weaker nations to his will, Taft preferred to use the buck. He believed he could convince smaller developing nations to support the United States by investing American dollars into their economies. **"Dollar diplomacy,"** as pundits dubbed it, was intended to make allies as well as easy money for American investors.

Dollar Diplomacy Fails

Taft put his new policy to the test in Manchuria. In 1909, he offered to purchase and develop the Manchurian Railway to prevent Russia and Japan from seizing control of it and colonizing north China. Unfortunately, both powers refused to hand over the railway to the United States, and the deal collapsed. The United States went on to dump millions into several unstable Latin American countries, such as Honduras, Nicaragua, Cuba, and the Dominican Republic. Eventually, occupation troops had to be sent to protect those investments. In short, Taft's dollar diplomacy failed miserably.

MORE TRUST-BUSTING

After the failure of dollar diplomacy, Taft devoted himself instead to domestic matters and made trust-busting his top priority. Amazingly, he filed eighty lawsuits against monopolistic trusts in just four years, more than twice as many as Roosevelt had filed in almost eight years. In 1911, the Supreme Court used the previously neglected Sherman Antitrust Act when it dissolved John D. Rockefeller's **Standard Oil Company** for "unreasonably" stifling the competition. Taft also famously filed a suit against J. P. Morgan's **U.S. Steel Corporation** later that year, a move that infuriated Theodore Roosevelt, who had helped the company in the past.

THE PAYNE-ALDRICH TARIFF

Many progressive Republicans hoped Taft would keep his campaign promise and reduce the protective tariff. Taft tried but didn't have enough political clout to prevent conservatives within the party from repeatedly amending the bill for a lower tariff. By the time the **Payne-Aldrich Tariff** reached the president, conservatives had made so many amendments to keep certain tariffs high that the overall tariff rate remained practically unchanged. Taft signed the bill in 1909 anyway and then strangely proclaimed it to be the best bill Republicans had ever passed. Outraged, progressives denounced both the tariff and the "traitor" Taft.

THE BALLINGER-PINCHOT AFFAIR

Taft further alienated supporters when he fired **Gifford Pinchot** for insubordination. Pinchot was the head of the Forest Service. A progressive, popular conservationist, and personal friend of Roosevelt's, Pinchot had opposed Secretary of the Interior **Richard Ballinger**'s decision to sell public wilderness lands in Alaska and the Rocky Mountains to corporate developers. The president furthermore refused to reinstate Pinchot even after Roosevelt and several prominent Republicans appealed on his behalf. The 1910 **Ballinger-Pinchot Affair** thus blackened Taft's public image and made him many enemies within his own party.

ROOSEVELT RETURNS WITH NEW NATIONALISM

Feeling betrayed by his one-time friend turned foe, Roosevelt left retirement in 1910 and dove back into politics to wrest back control of the Republican Party. During the following two years, he denounced Taft in scores of speeches delivered throughout the country. He also took the opportunity to promote his **New Nationalism** program, which entailed:

- Greater government regulation of business
- A graduated income tax
- Tariff reform
- A strong central government that acted in defense of the public interest

The former Rough Rider took charge of the fledgling National Progressive Republican League within the Republican Party, trying to win the party's nomination for president in 1912. Divided, but still dominated by powerful pro-business conservatives, delegates at the nominating convention eventually chose to stick with Taft.

The Election of 1912

Roosevelt thundered out of the convention still determined to win a third term. He took with him his Progressive allies and founded a new **Progressive Party**. Ultimately, four candidates ran for the White House in 1912:

- **William Howard Taft** for the Republicans
- **Theodore Roosevelt** for the Progressive Republicans
- **Woodrow Wilson** for the Democrats
- **Eugene V. Debs** for the Socialists

In the end, Roosevelt's Bull Moose Party split the Republican Party and allowed Wilson to win an easy victory. Wilson received 435 electoral votes to Roosevelt's eighty-eight and Taft's eight. Surprisingly, Debs managed to win nearly a million popular votes.

> The Progressive Republican Party quickly became known as the **Bull Moose Party** after Roosevelt claimed to be as politically strong "as a bull moose" to run against Taft and Wilson. Women's suffrage was an integral platform of the Bull Moose Party; in fact, the rules of the party stipulated that four women were to be members of the Progressive National Committee.

Wilson's First Term

Even though Woodrow Wilson had promised a new form of progressivism and foreign policy during his campaign in 1912, his policies ultimately resembled those of his predecessors. In other words, he continued to use federal power to regulate big business and protect consumers while exerting American power in Latin America.

NEW FREEDOM PROGRESSIVISM

During the 1912 campaign, Roosevelt and Wilson offered different kinds of progressivism. Wilson countered Roosevelt's New Nationalism with his own **New Freedom** plan. New Freedom championed states rights, a limited federal government, and support for small businesses. During his two terms in office, however, Wilson compromised and incorporated many elements from New Nationalism into the New Freedom plan.

Economic and Business Changes

Wilson and progressives passed a variety of economic and business reforms, including:

- **The Underwood-Simmons Tariff** in 1913, which lowered protective tariffs

- **The Glass-Owen Federal Reserve Act**, also in 1913, which established a system of 12 regional Federal Reserve Banks. Each of the Federal Reserve Banks came under the oversight of a **Federal Reserve Board.** This gave the federal government greater control over the U.S. banking system.

- **The Clayton Antitrust Act** in 1914, which outlawed unfair business practices

- **The Federal Trade Commission Act** in 1914, which created the **Federal Trade Commission (FTC)**, a federal regulatory agency with the power to investigate and prosecute businesses engaged in illegal practices. The FTC, with its broader powers, replaced the **Bureau of Corporations** instituted under Roosevelt and served as the foundation of Wilson's antitrust policies.

Wilson's Other Reforms

Other progressive reforms included child labor legislation, aid to farmers, and the institution of an eight-hour workday for railroad employees. In addition, Wilson pleased progressives in 1916 by nominating Louis D. Brandeis to the Supreme Court. A committed progressive, Brandeis was also the Supreme Court's first Jewish member.

*Congress and the states ratified the **Sixteenth Amendment** in 1913 to establish the first federal income tax. The revenue generated from the tax offset the losses from the lower protective tariff. That same year Congress also ratified the **Seventeenth Amendment** to allow the electorate to elect their senators directly.*

WILSONIAN FOREIGN POLICY

Wilson envisioned the United States as a moral leader and force for democracy in the world and championed **"missionary diplomacy"** as opposed to Taft's "dollar diplomacy." Despite its strong idealistic underpinnings, Wilson's foreign policy differed very little from Taft's.

U.S. Intervention in Mexico

In 1913, Wilson denounced **Victoriano Huerta**'s revolutionary government in Mexico. This government had seized power and deposed the rightfully elected president. After a year of tense relations, Wilson finally decided to challenge Huerta's regime by sending U.S. troops to invade the Mexican port of **Veracruz**. Another revolutionary named **Venustiano Carranza** capitalized on the American invasion to overthrow Huerta and win the support of the United States. In retaliation, Mexican national hero **Pancho Villa** launched attacks on Americans in New Mexico and Arizona; the United States withdrew its forces from Mexico in 1917.

U.S. Presence in the Caribbean

Wilson sent troops to the following locations:

- **Nicaragua** in 1914 to continue Taft's occupation to ensure political and economy stability

- **Haiti** in 1915 to suppress a revolution

- **Dominican Republic** in 1916 to prevent a revolution

- **Danish West Indies** in 1917 after the United States purchased the islands from Denmark and renamed them the U.S. Virgin Islands

World War I Erupts

Although the United States willingly became involved in disputes and conflicts in the Western Hemisphere, Wilson hoped to avoid involving the United States in the Great War that engulfed Europe in 1914. Several events ultimately forced the United States to enter the war.

THE ASSASSINATION OF ARCHDUKE FRANZ FERDINAND

On June 28, 1914, a Serbian nationalist assassinated **Archduke Franz Ferdinand,** heir to the Austro-Hungarian Empire, in Sarajevo. Austria-Hungary declared war on Serbia following the assassination, prompting every other major European power to choose sides in the largest-scale war the world had ever experienced. Great Britain, France, Russia, Italy, and Japan formed the **Allied Powers** on one side, and Germany, Austria-Hungary, and Turkey formed the Central Powers on the other.

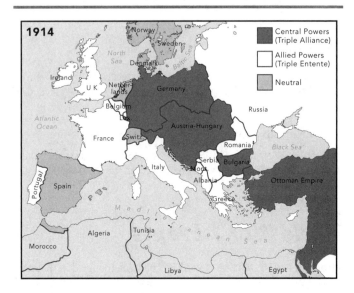

AMERICAN NEUTRALITY

Wilson tried to keep the United States neutral during the initial years of the war. Even though geography provided a natural buffer, war propaganda eventually crossed the Atlantic and split American public opinion. Moreover, the traditional American policy of neutral trading ultimately collapsed as Britain's blockade of Germany forced the United States to trade mainly with the Allies.

U-BOATS, THE LUSITANIA, AND THE SUSSEX

In response to the British blockade, Germany blockaded England with its deadly fleet of submarines, or **U-Boats**. While the United States objected to this expansion of the war zone, the situation did not become a crisis until the Germans sank the British passenger ship *Lusitania* on May 7, 1915. 1,198 people died in the *Lusitania* attack, including 128 Americans. Wilson and the German government negotiated to maintain relations after this incident and again after a 1916 attack on the French passenger ship *Sussex*.

The Zimmerman Note

Despite earlier pledges, the Germans began attacking both neutral and Allied ships in an unrestricted submarine warfare campaign in 1917 to strangle Britain economically. Wilson had no choice but to cut all diplomatic ties with Germany. Then, in February 1917, the British disclosed the contents of an intercepted German telegram promising to expand Mexican territory if Mexico invaded the United States. This **Zimmerman Note** outraged Americans, who put more pressure on Wilson to declare war on Germany.

WILSON DECLARES WAR

Unrestricted submarine warfare combined with Germany's blatant disregard for American sovereignty and territorial integrity ultimately forced Wilson to ask Congress to declare war in April 1917. Congress overwhelmingly consented to join the Allies against Germany, Turkey, and Austria-Hungary.

Mobilizing the United States for War

After deciding to enter the war, the Wilson administration immediately took several steps to gather the resources necessary to fight. The U.S. government funded the war by selling **Liberty Bonds** and collecting billions of dollars in new taxes.

Passed in 1917, the *Selective Service Act* established a nationwide draft and required all able-bodied men between the ages of twenty-one and thirty to register (the draft was later expanded to all men between eighteen and forty-five). The military drafted almost 3 million men to prepare for World War I.

WAR BOARDS

In 1916, the **Army Appropriation Act** established the **Council of National Defense** to oversee production of food, fuel, and railroads during the war. The council, in turn, created the following:

- **The War Industries Board**, headed by **Bernard Baruch**, organized and coordinated military purchases beginning in 1917. The board had extensive powers over U.S. production.

- **The National War Labor Board** settled disputes between labor and industry starting in 1918. Under pressure from the labor-friendly board, industries granted concessions such as an eight-hour workday and the right to bargain collectively.

COMMITTEE ON PUBLIC INFORMATION

Journalist George Creel headed the **Committee on Public Information** to produce propaganda in favor of the war effort. In addition to distributing films and printed material, the committee also had considerable control over information about the war that appeared in the popular press.

ESPIONAGE AND SEDITION ACTS

The **Espionage Act** of 1917 and the **Sedition Act** of 1918 effectively banned public criticism of governmental policy during the war. More than 1,000 people received convictions under these acts, which the Supreme Court upheld in 1919. Many of those convicted had ties to the growing Socialist party, including anti-war labor leader and presidential candidate **Eugene V. Debs**.

> Significant public opposition to German culture intensified in the United States during the war. Even though many German-Americans supported the war against Germany, many Americans still looked upon them as potential traitors. As a result, many companies fired their German-American employees, especially those who worked in war-related industries.

1901–1920

DOMESTIC LABOR

The war also brought changes in the domestic labor force. The flow of millions of working men into the armed forces and a reduction in immigration resulted in a labor shortage. To fill that gap, white women, African Americans, and workers of other races and ethnicities took jobs formerly held by white men.

Women in the Labor Force

During the war, women took jobs previously held by men, such as working on loading docks, operating heavy machinery, and working on the railroads. Some women even joined labor unions, although the American Federation of Labor (AFL) frequently opposed the entry of women into the work force. Most women only held their new jobs for the duration of the war.

The Nineteenth Amendment

During the war, suffragists increased the intensity of their campaign for the right to vote. Leaders included **Alice Paul**, who led the militant **National Woman's Party** and **Carrie Chapman Catt**, who took over the more moderate **National American Woman Suffrage Association** in 1915. Women's roles in the labor force ultimately helped Congress and the states to ratify the **Nineteenth Amendment**, which granted women the right to vote in 1920.

African Americans in the Labor Force

Many African Americans migrated from the South to urban areas in the North during the war years to take advantage of the labor shortage. This influx began the **Great African American Migration**, in which roughly 10 percent of all black southerners relocated to the North. Additionally, cotton-crop destruction by boll weevils and high unemployment rates in the South escalated the migration.

The United States in World War I

World War I had devastating repercussions for many nations. Although the United States had entered the war late, the nation still suffered major casualties. Some 112,000 American soldiers died in World War I, half from influenza and half from the fighting itself. Among all nations involved, some 10 million soldiers died. New military technologies and the use of trench warfare contributed to the high casualty rates.

*In November 1917, **Vladimir Lenin** and the **Bolshevik Party** overthrew a months-old, provisional republican government in Russia. The new communist government quickly arranged a peace settlement with Germany and effectively dropped out of the war. This allowed Germany to shift all its resources in the East to the Western front to fight France, Britain, and the United States.*

EFFECT OF U.S. FORCES

General John J. Pershing commanded the American Expeditionary Force sent to assist the British and French in Europe in 1917. U.S. forces, however, did not participate in any major fighting until 1918, when they helped achieve an Allied victory at the **Second Battle of the Marne**. Their defensive units defeated, German officials ultimately signed an armistice in November 1918.

THE FOURTEEN POINTS

On January 8, 1918, Wilson delivered a speech to a joint session of Congress that set forth, in a series of **Fourteen Points**, the aims for which he considered the United States to be fighting. Five of the points called for:

- Freedom of the seas
- Armament reduction
- Open diplomacy
- Free trade
- Impartial negotiation regarding colonial claims

Eight other points set forth recommendations for the institution of new national boundaries in the conquered Ottoman and Austro-Hungarian empires. The last point advocated an association of nations, or **League of Nations**, to mediate future disputes and protect countries' "political independence and territorial integrity."

THE PARIS PEACE CONFERENCE

In December 1918, the major combatants met at a peace conference in Paris. Wilson, Georges Clemenceau from France, David Lloyd George from Britain, and Vittorio Orlando from Italy made up the so-called **Big Four** that dominated the negotiations. On June 28, 1919, all sides signed the **Treaty of Versailles**, despite Germany's objection that the treaty would destroy its economy. The settlement required the following stipulations of Germany:

- Accept full responsibility for the war
- Pay $33 billion in reparations for the entire cost of the war
- Accept a foreign troop presence for fifteen years
- Cede some of its territory
- Abandon its colonies overseas

The Treaty of Versailles also divided the former Ottoman Empire in the Near and Middle East between Britain and France and established Wilson's League of Nations.

U.S. CONTROVERSY OVER THE TREATY

Wilson presented the Treaty of Versailles to the Senate in the summer of 1919 but encountered intense opposition. Republican Senator **Henry Cabot Lodge** and his **"reservationist"** allies denounced the treaty primarily because he disliked the League of Nations. Another group of **"irreconcilables"** objected to any American participation in the League. To gather public support, Wilson began a cross-country speaking tour, which was cut short in September 1919 when he fell ill. He later suffered a serious stroke that ruined any chance of the Senate ratifying the treaty. Congress formally declared the war over simply by passing a joint resolution in 1920.

Timeline

1900	Republican president William McKinley is reelected. His vice president is Theodore Roosevelt.
1901	On September 6, an anarchist shoots McKinley during the Pan American Exposition. McKinley dies several days later, and Theodore Roosevelt becomes president.
1902	The Anthracite Coal Strike begins in May. It ends in October after the sides agree to submit to arbitration by a Roosevelt-appointed commission. The resolution of the strike results in Roosevelt's phrase "square deal."
	Roosevelt prosecutes the Northern Securities Company, charging it with violation of antitrust legislation. Two years later, the Supreme Court upholds the Sherman Antitrust Act, ordering Northern Securities to dissolve.
1903	Congress creates the Department of Commerce and Labor, containing a Bureau of Corporations to investigate businesses conducting interstate commerce.
	W.E.B. Du Bois publishes *The Souls of Black Folk*.
1904	Japan attacks the Russian fleet stationed at China's Port Arthur, beginning the Russo-Japanese War.
	Roosevelt wins reelection.
	Roosevelt announces his "Roosevelt Corollary" to the Monroe Doctrine, giving the United States leave to involve itself in the domestic affairs of countries in the Western Hemisphere.
1906	Upton Sinclair publishes *The Jungle*.
	The Hepburn Railroad Regulation Act expands the mandate of the Interstate Commerce Commission.
	The Meat Inspection Act requires federal inspectors to examine meat.
	The Pure Food and Drug Act applies federal regulations to the sale of medicine and foods.
1908	Republican William Howard Taft wins the presidency.
1909	National Association for the Advancement of Colored People (NAACP) is founded.
1910	Congress passes the Mann-Elkins Act, expanding the powers of the Interstate Commerce Commission (ICC).
	Jane Addams publishes *Twenty Years at Hull House*.

1911	A fire breaks out at the Triangle Shirtwaist Company in New York City. The blaze, which kills 146 workers, helps gain support for fire codes, labor laws, and workplace regulation.
	The Taft administration initiates an antitrust suit against U.S. Steel, angering Theodore Roosevelt.
1912	Roosevelt runs for president as head of the "Bull Moose" Party, splitting the Republican vote with Taft, the Republican party's nominee, and allowing for the victory of Democratic challenger Woodrow Wilson.
1913	The ratification of the Sixteenth Amendment to the Constitution allows for a federal income tax.
	The Seventeenth Amendment to the Constitution is ratified, which institutes popular election of U.S. senators.
	Wilson signs the Glass-Owen Federal Reserve Act, establishing a system of regional Federal Reserve Banks under the oversight of a Federal Reserve Board.
1914	A Serbian nationalist assassinates Archduke Franz Ferdinand, the heir to the Austro-Hungarian Empire, leading to the start of World War I in Europe.
	The Panama Canal opens, linking the Atlantic and Pacific Oceans across the Isthmus of Panama.
	The Federal Trade Commission (FTC) is created to regulate businesses practices.
	The Clayton Antitrust Act passes, outlawing practices like interlocking directorates in large corporations and price discrimination.
	U.S. troops invade the Mexican port of Veracruz.
1915	Germans sink the *Lusitania*, killing 1,198 people, including 128 Americans.

1901–1920

1917	Germany begins unrestricted submarine warfare. Following that development, Wilson breaks diplomatic relations with Germany.
	The British relate the Zimmerman Telegram to Wilson, soon sparking the United States' entry into World War I.
	The United States declares war on Germany.
	The Selective Service Act establishes a nationwide draft.
	The Espionage Act passes. The Sedition Act passes in 1918. Both acts target public criticism of government policy.
	In Houston, Texas, a deadly clash occurs between black soldiers and the police. The incident results in the execution of nineteen black soldiers.
	The Bolshevik Party overthrows a provisional republican government in Russia. The new government arranges a peace with Germany in March of the following year, and exits the war.
1918	Wilson delivers his Fourteen Points to Congress. The speech, which sets forth the aims Wilson considers the United States to be fighting for, includes a proposal for the League of Nations.
	The Sedition Act is passed.
	The Second Battle of the Marne marks a turning point in World War I. In November, German officials sign an armistice.
1919– 1920	In the "Red Scare," Attorney General A. Mitchell Palmer and his assistant John Edgar Hoover organize raids in which authorities arrest alleged radicals.
1919	The ratification of the Eighteenth Amendment orders prohibition.
	At the end of the peace conference in Paris, all remaining participants in World War I sign the Treaty of Versailles, despite Germany's objections about the extremely punitive nature of the pact.
	Wilson presents the Treaty of Versailles to the Senate, where the document encounters opposition.
	The "Red Summer" sees race riots in many U.S. cities, including Washington, D.C., and Chicago.
	Steel workers strike for union recognition and an eight-hour day. Workers return to their jobs four months later, without the concessions.
1920	The ratification of the Nineteenth Amendment gives women the right to vote.

CHAPTER 13

The Roaring Twenties: 1920–1929

||||||||||||||||||||||||||||||||||||||||||||||||||||||||

The popular images of the twenties—late-night jazz sessions, sequined flappers doing the Charleston, and dapper young men drinking bathtub gin in smoky speakeasies—gave rise to its various nicknames, such as the "Roaring Twenties," the "Jazz Age," and the "Era of Excess." Automobiles, airplanes, radio, movies, mass consumerism, advances for women, and new concepts of morality also pushed Americans into the modern era.

On the other hand, many Americans opposed the headlong rush into modernity and struggled to reassert older, more conservative Protestant values. Republicans, for example, dominated domestic and foreign policy issues and underscored the new American isolationism by refusing to join the League of Nations. They also succeeded in passing stricter immigration laws, as well as the Eighteenth Amendment prohibiting the sale and consumption of alcohol. Membership in the Ku Klux Klan and fundamentalist Christian organizations also skyrocketed to combat immigration, the rise of black nationalism, and new scientific theories that challenged established religious beliefs.

Political Conservatism and Prosperity

Tired of war and the political squabbling that had characterized the final years of Woodrow Wilson's presidency, Americans craved stable leadership and economic prosperity in the 1920s. Weary voters elected three probusiness conservative Republican presidents in the 1920s: **Warren G. Harding, Calvin Coolidge**, and **Herbert Hoover**. As a result, continuity—rather than change—characterized the political climate of the 1920s.

WARREN G. HARDING AND NORMALCY

Republican candidate **Warren G. Harding** promised voters a return to **"normalcy"** if elected president in 1920. Disillusioned by the upheaval of World War I, most Americans found Harding's cautious and conservative politics compelling. His popular image as a small-town newspaper editor from the Midwest combined with his consistently neutral policies contributed to his overwhelming victory over Democratic opponent James Cox.

During his three years in office, Harding supported big business, relaxed government control over industry, and promoted high tariffs on imports.

Resistance to the League of Nations

In order to restore stability both at home and abroad, Harding adopted several measures to reduce the country's international commitments. He signed several peace treaties with Germany, Austria, and Hungary soon after taking office and proposed an arms-reduction plan for a new Europe. In doing so, Harding sidestepped the extremely controversial issue concerning American membership in the **League of Nations** that had plagued Woodrow Wilson. Harding's plan allowed the United States to focus more fully on domestic matters while taking a backstage role in the reconstruction of Europe.

1920–1929

Scandal

President Harding gave many of the top cabinet positions and civil service jobs to his old chums from Ohio. Unfortunately for the president, the **"Ohio Gang"** quickly sullied Harding's name by accepting bribes, defrauding the government, and bootlegging. In fact, grand juries indicted several of Harding's appointees; a few even received prison sentences. The chain of unending scandals prompted many Americans to questions Harding's own integrity and ability to lead.

The **Teapot Dome scandal** shocked Americans most of all. In 1923, journalists discovered that Harding's secretary of the interior, **Albert B. Fall**, had illegally authorized private companies to drill for oil on public lands. Investigators later determined that these companies had bribed the nearly bankrupt Fall to ignore their actions while they drilled. The naïve Harding escaped implication in the scandal only when he died unexpectedly of a heart attack in 1923. Although the nation expressed grief over his death, more scandals continued to surface throughout the decade and continued to tarnish Harding's reputation.

CONSERVATIVE CALVIN COOLIDGE

The quiet vice president **Calvin Coolidge** entered the White House following Harding's death in 1923. His reserved demeanor, moral uprightness, and distance from the Harding scandals allowed him to win the presidency in his own right the following year in the election of 1924. Although "Silent Cal" Coolidge's personality and public persona differed greatly from Harding's, the two men thought along the same lines politically. Coolidge continued to support big business, propose higher tariffs, and push for deregulation of business and the economy. As a result, his victory in 1924 marked the demise of Progressivism.

THE PRESIDENCY OF HERBERT HOOVER

Like Harding and Coolidge, **Herbert Hoover** won the presidency in 1928 on a platform for big business and against big government. Having grown accustomed to the prosperity associated with previous conservative presidents, Americans rejected Democratic candidate Alfred E. Smith and voted for Hoover.

Hoover's inflexible conservatism ultimately prevented him from facing the impending economic crisis. The European demand for American exports had dropped, farmers were more and more in debt, and Americans were continuing to live extravagant lifestyles, primarily on credit.

Prohibition and the Rise of Organized Crime

The **Eighteenth Amendment** took effect in January 1920, banning the manufacture, sale, and transport of all intoxicating liquors. Referred to by supporters as "the noble experiment," Prohibition succeeded at lowering the consumption of alcohol, at least in rural areas. At the same time, the amendment created a lucrative black market for alcohol sales. Illegal, or **bootlegged**, liquor became widely available in cities. Typically, smugglers brought this liquor into the United States from other countries, while other Americans produced it in small homemade stills. "**Speakeasies**," illegal bars where men and often women drank publicly, opened in most urban areas.

GANGSTERS AND RACKETEERS

While Prohibition did not necessarily lead to criminal activity and the formation of gangs, both of which existed long before, it did provide criminals with a financially rewarding new business. "**Scarface**" **Al Capone** emerged as the best-known gangster of the era. He moved to Chicago in 1920 and soon became the city's leading bootlegger and gambling lord, protecting his empire with an army of gunmen. Capone's profits reached approximately $60 million annually by 1927. Although authorities generally tolerated bootleggers and speakeasies at first, they cracked down on the gangsters when a Chicago bootlegging gang disguised as police officers gunned down members of a rival gang in the **St. Valentine's Day Massacre**. Authorities eventually prosecuted Capone in 1931 for federal income tax evasion.

PROHIBITION REPEALED

Because of the widespread availability of black-market liquor, federal authorities had trouble enforcing Prohibition. Still, President Herbert Hoover wanted to continue the morally worthy "experiment" in spite of growing opposition from the general public. Congress eventually passed the **Twenty-First Amendment** in 1933 to repeal Prohibition.

The Culture of Modernism

The expansion of radio broadcasting, the boom of motion pictures, and the spread of consumerism united the nation culturally. At the same time, these changes contributed to the breakdown of America's traditional vision of itself. As a result, a new national identity began to form.

THE IMPACT OF RADIO

The popularity of radio soared during the 1920s, bringing Americans together and softening regional differences. With the arrival of the first developed radio station in 1920, the format of radio programming changed dramatically, expanding to include news, music, talk shows, sports broadcasts, political speeches, and advertising. The American public eagerly welcomed radios into their homes, signaling their openness to a changing culture. By simply turning on the radio, they received standardized information transmitted through national broadcasts. They also encountered advertising campaigns designed to change their spending habits and lifestyles.

THE RISE OF MOTION PICTURES

The American movie industry began in New York City, but when it moved to California in 1915, a true entertainment revolution began. By 1929, nearly every citizen attended the movies weekly, eager to see the latest comedy, thriller, and western. As movie attendance rose, so did the fame of the actors and actresses who performed in them. The "movie star" soon became a figure of glamour and fame.

MASS PRODUCTION AND THE AUTOMOBILE

Mass production allowed **Henry Ford** and his **Ford Motor Company**—the industry leader during the 1920s—to sell cars at prices that the working class could afford. This vastly increased the automaker's market. Cars made on an assembly line could be produced approximately ten times faster than cars assembled using more traditional means. The rapid increase in the supply of new cars combined with dramatically lower prices led to a vast increase in the total number of cars sold. Throughout the course of the decade, the number of cars on American roads tripled to 23 million.

Car ownership changed the way many people experienced American life. Owning cars allowed Americans in rural areas to take advantage of the amenities of nearby cities. Many smaller towns simply disappeared as increased competition closed numerous small businesses.

> Americans loved cars so much that automobile manufacturing had become the most productive industry in U.S. history by 1930. Roughly one in five people owned cars when the Great Depression hit.

AVIATION

Other modes of transportation also progressed in the 1920s. On May 21, 1927, **Charles Lindbergh** completed the first successful solo flight across the Atlantic. The American public celebrated the flight as a triumph not only of individual heroism but also of technological advancement. This flight foreshadowed the emergence of the commercial airline industry, which would boom in the ensuing decades.

MODERNIST LITERATURE

Intrigued by what they saw as the fast-paced, fractured, unmoored modern world around them, writers in the 1920s struggled to develop a new type of language for expressing a new type of reality. Poets and fiction writers used new techniques such as **free verse** and **stream of consciousness** to capture the national mood.

Free verse is a form of poetry without a set scheme of rhyme or meter. Stream of consciousness is a literary style in which writers try to give a literary representation of characters' actual thought processes.

The Lost Generation

Some of the most prominent American writers of the 1920s actually lived in Europe. Known collectively as the **Lost Generation**, writers such as Ernest Hemingway, Gertrude Stein, Ezra Pound, and Harold Stearns penned bitter commentaries on postwar America. Cynical about the country's potential for progress and about what they perceived to be misappropriated values, these writers found community abroad and produced some of the most creative literature and poetry in American history.

The Southern Renaissance

In the South, authors dealt with their regions' own transformation from a traditional society to one more influenced by changes in the wider American culture. Bible Belt authors, for example, found abundant material in the struggles of individuals who did not want to relinquish their agrarian lifestyles to modernism. Prominent writers of this movement included William Faulkner, Thomas Wolfe, Alan Tate, and Ellen Glasgow.

Mississippi native William Faulkner received the Nobel Prize for Literature in 1949 for his modernist novels The Sound and the Fury, Light in August, *and* As I Lay Dying. *Faulkner mined the emotional depths of the American South and succeeded in both humanizing and mythologizing the tragedy of southern history. Many literary scholars consider him the most important American writer of the twentieth century.*

Resistance to Modernity

THE RED SCARE

Americans feared communist and socialist ideas in the wake of the Russian Revolution of 1917. In late 1919, communist fears picked up steam, and in January 1920, police across the nation seized more than 6,000 suspects in a raid to find and expel suspected communists. The government deported many socialists, including several in the New York legislature. Fortunately, the worst of the **Red Scare** had passed by 1921.

THE EMERGENCY IMMIGRATION ACT

Compelled by imagined threats of foreign influences on American values and the rapidly rising rates of postwar immigration in 1920 and 1921, Congress passed the **Emergency Quota Act of 1921**. The act restricted new arrivals of immigrants to 3 percent of foreign-born members of any given nationality. The **Immigration Act of 1924** reduced this number further to 2 percent.

Both the Emergency Quota Act of 1921 and the Immigration Act of 1924 blatantly favored northern and western Europeans and limited the influx of darker-skinned Catholics from southern and eastern Europe. The act also banned immigrants from East Asia.

THE SACCO AND VANZETTI TRIAL

The trial of two Italian anarchists, **Nicola Sacco** and **Bartolomeo Vanzetti**, illustrated Americans' intolerance for foreign ideas and individuals. Tried and convicted for robbery and murder in Massachusetts in 1920, Sacco and Vanzetti faced an openly bigoted judge who failed to give the defendants a fair trial. Although protesters rallied behind them for six years, Sacco and Vanzetti never received a retrial, and state authorities executed them in 1927.

THE KU KLUX KLAN

The **Ku Klux Klan** reemerged in the 1920s as a misdirected effort to protect American values. Unlike the Klan of the nineteenth century, which had terrorized blacks in the South, the new KKK of the 1920s had a strong following among white Protestants throughout the country. It targeted blacks, immigrants, Jews, Catholics, and other minority groups that threatened the KKK's homogenous values and identity.

Through the course of the decade, the Klan gained a significant amount of political power, exerting both direct and indirect influence on state politics throughout the country. However, by the end of the 1920s, the Klan attracted considerable negative publicity, which, combined with the diminished threat of immigration, led to its downfall.

THE SCOPES TRIAL

In 1925, a Tennessee court tried high school biology teacher **John Scopes** for teaching the theory of evolution in his classroom in spite of a prohibitory state law. Protestant leaders like **William Jennings Bryan** (a three-time Democratic candidate for president) spoke out against evolution, while Scopes's famed defense attorney **Clarence Darrow** tried to ridicule Christian fundamentalism. Clarence Darrow hounded and ridiculed William Jennings Bryan on the witness stand so extensively that some blame Darrow for Jenning's death from a stress-related illness several days after the trial concluded.

The so-called **Scopes "Monkey" Trial** captured the nation's interest. Although the court found Scopes guilty of violating the law, it only fined him $100. The high-profile trial illustrated the growing tension between tradition and progress.

Impact of Black Culture

As Americans became interested in the new musical sounds coming from cities such as New Orleans, New York, St. Louis, and Chicago, jazz music became the rage of the decade, typifying the fluidity and energy of the era. African Americans also captured their culture in literature and art. Many whites became fascinated by the image of the black American that emerged during the 1920s.

NEGRO NATIONALISM

Marcus Garvey led the "Negro Nationalism" movement, which celebrated the black experience and culture. As the leader of the **United Negro Improvement Association (UNIA),** Garvey advocated for the establishment of a Negro republic in Africa for exiled Americans. He argued that racial prejudice ran too deep in white American attitudes to ever be satisfactorily fixed and that black Americans should flee to their ancestral lands. Garvey's influence lessened after he went to prison in 1925 for federal mail fraud. His deportation to Jamaica in 1927 effectively ended his power within the African-American community.

THE NAACP

The National Association for the Advancement of Colored People (NAACP), established in 1910, remained active in the 1920s. Unlike the UNIA, the NAACP sought to resolve the racial issues in American society. The organization focused specifically on the dissemination of information and the implementation of protective legislation. In 1922, for example, the NAACP succeeded in getting a bill passed that helped end lynching. Although the bill remained mired in the House of Representatives for three years, public attention surrounding the bill helped reduce the number of lynchings in the United States.

THE HARLEM RENAISSANCE

The **Harlem Renaissance** was one of the major African-American cultural and artistic movements during the era. Black authors depicted experiences from urban Manhattan to rural Georgia and included Claude McKay, Langston Hughes, Zora Neale Hurston, and Alain Locke. Their poems and narratives not only captured the diversity of the African-American experience but also highlighted the rich culture of black America.

JAZZ

The growth of **jazz** music in the 1920s coupled the cultural expression of black Americans with mainstream culture by tapping into the emerging spirit of youth, freedom, and openness. The jazz movement also dissolved many traditional racial barriers in music, allowing young musicians of all races to collaborate and forge individual avenues of expression.

Emergence of the "New Woman"

Women's roles changed at an unprecedented rate. Oppressive taboos such as those against smoking, drinking, and sexually provocative behavior slackened during the decade as women sought more freedom and self-expression. Some women began experimenting with new styles of dress, danced more, and discussed sex openly and freely. However, historians note that most women in the 1920s still adhered to traditional gender roles and customs despite the new freedoms and morality.

SUFFRAGE AND THE NINETEENTH AMENDMENT

After the **Nineteenth Amendment** granted women the right to vote in 1920, former suffragettes formed the **League of Women Voters** to educate American women about candidates, issues, and the political process. Although some Americans feared the political leanings of the new electoral contingency, the addition of women voters had very little impact on voting trends because many women did not exercise their newly earned right to vote.

Many immigrant and southern women, for example, often chose not to vote because they didn't want to challenge the traditional authority of their husbands. On the other hand, those who did vote showed little solidarity in their commitment to the advancement of women in society. Activists like **Alice Paul** of the newly formed Woman's Party lobbied for feminist goals, such as equal rights and greater social justice. The majority of American women, however, still found such radical feminism distasteful and instead chose to fight for moderate and gradual reform through established parties.

Division within the women's movement ultimately led to the defeat of the **Equal Rights Amendment (ERA)**. Proposed in 1923, the ERA would have granted men and women equal legal rights. Female lobbyists did succeed in convincing Congress to pass other significant laws to help women. For example, the **Sheppard-Towner Act** passed in 1921 awarding federal funds for healthcare to women and infants. Unfortunately, such protective legislation and social welfare programs suffered without legislators' vigilant care, and Congress eventually abandoned the Sheppard-Towner program in 1929 to cut costs. Most other legislative efforts concerning women met similar fates.

> *Although more and more women began working outside the home throughout the 1920s, they filled primarily service and clerical jobs. Women had few professional opportunities, because social norms still dictated that they should be homemakers above all else. Most working women kept their jobs only until marriage.*

FLAPPERS

Flapper women became the icon of the 1920s with their short "bobbed" hair, makeup, dangling jewelry, short skirts, and zest for modernity. Unlike the women of previous generations, flappers drank, smoked, danced, flirted, and caroused with men freely and easily. Even though very few women actually became flappers, the image appealed widely to the filmmakers, novelists, and advertisers who made them famous. Thrust into the limelight, flappers helped transform Americans' conservative conceptions of propriety and morality.

The Stock Market Crash of 1929

The prosperity of the 1920s finally ended when the **"bull market"** suddenly showed the strain of overvaluation in the fall of 1929. The value of the stock market had more than quadrupled during the 1920s primarily because Americans had purchased stock **"on margin"** by using the *future* earnings from their investments to buy even more stock. Even though buying stock on margin grossly distorted the real value of the investments, most people naively assumed the market would continue to climb. Therefore, they funded their lavish lifestyles on credit.

When the market buckled and stock prices began to slip, brokers made **"margin calls"** requesting investors to pay off the debts owed on stock purchased on margin. Unfortunately, most people didn't have the cash to pay back the brokers. Instead, they tried to sell all their investments quickly to come up with the extra money. The surge in stock dumping eventually caused the most catastrophic market crash in American history on **Black Tuesday**: October 29, 1929. In spite of attempts by major investors to bolster the rapidly declining market, Black Tuesday marked the beginning of the rapid economic collapse known as the **Great Depression**.

1920-1929

Timeline

1919	The Red Scare begins.
1920	Prohibition begins with the Eighteenth Amendment.
	Women earn equal suffrage in the Nineteenth Amendment.
	Former suffragettes form the League of Women Voters.
	Warren G. Harding is elected president.
1921	Congress passes the Emergency Quota Act.
	Congress passes the Sheppard-Towner Act.
1923	The Teapot Dome scandal shocks Americans.
	Harding dies and Vice President Calvin Coolidge becomes president.
	The Equal Rights Amendment (ERA) is proposed.
1924	Coolidge is elected president.
	Congress passes the Immigration Act of 1924.
1925	Biology teacher John Scopes is tried for teaching evolution.
1927	Charles Lindbergh completes the first solo flight across the Atlantic.
	Nicola Sacco and Bartolomeo Vanzetti are executed.
1928	Herbert Hoover is elected president.
1929	Al Capone is prosecuted for tax evasion.
	The stock market crashes on Black Tuesday.

1920–1929

CHAPTER 14

The Great Depression and the New Deal: 1929–1939

||||||||||||||||||||||||||||||||||||||||||||||||||||||||||||||||||||||||||

The New Deal marked a major turning point in American history. Never before had the federal government become so involved in the daily lives of ordinary people. Unlike his Republican predecessor Herbert Hoover, Roosevelt and the New Dealers tried to directly help as many people as conservatives in Congress and the Supreme Court would permit. Much historical evidence suggests that had Roosevelt not been elected president, the Depression would have been much worse. The Canadian economy, for example, remained virtually unchanged during the entire ten-year period after the Crash of 1929 due to the relatively conservative government's policies of nonintervention.

The New Deal ultimately failed to end the Depression. Hunger, home-lessness, and unemployment still affected millions of Americans even as late as December 1941, when the United States entered World War II. Many historians and economists have suggested that the New Deal would have been more successful had Roosevelt put even more money into the economy. Only after the surge in demand for war munitions, ships, tanks, and airplanes did the economy finally right itself and leap forward.

The Depression Begins

The "Roaring Twenties" came to a crashing halt in 1929. By late October, more and more people had pulled their money out of Wall Street. Consequently, the Dow Jones Industrial Average fell steadily during a ten-day period until it finally crashed completely on October 29, 1929. This day came to be known as **"Black Tuesday."**

On Black Tuesday, investors panicked and dumped an unprecedented 16 million shares. The practice of buying on margin had destroyed Americans' credit and only made the effects of the **Crash of 1929** (or **Great Crash**) worse. Within only one month's time, American investors had lost tens of billions of dollars.

CAUSES OF THE DEPRESSION

Although the 1929 stock-market crash had acted as the catalyst, a confluence of several factors actually caused the Great Depression.

A Changing Economy

The foundation of the American economy slowly shifted from heavy industrial production to mass manufacturing. In other words, whereas most of America's wealth had come from producing iron, steel, coal, and oil at the end of the nineteenth century, manufacturing consumer goods like automobiles, radios, and other goods formed the basis of the economy in the twentieth century. As Americans jumped on the consumer bandwagon, more and more people began purchasing goods on credit, promising to pay for items later.

When the 1920s economic bubble burst, creditors had to absorb the cost of millions in bad loans that debtors couldn't repay. Moreover, policymakers found it difficult to end the Depression's vicious circle—Americans couldn't buy goods until they had jobs, but no factories wanted to give people jobs because they couldn't sell goods to a penniless population.

Buying on Margin

Americans had also purchased millions of dollars in stock on credit. Investors could purchase a share of a company's stock, and then use the *projected* earnings of that stock to buy even more. Not surprisingly, many people abused the system to invest huge sums of imaginary money that existed only on paper.

Overproduction in Factories

Overproduction in manufacturing also contributed to the economic collapse. Factories produced more and more popular consumer goods in an effort to match demand during the 1920s. Output soared as more companies utilized new machines to increase production, but workers' wages remained relatively stagnant throughout the decade. Eventually, the price of goods plummeted when factories began producing more goods than people demanded.

Overproduction on Farms

Farmers faced a similar overproduction crisis. Increasing debt forced many of them to plant more and more profitable cash crops such as wheat every year. Unfortunately, wheat depletes the soil's nutrients and renders it unsuitable for planting over time, but impoverished farmers couldn't afford to plant any other crop. Harvesting more wheat only depressed prices and forced them to plant even more the next year, which perpetuated the cycle.

Bad Banking Practices

Poor banking practices didn't help the situation. Many twentieth-century banks were little better than the fly-by-night variety of the previous century, especially in the rural areas of the West and South. The federal government didn't regulate the banks, and Americans had nowhere to turn to lodge complaints against bad banks. In fact, the majority of people had no idea what happened to their money after they handed it over to bankers.

Many bankers capitalized on the bull market to buy stocks on margin with customers' savings. This money simply vanished when the market collapsed, and thousands of families lost their entire savings in a matter of minutes. Hundreds of banks failed during the first months of the Depression, which produced an even greater panic and rush to withdraw private savings.

Income Inequality

Income inequality—the greatest in American history—made the Depression extremely severe. At the end of the 1920s, the top 1 percent of Americans owned more than a third of all the nation's wealth, while the poorest 20 percent of people owned a meager 4 percent of the wealth. The middle class, meanwhile, had essentially shrunk into nonexistence. As a result, only a few Americans had vast amounts of wealth while the rest lived barely above the poverty level.

Old War Debts

The aftermath of World War I in Europe played a significant role in the downward spiral of the global economy in the late 1920s. According to the Treaty of Versailles, Germany owed France and England impossible sums in war reparations. France and England in turn owed millions of dollars to the United States. Starting in Germany, a wave of Depression spread through Europe as each country became unable to pay off its debts. As a result, the Great Depression affected the rest of the industrialized world.

Hoover's Response

1929–1939

President **Herbert Hoover** and other officials downplayed the crash at first. They claimed that the slump would be temporary, and that it would clean up corruption and bad business practices within the system. Wall Street might not boom again, but it would certainly be healthier. The Republican president also believed that the federal government shouldn't interfere with the economy. In fact, he argued, if American families steeled their determination, continued to work hard, and practiced self-reliance, the United States could quickly pull out of the "recession."

THE RECONSTRUCTION FINANCE CORPORATION

Instead of tackling the problem pro-actively, Hoover took an indirect approach to jump-starting the economy. He created several committees in the early 1930s to assist American farm and industrial corporations. In 1932 he also approved Congress's **Reconstruction Finance Corporation** to provide loans to banks, insurance companies, railroads, and state governments. He hoped that federal dollars dropped into the top of the economic system would help all Americans as the money "trickled down" to the bottom. Individuals were not eligible for RFC loans. Hoover refused to lower the steep tariffs and shot down all "socialistic" relief proposals, such as the **Muscle Shoals Bill** drafted to harness energy from the Tennessee River.

> The Crash of 1929 caused a panic that rapidly developed into a depression the likes of which Americans had never experienced. Millions lost their jobs and their homes as most factories laid off workers in the cities to cut production and expenses. Shantytowns, or **"Hoovervilles,"** filled with the homeless and unemployed, sprang up overnight in cities throughout America.

THE DUST BOWL

The Depression also hit farmers hard, especially those in Colorado, Oklahoma, New Mexico, Kansas, and the Texas panhandle. Years of farming wheat without alternating crops to replenish the soil had turned the earth into a thick layer of barren dust. Depressed crop prices due to overproduction also forced many farmers off their fields. Unable to grow anything, thousands of families left this **Dust Bowl** region in search of work on the West Coast. Author John Steinbeck immortalized the plight of these farmers in his 1939 novel *The Grapes of Wrath*.

THE BONUS ARMY

Middle-aged World War I veterans were also among the hardest hit. In 1924, Congress had agreed to pay veterans a bonus stipend to be collected in 1945. As the Depression worsened, more and more of the veterans demanded their bonuses early. When Congress refused to pay up, more than 20,000 vets formed the

"**Bonus Army**" and marched on Washington, D.C., in the summer of 1932. They set up a giant, filthy Hooverville in front of the Capitol and were determined not to leave until the government paid them. Hoover eventually ordered General Douglas MacArthur (of World War II fame) to forcibly remove the Bonus Army. Federal troops used tear gas and fire to destroy the makeshift camp in what the press dubbed the **Battle of Anacostia Flats**.

> President Hoover's inability to recognize the severity of the crisis or the potential for disaster only worsened the Depression. Many historians and economists believe that Hoover could have dampened the effects of the Depression had he only regulated the finance sector of the economy and provided direct relief to the unemployed and homeless.

THE ELECTION OF 1932

The brutal treatment of America's war heroes further convinced people that Hoover simply didn't have the gumption or knowledge to resolve the economic crisis. Instead, all eyes focused on the optimistic Democrat, Governor **Franklin Delano Roosevelt (FDR)** of New York. A distant cousin of former president Theodore Roosevelt, FDR promised more direct relief and assistance rather than benefits for big business. Republicans nominated Hoover for a second term in the election of 1932 but couldn't compete with the Democrats. In the end, Roosevelt soundly defeated Hoover, carrying all but six states.

1929–1939

FDR and the First New Deal

Roosevelt's policies did much to get Americans back on their feet. The New Deal not only provided **relief**, **recovery**, and **reform**, but it also drastically changed the federal government's role in politics and society. His successful application of John Maynard Keynes's economic theories transformed Democrats into social-welfare advocates. Even decades after the Great Depression, these politicians would fight for more government intervention in the economy, redistribution of wealth, and aid for the neediest.

THE FIRST HUNDRED DAYS

Americans had voted for Franklin Delano Roosevelt in the election of 1932 on the assumption that the Democrat would spur Washington to dole out more federal assistance. True to his word, the new president immediately set out to provide relief, recovery, and reform in his bundle of programs, collectively known as the **New Deal**.

Roosevelt drew much of his inspiration for the New Deal from the writings of British economist **John Maynard Keynes,** who believed that government deficit spending could prime the economic pump and jump-start the economy. With the support of a panicked Democratic Congress, Roosevelt created most of the **"alphabet agencies"** of the **First New Deal** within his **First Hundred Days** in office.

Banking Relief and Reform

On March 6, 1933—just two days after becoming president—Roosevelt declared a five-day national **bank holiday** to temporarily close the banks. Roughly 9,000 banks had closed during each year of the Depression under Hoover, and the new president hoped that a short break would give the surviving banks time to reopen on more solid footing. Congress also passed Roosevelt's **Emergency Banking Relief Act**, which gave Roosevelt the power to regulate banking transactions and foreign exchange, and the **Glass-Steagall Banking Reform Act** of 1933, which protected savings deposits. The act created the **Federal Deposit Insurance Corporation (FDIC)** that insured individuals' savings of up to $5,000 (today, deposits of up to $100,000 are insured). The act also forbade banks from investing in the stock market and regulated lending policies.

After resolving the banking crisis, Roosevelt broadcast the first of his radio "fireside chats" to over 50 million listeners to encourage Americans to redeposit their money in the new banks. The fireside chats were a large reason for Roosevelt's popularity; they allowed Americans to feel a real sense of connection with the president.

1929-1939

The Civilian Conservation Corps (CCC)

Congress also created the **Civilian Conservation Corps (CCC)** in March 1933. Commonly known as the CCC, the corps hired unemployed young men to work on environmental conservation projects throughout the country. For thirty dollars a month, the men worked on flood control and reforestation projects, improved national parks, and built many public roads. Approximately 3 million men worked in CCC camps during the program's nine-year existence.

The Federal Emergency Relief Administration (FERA, CWA)

The so-called "Hundred Days Congress" also created the **Federal Emergency Relief Administration (FERA)** in May 1933. During the course of the Depression, FERA doled out $500 million to the states. The administration assigned roughly half of this money to bail out bankrupt state and local governments. States matched the other half (three state dollars for every one federal dollar) and distributed it directly to the people. Over the years, FERA gave more than three billion dollars to the states. In addition, FERA created the **Civil Works Administration (CWA)** to create temporary labor jobs to those most in need.

The Agricultural Adjustment Administration (AAA)

Roosevelt encouraged the creation of the **Agricultural Adjustment Administration (AAA)** to assist farmers. The AAA temporarily reset production quotas for farm commodities, including corn, wheat, rice, milk, cotton, and livestock. The AAA also subsidized farmers to reduce production so that prices would eventually rise again.

Congress also passed the **Farm Credit Act** to provide loans to farmers in danger of bankruptcy.

The Tennessee Valley Authority (TVA)

May 1933 heralded the creation of the **Tennessee Valley Authority (TVA)** as well. Congress created the TVA to modernize and reduce unemployment in the Tennessee River Valley, one of the poorest regions in the country even before the Depression.

The TVA hired local workers to construct a series of dams and hydroelectric power plants that brought cheap electricity to thousands of people. The public corporation also created affordable employee housing, manufactured cheap fertilizer, and drained thousands of acres for farming.

The National Industrial Recovery Act (NRA, PWA)

Roosevelt and Congress attempted to revive the economy as a whole with the **National Industrial Recovery Act** in 1933. The act created two administrations:

- **The National Recovery Administration (NRA)**, which stimulated industrial production and improved competition by drafting corporate codes of conduct. The administration also sought to limit production of consumer goods to drive prices up.

- **The Public Works Administration (PWA)**, which constructed public roads, bridges, and buildings. In accordance with Keynesian economic theories, Roosevelt believed that improving public infrastructure would prime the pump and put more money into the economy.

RESTRUCTURING AMERICAN FINANCE

Roosevelt spurred Congress to establish new regulations on the financial sector of the economy. After taking office, Roosevelt took the country off the gold standard, which had previously allowed citizens and foreign countries to exchange paper money for gold anytime they wanted. He also ordered Americans to hand over their stockpiles of gold to the U.S. Treasury in exchange for paper dollars. Roosevelt also created the **Securities Exchange Commission (SEC)** to regulate trading on Wall Street and curb the wild speculation that had led to the Crash of 1929.

THE INDIAN REORGANIZATION ACT

Native Americans also received federal assistance. In 1934, Congress passed the **Indian Reorganization Act** to promote tribal reorganization and give federal recognition to tribal governments. More important, nearly 100,000 young Native American men participated in relief programs, such as the Civilian Conservation Corps, PWA, and WPA.

The Indian Reorganization Act changed relations between the various tribes and federal government because it reversed the 1887 Dawes Severalty Act. The Dawes Act had weakened tribal affiliations by stipulating that only individual Native Americans—not tribal councils—could own land. Unfortunately, despite Roosevelt's efforts to alleviate Native American suffering, the Indian Reorganization Act accomplished very little. Some tribes had difficulty understanding the terms of the new treaty, for example, while tribes like the Navajo simply rejected it.

	Legislation/Policy/Program	How It Helped
First New Deal		
March 9, 1933	Emergency Banking Relief Act	Relief
March 31, 1933	Civilian Conservation Corps (CCC)	Relief and Recovery
April 19, 1933	The United States goes off the Gold Standard	Recovery and Reform
May 12, 1933	Federal Emergency Relief Administration (FERA)	Relief
May 12, 1933	Agricultural Adjustment Association (AAA)	Relief and Recovery
May 18, 1933	Tennessee Valley Authority (TVA)	Relief, Recovery, and Reform
June 16, 1933	National Industrial Recovery Act (NIRA)	Relief, Recovery, and Reform
June 16, 1933	Public Works Administration (PWA)	Relief and Recovery
June 16, 1933	Glass-Steagall Banking Reform Act (w/FDIC)	Reform
November 9, 1933	Civil Works Administration (CWA)	Relief
June 6, 1934	Securities Exchange Commission (SEC)	Reform
June 18, 1934	Indian Reorganization Act (IRA)	Reform
Second New Deal		
May 6, 1935	Works Progress Administration (WPA)	Relief and Recovery
July 5, 1935	National Labor Relations Act (Wagner Act)	Reform
August 14, 1935	Social Security Act	Reform
February 29, 1936	Soil Conservation and Domestic Allotment Act	Relief and Recovery
September 1, 1937	United States Housing Authority (USHA)	Relief, Recovery, and Reform
February 16, 1938	Second Agricultural Adjustment Association (AAA)	Relief and Recovery
June 25, 1938	Fair Labor Standards Act	Reform

Opposition to the New Deal

Roosevelt and the New Deal faced opposition from critics on both ends of the political spectrum. Politicians on the right referred to the New Deal as "Creeping Socialism" because they believed it threatened to subvert American capitalism. Others on the far left claimed that Roosevelt and New Dealers had not done enough to help people or stabilize the economy. They regarded capitalism as a dying system and believed that FDR had made misguided and futile attempts to salvage the doomed enterprise.

CRITICS FROM THE RIGHT

Conservative critics of the New Deal feared that FDR would open the gates to the leftist movements that had already gained footholds throughout the world. In 1934, the **American Liberty League,** led by former Democratic presidential hopeful **Al Smith** and funded by the Du Pont family, claimed that FDR wanted to destroy free-enterprise capitalism and pave the way for communism, fascism, or both in America. Big business generally opposed the New Deal, too, out of fears that the federal government would support organized labor.

CRITICS FROM THE FAR LEFT

The New Deal faced nearly as much criticism from the progressive left as from the conservative right. Some ultraliberals, for example, thought that FDR's New Deal conceded too much to the wealthy and failed to resolve the problems in the financial sector.

1929–1939

Father Charles Coughlin

A Catholic priest named **Charles Coughlin** became one of the most recognizable opponents of the New Deal when he began broadcasting his criticisms on a weekly radio program. He became so popular that he amassed a following of 40 million listeners within just a few years. He blamed the Depression primarily on crooked Wall Street financiers and Jews and campaigned for the nationalization of the entire American banking system.

Huey P. Long

Senator **Huey P. "Kingfish" Long** of Louisiana also condemned the New Deal. He believed that income inequality had caused the Depression, and he promoted his **"Share Our Wealth"** program, or **"Every Man a King"** program, to levy enormous taxes on the rich so that every American family could earn at least $5,000 a year. He enjoyed enormous popularity during the first few years of Roosevelt's first term but was assassinated in 1935.

Francis E. Townsend

Radio personality **Dr. Francis E. Townsend** also believed he had the solution to drastically reduce poverty. Townsend proposed that the government pay senior citizens approximately $200 every month on the condition that recipients had to spend all their money in order to put money back into the economy. He and Father Caughlin created the **National Union for Social Justice** and even ran as a candidate for the presidency in 1936.

Soviet Russian agents in the United States actually launched a "popular front" campaign to actively support FDR and the New Deal. An unprecedented number of people joined the American Communist Party during this decade as well. Yet, many socialist activists denounced the New Deal because they believed it was still too conservative.

The Second New Deal

FDR responded to many of these critiques with a second bundle of New Deal legislation. Known simply as the **Second New Deal**, Congress passed this follow-up wave of legislation between 1935 and 1938.

The Second New Deal differed drastically from the First New Deal in that its legislation relied more heavily on **Keynesian-style deficit spending**. Keynes strongly believed that the government needed to increase spending during times of economic crisis in order to stimulate the economy. The acceptance of his ideas was in part due to complaints from critics like Huey Long but also simply because it was clear by 1935 that more Americans still needed federal relief assistance. Approximately half of the Second New Deal programs and policies were aimed at long-term reform.

THE WORKS PROGRESS ADMINISTRATION

Congress launched the Second New Deal with the **Works Progress Administration (WPA)** in 1935 in an effort to appease those like Senator Long who clamored for more direct assistance from the federal government. Similar to the Public Works Administration of the First New Deal, the WPA hired nearly 10 million Americans to construct new public buildings, roads, and bridges. Congress dumped over $10 billion into these projects in just under a decade.

THE SOCIAL SECURITY ACT

Congress also passed the **Social Security Act** in 1935. This act created a federal retirement pension system for many workers that was funded by a double tax on every working American's paychecks. It also created an unemployment insurance plan to temporarily assist those out of work, and made funds available to the blind and physically disabled. Finally, it stipulated that Congress would match federal dollars for every state dollar allocated to workers' compensation funds.

1929–1939

The 1935 Social Security Act was undoubtedly the most sweeping of the new laws. This was not only because it provided income to some of the most destitute but also because it forever changed the way Americans thought about work and retirement. People came to recognize retirement as something every working American should be able to enjoy. Still, the program was criticized for not extending pensions to enough people, particularly unskilled African Americans and women.

MORE HELP FOR FARMERS

Roosevelt provided more assistance to farmers. After the Supreme Court declared the Agricultural Adjustment Administration unconstitutional in 1936, Democrats immediately responded with the passage of the **Soil Conservation and Domestic Allotment Act** the same year. This act continued to subsidize farmers to curb overproduction and also paid them to plant soil-enriching crops (instead of wheat) or to not grow anything at all so that nutrients would return to the soil. In 1938, Congress created a **Second Agricultural Adjustment Administration** to reduce total crop acreage.

LABOR REFORM

Much of the Second New Deal legislation promoted organized labor and included these important acts:

- **The National Labor Relations Act**, or **Wagner Act**, passed in 1935, which protected workers' right to organize and strike

- **The Fair Labor Standards Act**, passed in 1938, which established a national minimum wage and a forty-hour work week in some sectors of the economy and the outlawing of child labor

Like the Social Security Act, these labor reforms also had a lasting effect. The 1935 Wagner Act paved the way for collective bargaining and striking. Within a year, fledgling labor unions had made great headway fighting for better hours and higher wages. For example, assembly-line workers in the General

Motors automobile factory used the Wagner Act to initiate a series of sit-down strikes (workers would sit at their stations and refuse to leave, preventing the company from hiring new "scab" workers). By 1937, the company had recognized their right to organize. The Fair Labor and Standards Act also helped promote concepts of minimum wages and child-labor laws.

*New federal protection for organized labor prompted many unskilled workers to unionize under the leadership of **John L. Lewis**, a ranking member of the American Federation of Labor. Lewis organized the **Committee of Industrial Organization** within the larger AFL framework, but tensions between the mostly skilled workers in the AFL and the unskilled workers in the CIO eventually split the two groups in 1937. The Committee of Industrial Organization then became the **Congress of Industrial Organizations** and remained independent until it rejoined with the AFL in 1955.*

THE ELECTION OF 1936

By the time the 1936 elections came around, Republicans barely stood a chance against FDR and the Democrats. The Democratic effort to provide relief, recovery, and reform had by this time become highly visible and had won the support of blacks (who voted Democrat for the first time in large numbers), unskilled laborers, and those in the West and South. Republicans nevertheless nominated moderate Kansas Governor **Alfred M. Landon** on an anti-New Deal platform. Not surprisingly, Roosevelt won a landslide victory—523 electoral votes to Landon's eight—and proved that Americans widely supported the New Deal.

The End of the New Deal

In 1938, the New Deal steamroller came to an end. A conservative Supreme Court put the brakes on federal control of the economy and Keynesian-style deficit spending. Roosevelt's own political greed, as well as the recession in 1937, also turned many Americans against the New Dealers.

LEGAL BATTLES

The Republican-dominated Supreme Court had begun to strike down several key pieces of First New Deal legislation in the mid 1930s. For example:

- *Schecter v. United States* in 1935 declared that the National Industrial Recovery Act violated the Constitution because it gave too many powers to the president and attempted to control *intra*state commerce rather than *inter*state trade.

- *Butler v. United States* in 1936 declared that the Agricultural Adjustment Administration also violated the Constitution because it unconstitutionally tried to exert federal control over agricultural production.

Roosevelt's Court-Packing Scheme

Roosevelt believed the NRA and AAA were crucial to reviving the American economy and feared that any more conservative rulings would cripple or even kill the New Deal entirely. Consequently, he petitioned Congress in 1937 to alter the makeup of the Court; he believed that the justices' old age might affect their ability to concentrate on their work. He also asked for the power to appoint as many as six new justices (to bring the total to fifteen) and for the authority to replace justices over the age of seventy.

FDR's **"court-packing scheme"** backfired. Instead of winning over Democrats and New Dealers in Congress, it had the opposite effect. Even Roosevelt's most ardent fans were shocked by the president's blatant disregard for the cherished tradition of separation of powers. Roosevelt repeatedly denied charges that he wanted to bend the entire federal government to his will and defended his proposal by arguing that aging justices sometimes couldn't perform their duties. The court-packing debate dragged on for several months before Congress and Roosevelt compromised on making minor reforms in the lower courts, while keeping the Supreme Court untouched and intact. Still, the political damage had been done. Roosevelt's plan to "pack" the Supreme Court with pro–New Dealers did more than anything else to turn Americans and other Democrats away from him and the New Deal.

THE ROOSEVELT RECESSION

Pressured by conservatives in Congress and even by ardent New Dealers in the cabinet, Roosevelt began to scale back deficit spending in 1937, believing that the worst of the Depression had passed. He drastically reduced the size of the Works Progress Administration, for example, and halted paying farmers federal subsidies.

The early retreat came too soon, and the economy buckled again in the resulting **"Roosevelt Recession."** The stock market crashed again in 1937, and the price of consumer goods dropped significantly. Contrary to conservative beliefs, the economy had not pulled far enough out of the Depression to survive on its own. Roosevelt tried to place the blame on spendthrift business leaders, but Americans didn't believe him. As a result, Democrats lost a significant number of seats in the House and the Senate in the 1938 congressional elections.

THE HATCH ACT

Republicans in Congress further weakened Roosevelt's power with the **Hatch Act** of 1939, which forbade most civil servants from participating in political campaigns. The act also forbade public office holders (i.e., Roosevelt and New Dealers) from using federal dollars to fund their reelection campaigns. Finally the act made it illegal for Americans who received federal assistance to donate money to politicians.

Conservatives hoped these measures would completely divorce the functions of government from the campaign frenzy and ultimately dislodge entrenched New Dealers who preyed on a desperate public for votes. Blamed for the Roosevelt Recession, for the president's plan to dominate the federal courts, and with their political base kicked out from under them, Democrats and the New Deal met their end in 1938.

Roosevelt's decision to scale back deficit spending in order to appease Republicans and conservative Democrats was a huge mistake. Even though the New Deal had significantly reduced poverty, hunger, and the unemployment rate, the economy was still not ready to stand on its own. This was the last straw for many voters. The Republicans' return in the midterm congressional elections of 1938 was the final blow that effectively killed the New Deal.

Timeline

1929	The stock market crashes.
1930	Congress passes the Hawley-Smoot Tariff.
1932	The Reconstruction Finance Corporation is created.
	The Bonus Army camps in Washington, D.C.
	Franklin D. Roosevelt is elected president.
1933	**First Hundred Days**

- Emergency Banking Relief Act

- Civilian Conservation Corps

- Federal Emergency Relief Administration

- Agricultural Adjustment Administration

- Tennessee Valley Authority

- National Industrial Recovery Act

- Public Works Administration

The Twenty-First Amendment is ratified (repealing the Eighteenth Amendment).

1934	Congress passes the Indian Reorganization Act.
	Roosevelt creates the Security Exchange Commission.
1935	**Second New Deal**

- Emergency Relief Appropriations Act

- W. P. A.

- Social Security Act

- National Labor Relations Act

- Resettlement Administration

- National Housing Act

The Committee for Industrial Organization (CIO) is created.

The Supreme Court ruled on *Schecter v. United States*.

1936	Roosevelt is reelected.
	The Supreme Court rules on *Butler v. United States*.

1937	Roosevelt tries to "pack" the Supreme Court.
	The Roosevelt Recession begins.
1938	The CIO becomes the independent Congress of Industrial Organizations.
1939	Congress passes the Hatch Act.

CHAPTER 15

World War II: 1939–1945

||||||||||||||||||||||||||||||||||||||||||||||||||||||||

World War II transformed the United States in nearly every way imaginable. After a decade of economic depression, the nation ventured across two oceans to take a lead role in defending the world for democracy. In the process, the United States converted its sickly economy into an industrial war machine. These tasks demanded a lot from the American people, who made tremendous sacrifices.

During the war, women and ethnic minorities also found new opportunities in the previously closed labor market. As a result, labor unions began to represent more and more of these new workers. At home and abroad, these unprecedented opportunities also presented a new set of challenges that would preoccupy political leaders throughout the rest of the twentieth century.

Precursors to War

World War I planted many of the seeds for World War II. Outstanding war debts in Great Britain and France—combined with the heavy reparations payments forced upon Germany—facilitated the rise of **fascism**. Meanwhile, the strong desire for **isolationism** in the United States prevented the American government from participating in international efforts to check the increasingly aggressive Germany, Italy, and Japan.

WAR DEBTS AND REPARATIONS

Outstanding debts created lasting problems for the major European powers because the British and French had borrowed heavily from the United States in the final two years of World War I. Under the terms of the Treaty of Versailles, both countries relied on war reparations from Germany to pay off their debts to the United States. During the 1920s, Germany could no longer keep up its payments, so the United States provided loans to the struggling nation according to the **Dawes Plan**. But the American economic crash in the early 1930s destabilized the already weak **Weimar Republic** in Germany. These adverse economic conditions encouraged the rise of fascism in Germany.

AMERICAN ISOLATIONISM

The European default on war debts only reinforced American isolationism. By the end of World War I, Americans had grown tired of war and had turned their attention away from international affairs. Despite the urgings of President Woodrow Wilson, Congress refused to join the League of Nations. Although American leaders managed to enter a number of international agreements, isolationist sentiments prevailed in the face of a growing international crisis.

1920s Diplomacy

The United States collaborated with the international community on disarmament. Alarmed by the rapid growth of the Japanese navy, the United States government held the Washington Armaments Conference in 1921 and cosigned the following treaties:

- **The Five-Power Naval Treaty**, which restricted the size of the American, Japanese, British, French, and Italian navies.

- **The Four-Power Treaty**, which required the United States, Japan, Great Britain, and France to maintain the territorial status quo in the Pacific.

- **The Nine-Power Treaty**, which bound the United States, Japan, Britain, France, Italy, Belgium, China, the Netherlands, and Portugal to respect the territorial integrity of China and abide by the Open Door Policy.

Roosevelt's Foreign Policy

Franklin Delano Roosevelt served as President Woodrow Wilson's secretary of the navy and endorsed an internationalist foreign policy in the late 1920s. Roosevelt supported the League of Nations and wanted to cancel European debts in order to stabilize the European economy. After becoming president in 1932, he promoted international cooperation (through trade) rather than military coercion. In order to accomplish this, he announced the **"Good Neighbor" Policy** in 1933 to reassure Latin American countries that the United States would not intervene in their internal affairs. He also formally recognized the Soviet regime in Russia in 1933.

*The **Nye Committee** in the Senate concluded that bankers and munitions-makers had convinced President Wilson to go to war and had profited as a result. The committee warned that the United States had to find ways to avoid making these mistakes again, prompting Congress to pass the Neutrality Act of 1935.*

The Neutrality Acts

Congress also passed several laws designed to prevent American involvement in another European war. The **Johnson Debt Default Act** of 1934 prohibited private loans to all governments that defaulted on their war debts. Congress then passed the **Neutrality Act of 1935** to prohibit the sale of arms and munitions to nations at war.

The following year, Congress renewed these provisions and also forbade American corporations from loaning money to belligerent nations. Congress enforced the **cash-and-carry** policy when it passed the **Neutrality Act of 1937**, which required nations at war to purchase American goods with cash and to use their own ships to transport them back to Europe.

THE RISE OF MILITARISM AND FASCISM OVERSEAS

Events overseas reinforced the American desire to maintain neutrality. By the early 1930s, militaristic and expansionist governments controlled Japan, Italy, and Germany. The League of Nations proved ineffective at stopping these countries as the world inched closer to war.

The Japanese Invasion of Manchuria and China

The first stirrings of war occurred when militarists seized political power in Japan in 1931. Almost immediately, the Japanese invaded Manchuria, an area of China in which Japan had economic interests. Neither the United States nor the League of Nations attempted to intervene. Over the next several years, Japan sought to assert its military power in East Asia with these actions:

- Bombing the Chinese city of Shanghai in 1932
- Withdrawing from the League of Nations in 1933
- Renouncing the Five-Power Naval Treaty in 1934
- Invading China's northern provinces in 1937

Italy and Ethiopia

Meanwhile, the nationalistic **Fascist Party** had maintained control over Italy under the leaders of **Benito Mussolini** since the 1920s. Beginning in the mid-1930s, Mussolini also flexed Italy's military might through these actions:

- Invading Ethiopia in northeastern Africa in 1935
- Withdrawing from the League of Nations in 1937
- Conquering the Kingdom of Albania in 1939

The Rise of Nazism in Germany

Transformations in Germany alarmed European leaders even more. The economic problems facing the country in the aftermath of World War I helped fascist **Adolf Hitler** rise to power as leader of the National Socialists, or **Nazi Party**. The Nazis appealed to many Germans by pointing out the injustices of the Treaty of Versailles and blaming the country's troubles on Jews and other "inferior" races.

After becoming Chancellor of Germany in 1933, Hitler recalled the country's representatives to the League of Nations and began to rearm the German military in violation of the Treaty of Versailles. Within a few years, Hitler had used his military power to expand German territory. In March 1936, for example, German troops had invaded the Rhineland, an area placed under French control at the end of World War I. The French offered no resistance. Two years later, Hitler announced the annexation, or **Anschluss**, of Germany and his native country of Austria.

The Munich Accords

In September 1938, Hitler demanded that Czechoslovakia grant Germany control of the **Sudetenland**, an area where many ethnic Germans lived but later agreed to meet with French and British envoys in Munich, Germany, to negotiate a peaceful settlement. Adopting a policy of **appeasement**, the British and French agreed to allow the annexation of the Sudetenland in exchange for Hitler's guarantee to halt territorial expansion.

Based on his accomplishments, British Prime Minister **Neville Chamberlain** triumphantly claimed he had secured "peace in our time." But the following March, Hitler broke the **Munich Accords** when he seized control of all of Czechoslovakia. Still, the British and French did nothing in the hope of avoiding another catastrophic war.

The Invasion of Poland

Emboldened by the inaction of France and England, Hitler then looked toward Polish land that had once belonged to Germany before World War I, even though the British and French had promised to assist Poland against German aggression. In August, Hitler signed a nonaggression agreement with the Soviet dictator **Joseph Stalin** to ensure that Russia would not assist Poland and then ordered the invasion of Poland on September 1, 1939. France and Great Britain honored their promise to Poland and immediately declared war on Germany.

Many historians consider the **Spanish Civil War** a "dress rehearsal" for World War II, because it involved many of the same countries. In 1936, the fascist General Francisco Franco began a rebellion against the Republican government of Spain. Germany and Italy supplied troops to the fascists, while the Soviet Union aided the pro-communist Loyalists. The United States, Britain, and France all declared their unwillingness to intervene. Some Americans went to fight anyway as part of the **Abraham Lincoln Brigade**, which joined citizens of several other countries to fight beside the Loyalists. Spain ultimately fell to the fascists on March 28, 1939.

War Erupts Abroad

The first two years of the war went well for Germany, Italy, and Japan. By the end of 1941, Germany and Italy had conquered much of Europe and planned to attack Great Britain and Russia. Japan continued to expand its influence in the Pacific and China, although to a lesser extent. The United States responded to these developments by increasing its aid to the Allies and by arming itself for the possibility of war.

THE ESCALATION OF THE WAR

The war in Europe began with Germany's invasion and conquest of Poland, but very little happened the following winter. This "phony war" ended in the spring of 1940, when Hitler began his European military campaign in earnest.

The Blitzkrieg

In the spring and summer of 1940, Hitler launched the Blitzkrieg, or "lightning war." This rapid series of successful invasions gave him control over much of Western Europe, including Denmark and Norway (in April), Belgium and the Netherlands (in May), and France (in June).

The Nazis established a pro-German regime in Vichy called Vichy France soon after the invasion. Meanwhile, the British gathered all their ships at Dunkirk and used them to return their troops to England.

> The Nazi-Soviet Pact of 1939 gave Stalin a brief opportunity to expand his reach in Eastern Europe without interference from Hitler. In fall 1940, the Soviets invaded the Baltic republics of Estonia, Latvia, and Lithuania, and then asserted control in Finland. In response, the United States established an embargo on arms shipments to Russia.

The Battle of Britain

Hitler next turned his attention to the British Isles. During the summer and fall of 1940, the Germans regularly bombed English cities in preparation for a possible invasion. Inspired by the speeches of their new Prime Minister Winston Churchill, Britons deepened their resolve to resist Nazi aggression. The British Royal Air Force took to the skies to counter the German attack and helped win the Battle of Britain. Hitler's defeat forced him to put off another invasion until a later date.

German Invasion of Russia

In the summer of 1941, Hitler broke the Nazi-Soviet pact and invaded the Soviet Union. Within four months, Hitler's armies had penetrated deep into Russia. But intense Russian resistance and bitter cold weather stopped the German advance in the winter.

The invasion of Russia proved to be Hitler's greatest blunder during the war. Opening a second front in Russia required the Nazis to divert considerable resources from the fighting in Western Europe for the remainder of the war. Moreover, Germany's invasion of Russia prompted Russia to form an alliance with Britain and later with the United States.

INCREASING AMERICAN INVOLVEMENT

Despite an official policy of neutrality, the United States became increasingly involved in the war overseas. The American people expressed a strong preference for the Allies, a preference derived partly from the United States' affinity with Great Britain. President Roosevelt also supported the Allies and undertook policies to aid their cause, but stopped short of entering the war. In doing so, he slowly unraveled the constraints established by the earlier Neutrality Acts.

Neutrality Act of 1939

After the invasion of Poland, President Roosevelt called a special session of Congress. He asked members to revise the previous neutrality acts that he had come to regard as mistakes. Congress obliged the president and authorized the sale of war goods to belligerent nations on a cash-and-carry basis in the **Neutrality Act of 1939**, though American ships still could not enter war zones or the ports of belligerents. Soon after, Roosevelt secretly circumvented the cash-and-carry policy when he provided the British with fifty destroyers in exchange for long-term leases on bases in British colonies in the Western Hemisphere.

War Preparedness

Concerned that the United States would be unprepared if it had to go to war, Roosevelt and Congress bolstered American defenses by increasing military spending almost tenfold in 1940. Additionally, they passed the **Burke-Wadsworth Conscription Act**, the first peacetime draft in United States history. All men aged 21 to 35 had to register for a year's worth of military service.

The Election of 1940

Roosevelt ran for an unprecedented third term against Republican challenger **Wendell Willkie** in 1940. When Willkie fell behind in the race, he accused Roosevelt of leading the country into war. Roosevelt responded by telling the American people, "Your boys are not going to be sent into any foreign wars." Roosevelt won the election by a landslide.

Lend-Lease

In March 1941, Congress enacted the **Lend-Lease** policy, which permitted the president to loan or lease arms to any nation considered vital to American defense. Britain and China received arms first, followed by the Soviet Union after Hitler's invasion.

> Roosevelt justified Lend-Lease to the American people in a **fireside chat** radio broadcast. He argued that supplying weapons to Great Britain was the same as loaning a garden hose to a neighbor whose house was on fire to prevent the fire from spreading.

Shipping in the Atlantic

The United States also increased its shipping activities in the Atlantic Ocean, where German **U-Boat** submarines had proven adept at sinking British ships. In order to help deliver aid to the Allies, President Roosevelt claimed the western Atlantic neutral territory, and then extended American patrols as far as Iceland in July 1941.

In September, a German U-Boat fired on an American destroyer, prompting Roosevelt to order American ships encountering German submarines to "shoot on sight." When another U-Boat sunk an American destroyer the following month, Congress quickly authorized the arming of all merchant vessels and began permitting American ships to enter combat zones and the ports of nations at war.

The Atlantic Charter

In August 1941, Roosevelt met with Churchill off the coast of Newfoundland, where the pair signed a set of "common principles" known as the **Atlantic Charter**. In addition to calling for the "final destruction of Nazi tyranny," the charter sought to establish the following:

* Self-rule for all peoples

* International economic cooperation

* Disarmament and a system of collective international security

* Freedom of the seas

GROWING TENSIONS BETWEEN THE UNITED STATES AND JAPAN

The United States also inched away from strict neutrality in Asia. When Japan invaded China in 1937, Roosevelt responded by calling for a "quarantine" of aggressor nations. In 1940, Japan began working with its allies to secure a foothold in Southeast Asia and the Pacific in order to secure important war materials such as rubber and oil. Japan widened the scope of its war through measures such as:

* Securing the right to build airfields in Indochina from the Vichy government

* Occupying French Indochina

- Signing the **Tripartite Pact** with Germany and Italy to form the **Axis** alliance

- Signing a nonaggression pact with the Russians in order to ensure the safety of its northern front in China

The American Response to Japanese Expansion

The United States responded to these actions by voicing its disapproval and pursuing economic policies meant to discourage Japan from further aggression. Congress and Roosevelt:

- Granted loans to China

- Refused to export arms to Japan

- Froze all Japanese assets in the United States

- Stopped exporting oil to Japan—a significant punishment, considering 80 percent of Japanese oil came from the United States

Roosevelt refused to lift the embargo until Japanese troops withdrew from China and Indochina. In Japan, Prime Minister Fumimaro Konoye sought a compromise, but militants led by War Minister **Hideki Tojo** pushed Konoye out of office. Japanese diplomats continued to negotiate with the United States while the military planned a strike on Allied bases in the Pacific. American intelligence learned of a forthcoming attack but did not know the target.

Pearl Harbor

On the morning of **December 7, 1941**, Japanese planes took off from aircraft carriers and attacked the American naval base at **Pearl Harbor**. Within two hours, the Japanese had sunk or damaged nineteen ships, destroyed scores of planes, and killed over 2,400 service members and civilians. The next day, President Roosevelt and Congress condemned the attack and declared war on Japan. Because of the Tripartite Pact, Italy and Germany then declared war on the United States on December 11, 1941. This prompted Congress to respond in kind.

Just after the attack on Pearl Harbor, Japanese Admiral Isoroku Yamamoto remarked, "I fear we have awakened a sleeping giant and filled him with a terrible resolve." Yamamoto's words proved true, as the atomic bombs that the United States dropped in retaliation wreaked massive devastation on their country.

The United States Enters the War

The Japanese had coordinated a campaign to cripple the Allied presence in the Pacific, so U.S. forces immediately went on the defensive upon entering the war. Within months, however, the Japanese had nevertheless succeeded in capturing several important Allied territories.

By the end of 1942, U.S. forces stopped the Japanese advance at several decisive battles and then went on the offensive. In battles on the Atlantic and in North Africa, the Americans helped the Allies stop the Germans as well, making Atlantic and Mediterranean waters safe for Allied ships. By early 1943, the tide had finally begun to turn in the Allies' favor.

WAR IN THE PACIFIC

Following the attack on Pearl Harbor, the Japanese quickly conquered Allied territory in the Pacific and East Asia. Japanese **Admiral Isoruku Yamamoto** believed that only quick victories would allow Japan to beat the Allies. The attack on Pearl Harbor had damaged—but not crippled—the American navy. This was because all of the American aircraft carriers in the Pacific Fleet had left Hawaii several days before the attack.

The Japanese Offensive

Japan followed up its attack on Pearl Harbor by capturing a succession of Allied outposts in the Pacific and in Asia. The Japanese quickly conquered:

- Guam, Wake Island, the Gilbert Islands

- Hong Kong and Singapore

- The Dutch East Indies (Indonesia)

- Burma

Pacific Naval Battles

1 Attack on Pearl Harbor	4 Raids into the Indian Ocean
2 Sinking of the Prince of Wales and Repulse	5 Battle of the Coral Sea
3 Java Campaign	6 Battle of Midway
	7 Guadalcanal Naval Battles
	8 Solomon Islands Naval Battles
	9 Battle of the Komandorski Islands
	10 Destruction of Truk
	11 Battle of the Philippine Sea
	12 Leyte Naval Battles
	13 Sinking of the Yamato
	14 Final destruction

The Philippines

Within hours of the attack on Pearl Harbor, Japanese planes also bombed U.S. airfields in the Philippines. Later that month, American forces under the command of **General Douglas A. MacArthur** abandoned Manila and retreated to the Bataan Peninsula. In March 1942, MacArthur escaped to Australia under orders from his superiors. The following month, American troops retreated to the island of **Corregidor.** The remaining American forces at Corregidor surrendered on May 6.

The Battle of the Coral Sea

The United States finally managed to halt Japanese advances at the **Battle of the Coral Sea** in early May 1942. The battle began when American forces encountered Japanese ships bound for New Guinea. The United States successfully turned the ships back. This victory prevented the deployment of Japanese troops sent to participate in an eventual invasion of Australia.

The Battle of Midway

The United States achieved another major victory over the Japanese at the **Battle of Midway** in June 1942. After American cryptologists had uncovered a secret Japanese plan to invade Hawaii, U.S. Navy commanders decided to intercept the Japanese fleet before it could attack. The Japanese lost all four of the aircraft carriers they brought to Midway, while the United States lost only one. The Japanese did not win another significant battle in the Pacific for the rest of the war.

U-BOATS AND THE BATTLE OF THE ATLANTIC

The United States also faced naval challenges in the Atlantic. "Wolf packs" of German submarines began menacing American shipping after the U.S. had declared war. U-Boats sunk hundreds of ships along the United States Atlantic coast and in the Caribbean throughout 1942. By the middle of 1943, the Allies effectively neutralized the dangers posed by U-Boats and won the Battle of the Atlantic.

1939–1945

THE ALLIED STRATEGY IN EUROPE

In Europe, the Allies had to decide when and where to strike the Germans and Italians. Stalin wanted the British and Americans to stage a cross-channel invasion of France as soon as possible in order to open a second major front and pull troops away from the Eastern. On the other hand, Churchill argued for smaller offensives around the edges to eventually build up to a full-scale invasion of Germany. After meeting with Churchill in Washington in 1942, Roosevelt opted for the British plan, which would get American troops into battle more quickly.

THE NORTH AFRICAN CAMPAIGN

American ground forces faced their first real test in the deserts of North Africa. German forces under **General Erwin Rommel** had penetrated British-controlled Egypt in the hope of capturing the Suez Canal. In October 1942, the British halted Rommel's advance at **el-Alamein** in Egypt. They then began pushing the Germans back across Libya. On November 8, 1942, **General Dwight D. Eisenhower** landed American troops in French Morocco to join British forces attacking Rommel. By May 1943, the Allies had forced the Germans out of North Africa and cleared the way for the invasion of Italy.

CASABLANCA

In January 1943, Roosevelt and Churchill met again in **Casablanca**, Morocco, to further discuss war plans. Both the Americans and British ultimately decided they needed more time to prepare for an invasion of France. However, they did agree to invade Italy via Sicily and accept only unconditional surrender from the Axis powers. They also agreed to launch major offensives in the Pacific.

War on the Home Front

World War II had a significant impact on the lives of all Americans. Over 15 million men and women served in the armed forces. Even though the fighting never directly affected civilians at home, it nonetheless transformed their lives. The demands of war production brought about a return to prosperity after a decade-long depression, increased membership in labor unions, ended many of the reform programs of the New Deal, and provided new opportunities for women and minorities.

WAR PRODUCTION AND THE ECONOMY

Most historians agree that World War II effectively ended the Great Depression. The demand for war materials drove up production, which in turn created jobs and put money in the hands of American workers. At the same time, the draft removed millions of men from the workforce. To meet the needs of the growing economy and conserve resources, the U.S. government poured money into war production, as well as established agencies to manage the **economic conversion** of industry. Additionally, the government established **price and wage controls** to prevent runaway inflation, rationed vital resources, and worked with **labor unions** to prevent slowdowns in production.

Government Spending During the War

By funneling money into war industries, the American government played an important role in the economic boom. The federal budget rose from $9 billion in 1939 to $100 billion in 1945. Roosevelt wanted to fund the war solely with tax increases, but conservatives in Congress would not comply. They reached a compromise by agreeing to pay for half of the war with revenue raised from increased taxes and the remainder by borrowing from the public. The federal government did this by issuing **War Bonds** throughout the war, and Americans purchased over $150 billion worth of bonds. Additional money came from banks and other financial institutions.

Economic Conversion

In order to manage the economic conversion, the United States moved quickly to organize and direct the national economy. In 1942, the government created the **War Production Board** to manage the conversion of private industry to war production. **"Dollar-a-year men,"** businessmen who moved to Washington, D.C., to work without pay, led a multitude of new agencies designed to oversee war production. As a result of these efforts, larger companies grew stronger because they could better handle mass production.

Price and Wage Controls

Americans had more money in their pockets, but the industrial commitment to war production meant that people could not spend their money on new housing, automobiles, or appliances. Because officials feared that scarcity of goods would create inflation, Congress created the **Office of Price Administration (OPA)** to set caps on prices, wages, and rents in 1942. By the end of the war, prices had risen 31 percent—only half as much as they had risen during World War I.

Rationing and Shortages

Consumer items such as sugar, gasoline, and meat also came in short supply. The government addressed these shortages by instituting a **rationing** program. Officials also encouraged the public to conserve precious resources for the good of the war effort. Some Americans, for example, planted **"victory gardens,"** in which they grew their own food. Others gathered old rubber and scrap metal to be recycled and reused as war materials.

Labor Unions

The government ensured that all new workers would automatically join unions. In exchange, labor leaders agreed to accept limits on wage increases and made a **"no-strike" pledge** for the duration of the war. As a result, membership in labor unions rose from about 10.5 million in 1941 to 15 million just four years later.

1939-1945

Cooperation between the government and labor occasionally broke down. Sometimes workers would strike without the approval of their unions. In 1943, a United Mine Workers strike led by **John L. Lewis** prompted Congress to pass the **Smith-Connally Act**. The law required a thirty-day cooling-off period before unions could strike and gave the president authority to seize war plants if necessary. States also passed additional laws to curtail the power of unions.

POLITICS DURING WARTIME

The federal government gradually became more and more conservative as the American economy improved. With the Great Depression over, New Deal reforms seemed less pressing and less necessary, and as a result, the 1942 elections led to the repeal of some Depression-era programs.

The End of Reform

Soldiers and war workers who had moved away from home could not cast their traditionally Democratic votes in 1942. This, plus general annoyance with wartime shortages and controls, helped increase Republican numbers in Congressional elections. Conservatives grabbed the opportunity to end or cut back popular New Deal programs, including:

- The Works Progress Administration (WPA)

- The Farm Security Administration

- The National Planning Resources Board

By the end of 1943, Roosevelt had acknowledged the changing priorities of Americans and announced that winning the war would take precedence over the New Deal.

The Election of 1944

Roosevelt sought reelection once again in 1944, and he ran against Republican Thomas E. Dewey from New York. Bowing to pressure from Democratic leaders, Roosevelt agreed to drop his vice president, Henry Wallace, and ran with the more moderate

Harry S Truman, who had chaired a Senate committee to investigate fraud and waste in war production. Roosevelt won with 432 electoral votes to Dewey's ninety-nine.

WOMEN AND THE WAR

The war emergency produced new opportunities for women in the workplace and the military. Women experienced unprecedented economic and social freedom as a result.

> Approximately 350,000 women served in the armed forces during the war. Roughly 200,000 of these women served in the **Women's Army Corps (WAC)**, the Navy's **Women Accepted for Volunteer Emergency Service (WAVES)**, and other military auxiliaries. The rest joined the Nurse's Corps.

Women in War Industries

During the Great Depression, women had been discouraged from seeking work for fear that they would steal jobs from men. But the new demand for labor during the war prompted the government and industries to recruit women to increase war production. The government's publicity campaign encouraged women to enter traditionally male manufacturing positions by producing famous images of **Rosie the Riveter**.

Their campaign was successful, and about 6 million women entered the workforce during the war, an overall increase of more than 50 percent. The number of women working in manufacturing increased 110 percent, and the percentage of married women in the workforce rose from 15 percent in 1940 to 24 percent in 1945.

AFRICAN AMERICANS AND THE WAR

The war also had a profound social impact on African Americans. Many joined the military and saw other parts of the country and the world for the first time. The demand for labor in northern and western industrial cities also prompted more than 5 million blacks to move out of the agricultural South and to the cities during the 1940s.

African Americans in the Military

One million African Americans served in the U.S. military during World War II. Most served in segregated units due to a military policy that remained largely intact throughout the war. The Red Cross even maintained separate blood supplies for whites and blacks. In 1940, however, the government ended segregation in all officer candidate schools except for those training air cadets. About 600 black pilots received their training at a special military flight school established at Tuskegee, Alabama. Many of these **Tuskegee Airmen** went on to serve in decorated combat units.

African-American Employment

In 1941, **A. Philip Randolph**, the head of the Brotherhood of Sleeping Car Porters, announced plans for a massive **March on Washington**. This march was to demand that the government require defense contractors to integrate their workforce and open more skilled-labor jobs to African Americans. Afraid of racial violence, Roosevelt convinced Randolph to cancel the march in exchange for creating the **Fair Employment Practices Commission**. During the war, the commission helped reduce black unemployment by 80 percent.

The Double V Campaign

Because the war against fascism implicitly criticized the racial theories of Nazi Germany, African Americans seized the opportunity to fight all forms of prejudice at home. The NAACP started launched the "victory at home, victory abroad" campaign, also known as the **Double-V Campaign**. As a result, NAACP membership during the war increased from 50,000 members to roughly 450,000. A new civil rights group founded in 1942, the **Congress of Racial Equality (CORE)**, also campaigned for desegregation by staging demonstrations and sit-ins around the country.

1939–1945

Race Riots

The influx of African Americans into the workforce and cities, combined with growing demands for equal rights, created serious tensions with white Americans. During 1943, 242 separate incidents of racial violence occurred in forty-seven different American cities, the most serious being the **Detroit Race Riots**, in which twenty-five African Americans and nine whites died.

NATIVE AMERICANS AND THE WAR

More than 25,000 Native Americans served in uniform during World War II, often in integrated units. Some of the most famous were the Native American **"Code-talkers"** who used their native languages to encode important military messages. Many Native Americans also worked as laborers alongside whites in various war industries. Those who left their reservations for military service or war work acquired new skills, came into close contact with whites for the first time, and discovered new opportunities in American society.

INTERNMENT OF JAPANESE AMERICANS

After Pearl Harbor, Americans grew deeply distrustful of Japanese Americans, many of whom lived on the West Coast. Although no Japanese American ever committed treason during the war, Roosevelt authorized the **internment** of all Americans of Japanese descent in "relocation centers" in early 1942.

Internment camps in the western interior of the United States eventually housed about 100,000 Japanese Americans, two-thirds of whom were American citizens. Prisoners had little time to make arrangements for their property before being deported to the camps, so many people lost homes and businesses. The Supreme Court upheld the order in 1944.

After much debate, in 1988, Congress decided to award $20,000 and an official apology to each of the roughly 60,000 surviving Japanese American internees.

Victory in Europe

In 1943, the Allies began their campaign to roll back the Axis in earnest. Churchill and Roosevelt ignored Stalin's request to engage the Germans on a second front and instead followed up on their success in North Africa by invading Italy. But a year later, the United States and Great Britain did attack in the West when they invaded France. The Allies pressed in on Germany from both sides, meeting in the spring of 1945 and forcing Germany's surrender.

THE ITALIAN CAMPAIGN

In July 1943, roughly 160,000 American and British troops invaded the island of Sicily. Unprepared to fight, the Italians quickly retreated to the Italian mainland. By the end of the month, the fascist regime had collapsed and Mussolini had fled to northern Italy. The Italian government soon surrendered unconditionally and even joined the Allies. Despite Hitler's eleventh-hour campaign to restore Mussolini to power, the Allies finally captured Rome in June 1944.

CAIRO AND TEHRAN

In November 1943, Roosevelt, Churchill, and Stalin met face to face for the first time. After conferring with Chinese leader **Chiang Kai-shek** in Cairo, Egypt, the Allies issued the **Declaration of Cairo**, which reaffirmed the demand for Japan's unconditional surrender, promised to return all Chinese territory occupied by Japan to China, and declared that the Korean peninsula would become an independent state free from outside control.

The **"Big Three"** leaders then proceeded to **Tehran**, Iran, to plan their final assault on the Axis powers. In Tehran, they agreed that the United States and Great Britain would invade France the following May, that the Soviet Union would begin fighting Japan once Germany had surrendered, and that all three countries would occupy Germany at the end of the war and establish a postwar security organization.

STRATEGIC BOMBING OVER EUROPE

American and British planes conducted a lengthy bombing campaign against military and industrial targets in Germany. By targeting cities such as Dresden and Berlin, bombers delayed German war production and disrupted transportation. These attacks also depleted the German air force, distracted the German military's attention from other fronts, and reduced Hitler's popularity amongst the German people.

D-DAY

In the middle of 1944, the Americans and British finished preparations to open a second front with a cross-channel invasion of France, dubbed **Operation Overlord**. The Germans prepared for an assault, but they mistakenly believed that the Allies would cross at the narrowest point in the English Channel and land at Pas de Calais, near the French-Belgian border. Instead, the roughly 150,000 Allied soldiers landed on the beaches of **Normandy**, France, on **D-Day**: June 6, 1944. Poor landing conditions, logistical errors, and German gun emplacements made the invasion difficult, but the Allies eventually secured the beach with the help of paratroopers dropped behind enemy lines the night before. Within two weeks, a million more Allied troops had landed in France.

THE ALLIED ADVANCE FROM THE WEST

The Allies pushed through France and toward Germany over the summer of 1944. The only real resistance posed by the Germans occurred at the **Battle of the Bulge**. By the end of the year, the Americans, British, and French in the West and the Russians in the East had effectively surrounded the Germans.

THE SURRENDER OF GERMANY

After successfully breaking through German lines at the Battle of the Bulge, American **General Omar Bradley** led his troops toward Berlin through central Germany, while the British swept through the North and the Russians approached from the East. Meanwhile, Adolph Hitler retreated to his underground bunker in Berlin and committed suicide on April 30. On May 2, Berlin fell to the Soviets, and within a few days, the Germans had unconditionally surrendered.

THE DEATH OF PRESIDENT ROOSEVELT

Even though he had conducted the war through an unprecedented three presidential terms and part of a fourth, Franklin Roosevelt did not live to see Germany defeated. After a lengthy illness, he died of a massive stroke on April 12, 1945. The nation's grief for the beloved president cast a shadow over the otherwise jubilant celebration for the victory in Europe. Roosevelt's vice president, **Harry S Truman**, immediately assumed office.

THE HOLOCAUST

The defeat of Germany also uncovered disturbing revelations about Hitler's **"final solution."** Even though the Nazis had announced their belief in the racial inferiority of Jews to "pure" Germans, American anti-Semitism and isolationism during the 1930s had prevented Roosevelt from changing immigration policies to welcome European refugees. As early as 1942, the U.S. government had received reports that Germany had detained Jews and other "impure" peoples in concentration camps, with the intention of systematically exterminating them. But many officials had dismissed such reports as preposterous. When the Allies liberated the camps in 1945, they found incontrovertible proof of genocide. As many as 10 million Jews and other minorities died in the **Holocaust**.

Victory in the Pacific

The Americans finally went on the offensive against the Japanese in the Pacific in mid-1942. The victories at Coral Sea and Midway had damaged the Japanese fleet and marked the start of an American campaign to roll back Japanese gains. U.S. forces succeeded every step of the way, despite intense and extremely bloody opposition from the Japanese at Guadalcanal, Iwo Jima, and Okinawa. The anticipation of a costly invasion of Japan inspired support for President Truman's decision to ultimately end the war by dropping two **atomic bombs**.

GUADALCANAL

The first major American offensive in the Pacific occurred in the Solomon Islands, east of New Guinea. On August 7, 1942, the First Marine Division attacked a Japanese installation building on an airfield on the island of **Guadalcanal**. It took American forces six months of brutal fighting to push the Japanese off the island and prevent them from building air bases from which to attack Australia and New Zealand.

THE AMERICAN OFFENSIVE IN THE PACIFIC

After Guadalcanal, the American military leaders put into action a two-pronged strategy that combined the recommendations of General MacArthur and **Admiral Chester Nimitz**. American troops in the South Pacific would move northward through New Guinea and retake the Philippines while naval forces would simultaneously sweep westward through the Pacific from Hawaii toward Japanese island outposts. The two would eventually meet and prepare for an invasion of Japan.

MacArthur in the South Pacific

American forces in Australia and New Guinea approached the Philippines by attacking Japanese-controlled territory in the South Pacific. In the **Battle of the Bismarck Sea**, which lasted from March 2 to March 3, 1943, U.S. forces sank eighteen enemy ships and discouraged the Japanese from shipping future rein-forcements to besieged islands. The victory allowed MacArthur's forces to reclaim the western Solomon Islands and the northern coast of New Guinea with the help of Australian troops.

Nimitz in the Central Pacific

Meanwhile, the Navy moved westward from the central Pacific. In November 1943, Admiral Nimitz began his **island-hopping campaign** by attacking Japanese bases in the Gilbert Islands. Over the next year, Nimitz moved westward across the Pacific. In 1944, he conquered the Marshall Islands in February, the Mariana Islands in June, and the western Caroline Islands in September.

Battle of Leyte Gulf

MacArthur met with Nimitz in October of 1944 at Leyte Gulf near the Philippines. In the **Battle of Leyte Gulf**, the largest naval battle in history, American forces effectively decimated what remained of Japan's navy. Japanese pilots in **"kamikaze"** units attacked U.S. battleships and aircraft carriers in suicide attacks.

Iwo Jima and Okinawa

Fighting grew more intense and more costly as American forces inched closer toward Japan. On February 19, 1945, U.S. Marines landed on the island of **Iwo Jima** only 750 miles from Tokyo. In roughly six weeks, U.S. troops secured the island at a cost of 7,000 dead and nearly twice that number wounded. On April 1, 1945, the Americans landed on the island of **Okinawa**, 370 miles from Tokyo. For nearly three months, 300,000 U.S. servicemen fought to secure the island. Once again, kamikaze pilots flew their planes into American ships. In the end, over 100,000 Japanese soldiers and about a third as many Okinawans died in the fighting. American troops suffered 50,000 casualties.

THE ATOMIC BOMB

The dropping of the terrifying atomic bomb marked the end of the war in the Pacific. President Truman's decision to drop two atomic bombs hastened an inevitable Japanese defeat and arguably saved thousands of American lives. His decision also ushered in the atomic age and changed the nature of modern warfare.

The Manhattan Project

The United States worked on developing an atomic bomb throughout the war. In 1939, famous physicist **Albert Einstein** warned Roosevelt that the Germans had experimented with nuclear fission in the hope of creating their own atomic bomb. Roosevelt therefore diverted military funds into a secret nuclear research program called the **Manhattan Project** in order to develop the weapon first.

Over 100,000 people worked on the secret project in thirty-seven locations throughout the United States. **Dr. J. Robert Oppenheimer** led the theoretical research team based in Los Alamos, New Mexico. On July 16, 1945, scientists witnessed the first explosion of an atomic bomb in the desert near Alamogordo, New Mexico.

Truman's Ultimatum

After becoming president, Harry Truman had little time to contemplate the ramifications of using a nuclear weapon to end the war, because he and military commanders feared that as many as 250,000 Allied troops would die in the invasion of Japan. Upon hearing of the successful test at Alamogordo, Truman issued an ultimatum to the Japanese by demanding that the Japanese surrender unconditionally before August 3, 1945, or face "utter devastation."

Hiroshima and Nagasaki

When the Japanese still failed to surrender, Truman authorized dropping the bomb. On August 6, 1945, the B-39 bomber *Enola Gay* dropped an atomic bomb on **Hiroshima**, Japan. The explosion flattened the city and killed 78,000 people instantly. By the end of the year, 70,000 more had died from radiation exposure. On August 9, the United States dropped a second atomic bomb on **Nagasaki**, Japan, killing more than 100,000 civilians.

Once the United States had established air bases within striking distance of Japan, American bombers had dropped thousands of conventional bombs over major Japanese cities. By the end of the war, U.S. forces had firebombed over sixty cities, destroyed Tokyo, and killed approximately 500,000 Japanese civilians. Still, Japanese rulers steadfastly refused to surrender, forcing Truman to consider using the atomic bomb to end the war.

1939–1945

Japanese Surrender

Truman's decision to use the bomb succeeded in averting an Allied invasion. After the bombing of Nagasaki, a peace faction assumed control of the Japanese government and surrendered unconditionally. On September 2, 1945, Japan signed a formal surrender on the deck of the battleship **USS Missouri** in Tokyo Bay.

Timeline

1921	Congress collaborates with the international community on disarmament with the Five-Power Naval Treaty, the Four-Power Naval Treaty, and the Nine-Power Naval Treaty.
1924	The United States provides loans to Germany in the Dawes Plan.
1931	Japan invades Manchuria.
1933	Roosevelt announces the Good Neighbor Policy.
1935	Italy invades Ethiopia.
	Congress passes the Neutrality Act of 1935.
1936	Congress passes the Neutrality Act of 1936.
	Spanish Civil War begins.
	Roosevelt is reelected.
1937	Congress passes the Neutrality Act of 1937.
	Japan invades China.
1938	Germany invades Austria.
	The Munich Conference is held in Germany.
1939	Germany invades Czechoslovakia.
	Hitler signs a nonaggression agreement in the Nazi-Soviet Pact.
	Germany invades Poland to begin World War II.
	Congress passes the Neutrality Act of 1939.
1940	Germany invades France, Denmark, Norway, the Netherlands, and Belgium.
	The British Royal Air Force counters the German attack in the Battle of Britain.
	The United States makes the Bases-for-Destroyers Deal with Great Britain.
	Roosevelt is reelected.

1941	Congress passes the Lend-Lease Act.
	Germany invades the Soviet Union.
	Roosevelt and Churchill sign the Atlantic Charter.
	Japan attacks Pearl Harbor.
	The United States enters the war.
	Randolph prepares the March on Washington.
	Roosevelt establishes Fair Employment Practices Commission.
1942	Japanese-Americans are forced into internment camps.
	Japan invades the Philippines.
	The Battle of the Coral Sea occurs.
	The Battle of Midway occurs.
	The United States invades North Africa.
	Congress of Racial Equality is founded.
	The first major American offense in the Pacific occurred at the Battle for Guadalcanal.
1943	Roosevelt and Churchill hold the Casablanca Conference.
	Allies invade Italy.
	The United States achieves victory at the Battle of Bismarck Sea.
	The "Big Three" plan their final assault on the Axis powers at the Tehran Conference.
1944	Allies invade Normandy on D-Day.
	Roosevelt is reelected.
	The Battle of the Bulge begins.
1945	Roosevelt dies.
	Truman becomes president.
	Germany surrenders.
	U.S. Marines invade Iwo Jima.
	Thousands die in the battle at Okinawa.
	The United States drops atomic bombs on Hiroshima and Nagasaki.
	Japan signs a formal surrender on the USS *Missouri* in Tokyo Bay.

CHAPTER 16

The Cold War: 1945–1963

||||||||||||||||||||||||||||||||||||||||||||||||||||||

Japan's surrender in 1945 brought World War II to a close, but Joseph Stalin threatened that peace when he seized control of most Eastern European states in the immediate postwar years. The Soviet Union's desire to spread communism alarmed American leaders, who willingly accepted the mantle of world leadership. Rivalry with the Soviet Union turned into an ongoing global confrontation known as the Cold War. And with the new technology of nuclear weapons, fear of total global destruction intensified.

Americans were also worrying about changes closer to home. They desperately wanted to avoid another Great Depression. Minorities in the United States, many of whom had joined the war effort against tyranny and oppression overseas, hoped to achieve freedom and equality at home by launching the civil rights movement. In the decades after World War II, American's focus was on fighting communism abroad, achieving prosperity, and winning freedom at home.

The Yalta Conference

As the Allies prepared for victory in Europe and Japan, they also laid plans for the postwar world. In separate conferences at **Yalta** and **Potsdam**, the United States, Great Britain, and Soviet Russia sought to avoid the mistakes of the post–World War I negotiations and prevent another world war in the future. These powers created a new organization more powerful than the League of Nations: the United Nations. Still, disagreements among the three produced mixed results over the postwar fates of both Germany and Poland.

PLANNING THE POSTWAR WORLD

In February 1945, Roosevelt, Churchill, and Stalin met in the Russian town of Yalta to discuss the postwar world. Stalin agreed to side against Japan in exchange for authority over areas controlled by China and Japan. At the end of the **Yalta Conference**, the three leaders released the **Yalta Declaration of Liberated Europe**, which affirmed the promises in the Atlantic Charter to ensure free democratic systems in postwar Europe. In addition, there were three points of discussion:

1. The establishment of a new international organization
2. The plans for occupied Germany
3. The fate of a liberated Poland

The United Nations

Roosevelt, Churchill, and Stalin endorsed a plan for the establishment of a new world body called the **United Nations (UN)**. Every nation would have a seat in the organization's General Assembly, but real power would reside with the smaller **UN Security Council**. The United States, the Soviet Union, Great Britain, France, and China would each have a permanent seat on the Security Council as well as veto power. At the end of April 1945, fifty nations met at the **UN Conference in San Francisco** to draft the charter for the United Nations. The U.S. Senate ratified the charter in July 1945.

The Partition of Germany

Discussions at Yalta also determined the fate of occupied Germany. Roosevelt, Churchill, and Stalin agreed to temporarily divide occupied Germany into four zones to be controlled by the United States, Great Britain, France, and the Soviet Union. The city of Berlin, located in the Soviet zone, would consist of four similar zones. The agreement, which anticipated the eventual reunification of Germany, provided no specific plan or timeline. Stalin requested that Germany pay $20 billion in reparations to the Allies, half of which would go to the Soviets, although the Reparations Committee never resolved the issue.

Poland

The Allies also discussed the future of Poland. At the Tehran Conference, Roosevelt and Churchill had agreed to let the Soviet Union annex eastern sections of Poland but refused Stalin's proposal to install a procommunist government. Instead, the pair wished to return the Polish government-in-exile that had operated out of London since Hitler's invasion in 1939. At Yalta, they agreed to allow both the old government and communists form a new provisional government for the duration of the war. Stalin promised free elections in Poland, but he set no specific deadline. Poles ultimately waited forty-five years before they could vote in free democratic elections.

POTSDAM

Shortly after Roosevelt's death, **President Truman** attempted to revisit the unresolved issues of the Yalta Conference. In April 1945, he met with the Soviets and accused them of breaking the agreements set at Yalta. That July, he met with Churchill and Stalin in Potsdam, Germany, in Russian-controlled territory. There, Truman accepted Stalin's proposed borders for Poland but refused to agree to reparations from the other Allied zones of Germany. In 1949, the Russian zone became the republic of East Germany, and the three remaining zones joined together to form the separate state of West Germany.

Not long after the war, Europe grew divided between democracy and communism. President Franklin D. Roosevelt had anticipated that rivalries between nations would lead to conflict. To compensate, he developed a plan for the **United Nations (UN)** that would force nations to cooperate and maintain peace. Both the United States and the Soviet Union agreed to join the UN. But, as members of the UN Security Council, both countries held a veto over UN actions. Thus, the Cold War held the UN hostage and rendered the organization relatively powerless.

*Winston Churchill described the division between the democratic west and the communist east as an **"iron curtain."** In the mid-1940s, no one knew if the iron curtain would remain in a fixed position or if it could change its location.*

The Cold War Begins

As soon as World War II ended, soldiers and their families anticipated a quick return to normality. Instead, the United States found itself in a new kind of war: the **Cold War**. In the aftermath of World War II, the United States and the Soviet Union stood alone as the two great world powers. While the Soviet Union appeared eager to spread communism across the globe, the United States sought to defend democracy.

UNITED STATES–SOVIET UNION RIVALRY

President Franklin D. Roosevelt hoped to work with Soviet leader Joseph Stalin, but Roosevelt's death prevented such a partnership. When Truman succeeded Roosevelt as president, he brought with him a reluctance to deal with Stalin, and soon Cold War tensions cooled relations between the United States and the Soviet Union. The Truman administration drastically expanded its role in the postwar world order. With the atomic bomb and a country relatively undamaged by World War II, American leaders created a new foreign policy based strictly on anticommunism.

The Berlin Airlift

Stalin's actions in Poland led many U.S. policymakers to believe that the Soviet Union would also try to expand into Western Europe. Therefore, the Truman administration took immediate steps to confront the Soviet empire. Truman authorized the creation of an intelligence organization called the **National Security Agency** as well as the **National Security Council** to advise him. When Stalin cut off western access to Berlin, Truman refused to back down. He ordered the Air Force to drop thousands of pounds of food, clothing, and other goods to West Berlin in the **Berlin Airlift**.

Containment

Truman built his foreign policy around U.S. diplomat **George Kennan**'s containment theory. Kennan believed that the Soviet Union wanted to expand, and that if the United States kept the Soviets within their current borders, communism would eventually collapse. Kennan argued that a patient policy of containment would allow the United States to defeat the Soviet Union without having to suffer any loss of life on the battlefield. The Truman administration quickly applied the containment theory as follows:

- Pledging to assist other countries fighting communist armies or revolutionaries in the **Truman Doctrine** in 1947. The first aid payments supported democratic governments in Greece and Turkey.

- Giving billions of dollars in aid to Western Europe according to the **Marshall Plan** in 1948. This aid improved the tattered economies of Western Europe and quieted communist movements. The plan also ensured that Western Europe would spend much of its aid money buying American goods.

- Forming the **North Atlantic Treaty Organization (NATO)**. NATO allied the United States with Canada, France, Great Britain, and other countries in Western Europe. Each NATO member pledged to support the others in the event of a Soviet invasion.

When Germany joined NATO in 1954, the Soviet Union formed its own treaty with the nations of Eastern Europe known as the **Warsaw Pact**.

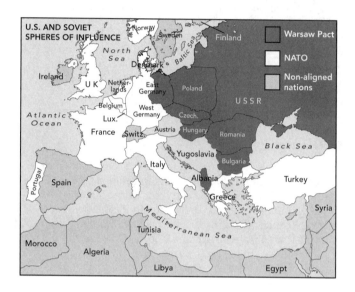

THE FOUNDING OF ISRAEL

Jews across the world had long sought their own independent state. In the twentieth century, they focused their effort on creating a state in British-controlled Palestine, their spiritual home. After the Holocaust, world sentiment began to increase in favor of a Jewish state in Palestine. Eventually, Palestinian Jews founded the independent Jewish state of Israel in 1948, and Truman offered diplomatic recognition. Despite some criticism, Truman believed in the Jewish right to a home state and also knew that the decision would prove popular during the upcoming presidential election.

The Korean War

Even though the Truman administration applied its containment strategy primarily in Europe, the first major battle in the Cold War occurred in East Asia as the Soviet Union and the United States backed different factions in the Korean civil war.

THE WAR BEGINS

After World War II, the United States and the Soviet Union had their own areas of influence on the Korean peninsula. Stalin installed a Soviet-friendly government in the north, while the American-backed **Syngman Rhee** controlled the southern half below the **Thirty-eighth Parallel**.

North Koreans Invade the South

In June 1950, North Korea launched an attack on the South. In accordance with containment and the Truman Doctrine, Truman immediately sent troops to protect South Koreans and managed to garner UN support for the mission. The initial fighting proved disastrous for the U.S. military, and by mid-September, the North Korean army had nearly conquered the entire peninsula.

Although Truman strongly advocated civil rights, Congress ignored or struck down many of his legislative proposals. After World War II, many African American soldiers remained bitter about having fought a war for freedom while serving in segregated units and reporting to racist officers. As president, Truman strongly believed that the military should be fully integrated. In July 1948, Truman issued an executive order banning racial discrimination in the armed forces. During the Korean War, African Americans fought side by side with white soldiers for the first time.

MACARTHUR'S INCHON LANDING

On September 15, 1950, General **Douglas A. MacArthur** launched a daring amphibious assault at Inchon near Seoul and then proceeded to drive back communist forces north of the Thirty-eighth Parallel. When U.S. troops reached the border between North and South, Truman ordered MacArthur to invade the North, hoping to wipe out communism in Korea altogether. In early October, MacArthur's troops entered North Korea and quickly trounced the communist forces.

Disaster on the Yalu River

As the U.S. army approached the Yalu River, which separated North Korea from China, Chinese troops swarmed into North Korea and quickly drove the U.S. soldiers back southward well into the territory MacArthur had just regained. U.S. General Matthew Ridgway eventually halted the U.S. retreat and pushed the Chinese forces back to the Thirty-eighth Parallel. By 1951, it was apparent both sides had stalemated each other, even though fighting continued for another two years.

TRUMAN FIRES MACARTHUR

After Ridgeway and American forces drove the Chinese north of the Thirty-eighth parallel, Truman decided to negotiate a peace settlement. But MacArthur couldn't stand the idea of cutting a deal with communists after so many men had died for so little gain. The general therefore ignored Truman's orders and demanded that China surrender or face a United States invasion.

Moreover, General MacArthur publicly criticized the president's decisions in the American press, especially since Truman refused to use nuclear weapons in Korea or in China. MacArthur's threats ended the peace negotiations and forced the stalemated war to drag on for almost two more years. Truman fired Mac-Arthur for his insubordination.

THE AFTERMATH OF KOREA

The Korean War finally ended after Eisenhower negotiated an armistice. After almost four years of war, North and South Korea had the same boundaries as before the war. Even though historians have dubbed the conflict America's "forgotten war," the Korean War killed roughly 33,000 Americans and injured more than 100,000. North Korea and China had over 1.5 million casualties.

The Korean War prompted the United States to implement **NSC-68**, a National Security Council report that called for a massive military buildup to wage the Cold War. NSC-68 tripled defense spending, as well as fueled anticommunism both at home and abroad.

The Cold War at Home

Truman had to balance his attention between the Cold War overseas and demobilization at home. However, just as life began to return to normal, fears of communist infiltration in the United States gripped American society.

DEMOBILIZATION

Demobilization from war to peace proved to be an uneasy process, as millions of G.I.s returned home hoping to find work. They wanted the millions of women who had joined the workforce during World War II to give up their jobs. Business leaders meanwhile pressured Truman to remove the government regulations Congress had enacted during the war, such as price controls and pro-labor laws. Workers, on the other hand, refused to give up their rights. A series of strikes broke out in the years following the war, including a railroad strike that almost completely paralyzed the nation.

The postwar turmoil eventually settled down. The Truman administration gradually ended price controls, and Americans began to spend the money they had saved during the war. The **GI Bill** provided veterans with money for education, housing, and job training. However, organized labor suffered when Congress passed the **Taft-Hartley Act** in 1947, which placed harsh restrictions on unions and limited the right to strike. Truman vehemently opposed the law, but Congress passed it over his veto.

TRUMAN'S FAIR DEAL

Truman's support of organized labor made up just one part of his domestic agenda that sought to expand Franklin Roosevelt's New Deal. His support was dubbed the **"Fair Deal,"** and included the following stipulations:

- Stronger civil rights laws, including a ban on racial discrimination in the hiring of federal employees

- A higher minimum wage

- Extension of Social Security benefits

- Funding of low-income housing projects

The Republican-dominated Congress rejected other more radical aspects of Truman's Fair Deal. Several Democrats, mostly from southern states, disagreed with Truman over his stance on civil rights. When Truman ran for reelection in 1948, a group of southern Democrats broke from the party. Calling themselves **Dixiecrats**, they nominated Senator **Strom Thurmond** for president. Although Truman won the election, he continued to face opposition from the Republican Congress and the southern wing of his own party.

THE SECOND RED SCARE

The fear of communism also spawned a **Second Red Scare** in the mid-1950s. Ordinary people began to believe that communist insurgents had infiltrated American institutions and suspected Hollywood actors, government officials, and even their own neighbors of being communist spies. Politicians capitalized on these fears and used anticommunism in their favor as a political tool to purge their enemies from office. Americans had grown more and more afraid of communism since the end of World War II for the following reasons:

- Communist forces under **Mao Zedong** had taken control of China in 1949. The so-called **Fall of China** meant that communists ruled the two largest nations on earth.

- Espionage trials had concluded that **Klaus Fuchs** and **Julius and Ethel Rosenberg** had given information about the atomic bomb to the Soviet Union.

- The Soviet Union had developed nuclear weapons.

- Communist forces had nearly overwhelmed American troops in Korea.

- U.S. officials had convicted former State Department official **Alger Hiss** of perjury.

Growing Suspicion

Although only a few hundred people belonged to the American Communist Party, government authorities began a comprehensive campaign to eradicate socialist influences in the United States. The **Federal Bureau of Investigation (FBI)** under the direction of J. Edgar Hoover, for example, began spying on people suspected of being communists. In Congress, the **House Un-American Activities Committee (HUAC)** also held widely publicized investigations of labor unions and other organizations suspected of harboring communist sympathizers.

> HUAC hearings hunting for communists in the Hollywood film industry prompted a group of ten Hollywood screenwriters to cry out that HUAC violated the First Amendment. In response, Hollywood film executives placed the writers, who came to be known as the **Hollywood Ten**, on a **blacklist**, or a list of suspected communists who shouldn't be hired. This blacklist grew over the next few years to include hundreds of Hollywood writers, directors, actors, producers, and other employees. Famous screen actor and future president Ronald Reagan helped authorities hunt suspected communists in the industry.

Government Action

Upon realizing that anticommunism played well with the American people, the Republican party criticized the Truman administration for being "soft on communism." As a result, Republicans in Congress passed two acts:

- **The Loyalty Acts**, which required federal employees to remove any worker who had any connection to a communist organization

- **The McCarran Act**, which forced communist groups to register their names with the attorney general and restricted immigration of potential subversives. Truman vetoed this, but Congress overruled him.

McCarthyism

Senator **Joseph McCarthy** from Wisconsin took anticommunism to new heights by holding public hearings in which he badgered witnesses and accused people of being communists. He never proffered any evidence and branded anyone who disagreed with him a communist. Despite this, his tactics made him extremely popular and won him national fame and reelection to the Senate.

McCarthy finally overstepped his reach in 1954 when he accused the U.S. Army of harboring communists. Aired on national television, the **Army-McCarthy Hearings** revealed McCarthy's vindictive behavior to millions of Americans across the country. The Senate censured McCarthy for his misconduct shortly after the hearings and effectively ended his career.

Prosperity and Consumerism

Domestic politics settled into a tame routine after the tumult of the Second Red Scare. An economic boom muted political divisions, and American society embraced an exploding consumer economy.

EISENHOWER'S DOMESTIC AGENDA

President **Dwight D. Eisenhower** loomed over the 1950s as the central political figure of the age. The economy soared, creating a level of affluence not seen before in American history. Additionally, Eisenhower worked to maintain the essential elements of the New Deal.

Dynamic Conservatism

In the 1952 election, Eisenhower defeated Democrat Adlai Stevenson. A moderate conservative, Eisenhower appealed to members of both parties, and partisan tensions decreased during his two terms in office. "Ike" Eisenhower championed **dynamic conservatism**, a philosophy that combined conservative fiscal policies with the social reforms of the New Deal. Policies included:

- Closer ties between government and business

- Reduction of federal spending, balancing the budget, ending wage and price controls, and lowering farm subsidies

- Expandsion of Social Security benefits and raising the minimum wage

- Funding of public works programs, including the **St. Lawrence Seaway** and the **Interstate Highway system**

Economic Boom

The **Gross National Product (GNP)** more than doubled between 1945 and 1960 as the economy grew stronger and stronger in the postwar years. Inflation stayed low, and the income of the average American household rose, allowing more people to buy expensive consumer goods. The economy thrived, for such reasons as:

- Government spending encouraged economic growth. Federal funding of schools, housing, highways, and military expenditures created jobs.

- Europe offered little competition to American levels of production. As the rest of the world recovered from World War II, the United States exported goods across the globe.

- New technologies like computers boosted productivity in many areas, including heavy industry and agriculture.

- Consumption increased. After the lean years of the Great Depression and World War II, Americans bought goods they couldn't previously afford. The **baby boom** also increased consumer needs.

The rising level of affluence in America left some people behind. Small farmers and residents of rural areas, for example, suffered hardship. The total number of farmers fell as prices steadily dropped. Many city dwellers, including African Americans and other minorities, often lived in poverty. Many industries cut jobs for unskilled workers, and racial discrimination often kept minorities out of other jobs.

CONSUMER CULTURE

Although rural and urban areas suffered during the 1950s, the suburbs boomed. Meanwhile, the postwar prosperity gave birth to a new consumer culture.

The Growth of Suburbs

As middle-class Americans grew wealthier, every family wanted a home of their own. Americans began spreading out of the cities and into the suburbs. Builders rapidly constructed suburbs like New York's Levittown, which consisted of nearly identical houses. Levittown and other suburban developments often excluded African Americans.

The Consumer Culture

During the 1950s, industrial jobs began to disappear, while white-collar jobs in industries like advertising and finance increased. The newly expanded industry of advertising encouraged Americans to buy new goods such as televisions, cosmetics, and frozen TV dinners. The consumption of consumer goods soon became one of the driving forces behind the American economy. Shopping malls consequently sprouted in suburbs across the United States. When Americans could not afford a purchase, they relied on credit, a psychology that differed greatly from the thrift and financial conservatism of the previous generation that had come of age during the Great Depression.

Critics of the Postwar Culture

Not everyone approved of the changing American culture. Some artists and writers began to challenge the culture of suburbs,

*The United States also became a nation of automobile owners. Americans could buy cars on credit, and auto manufacturers introduced new models every year to encourage people to replace their old cars. The **Interstate Highway Act** of 1956 created a uniform system of roads across the country. As a consequence, countless fast food restaurants and hotel chains popped up along the nation's highways.*

nonindustrial jobs, and interstates. For example, William H. Whyte's *The Organization Man* argued that American business had lost its enterprising spirit. Whyte believed that instead of encouraging innovation, white-collar jobs stifled creativity by forcing workers to conform to company norms. Many Americans extended this argument to apply to the suburbs. Critics argued that the suburbs lacked the cultural institutions and ethnic diversity of the cities; rather, suburbanites focused on matching the consumption of their neighbors.

A literary group known as the **Beats** challenged the conformity of the times. The Beats rejected mainstream culture and embraced spontaneity and individuality in personal behavior. "Beatnik" Jack Kerouac and his 1957 novel *On the Road* typified the movement.

*American youth began to challenge conformity during this time period. Young people embraced **rock 'n' roll**, a sexually charged type of music that crossed racial boundaries by blending African-American rhythm and blues with white country music. Top performers included Chuck Berry, Elvis Presley, and Bill Haley.*

The Civil Rights Movement Begins

Although many Americans prospered during the 1950s, African Americans experienced few benefits from the economic boom. **Jim Crow laws**—laws that enforced segregation throughout the South—continued to exist, while the Eisenhower administration expressed little interest in civil rights. A landmark Supreme Court decision in the mid-1950s, however, sparked a massive **civil rights movement** that ultimately reshaped American society. Historians identify several factors that led to the rise of African-American protest during the 1950s and 1960s:

- Experiences in World War II had offended many African Americans' sense of justice. The United States had fought a war for freedom abroad but had ignored civil rights at home.

- A black middle class began to emerge. This class consisted of doctors, ministers, lawyers, and teachers, who also acted as community leaders. The civil rights movement relied heavily on these men and women.

- University enrollment began to increase after World War II. African-American college students formed networks of activism that eventually helped end segregation.

BROWN V. BOARD OF EDUCATION

For decades, the **National Association for the Advancement of Colored People (NAACP)** had issued court challenges against segregated schooling. In 1954, the Supreme Court, under the stewardship of Chief Justice **Earl Warren**, unanimously struck down segregated education with its landmark decision in *Brown v. Board of Education of Topeka, Kansas*. The decision overturned the notion of "separate-but-equal" previously established by *Plessy v. Ferguson* in 1896.

Unfortunately, very little changed after the ruling. The predominantly black schools still lacked the resources and money of white schools. President Eisenhower refused to voice support for the *Brown* v. *Board of Education* decision.

School Desegregation

Across the South, racist whites campaigned vigorously against the Court's decision. Many school districts desegregated as slowly as possible, and some whites even shut down their schools rather than admit black students. A showdown over school integration occurred in Little Rock, Arkansas, in 1957, when an angry mob of whites prevented a group of nine African Americans from entering Little Rock's Central High School. Arkansas Governor Orval

Faubus supported the mob but eventually backed down after Eisenhower reluctantly sent army troops to escort the **"Little Rock Nine"** to class. Eisenhower's decision demonstrated that federal government supported desegregation.

THE MONTGOMERY BUS BOYCOTT

Having won desegregation in schools, African-American activists began to challenge other Jim Crow laws as well. The first major burst of activism occurred in Montgomery, Alabama, after police had arrested black resident **Rosa Parks** for refusing to give up her seat on a city bus to a white man in December 1955. NAACP attorneys immediately filed a lawsuit against the city, while the African-American community boycotted the bus service.

The Rise of Martin Luther King, Jr.

A young, charismatic preacher named **Martin Luther King, Jr.**, who empowered the civil rights movement with powerful rhetoric and skillful, nonviolent tactics, mobilized Montgomery's religious community behind the bus boycott. King's eloquence eventually won the movement national support. Within a year, Montgomery city officials agreed to desegregate its bus system.

> The Montgomery movement exposed the potential power of ordinary African Americans. Consequently, communities throughout the South began mobilizing to end Jim Crow laws. Racists organized themselves as well, hoping to stem the tide of social change.

The Cold War in the Fifties

The Cold War moved in two directions during the 1950s. On the one hand, the United States and the Soviet Union moved closer together. After Stalin died in 1953, Eisenhower reached out to the new, more moderate Soviet leader **Nikita Khrushchev**. Eisenhower and Khrushchev began a dialogue about ending the arms race and reducing nuclear weapons. In other ways, however, Cold

War tensions increased. The development of new technologies and weapons threatened the peace with new methods of destruction. As a result, Eisenhower's administration adopted a newer and more aggressive foreign policy.

THE NEW LOOK AND MASSIVE RETALIATION

Eisenhower and his secretary of state, **John Foster Dulles**, promised a new type of foreign policy. They sought to contain the Soviet Union, but they also wanted to "roll back" communism and liberate Eastern Europe. The new foreign policy also relied on covert CIA operations to prevent communist groups from taking power in strategic countries. Additionally, Eisenhower sought to reduce spending on conventional weapons and increase spending on nuclear weapons, believing that nuclear weapons provided "more bang for the buck," a policy known as the **New Look**. Dulles promised to respond to Soviet aggression with **massive retaliation**, i.e., a devastating nuclear attack.

THE COLD WAR IN THE THIRD WORLD

The Eisenhower administration devoted much attention to preventing communism in the third world, or areas outside of American or Soviet spheres of influence. In fact, Eisenhower and Dulles often used the **Central Intelligence Agency (CIA)** to topple unfriendly governments or combat communist revolutionaries. For example, the CIA prevented a coup from deposing the corrupt shah, or king, of Iran in 1953; engineered a coup against a popularly elected socialist government in Guatemala in 1954; and invaded Cuba in 1961 after communist Fidel Castro seized power.

The Suez Crisis

In 1956, Dulles froze American aid in Egypt when Egyptian president **Gamal Abdel Nasser** voiced his intention to accept aid from communist countries. Nasser responded to Dulles's actions by seizing the **Suez Canal**, jointly owned by Great Britain and France. When Great Britain, France, and Israel attacked Egypt in order to take back the Suez Canal, an outraged Eisenhower refused to sell them the oil they needed to maintain their economies. Unable to risk angering the United States and thus endanger their oil supply, they withdrew and allowed UN peacekeeping forces to stabilize the region.

Vietnam Troubles

Eisenhower also faced a growing crisis in Southeast Asia, where France had struggled to maintain control of their colonies since the end of World War II. In Vietnam, for example, rebels led by procommunist **Ho Chi Minh** declared their independence from France after seizing the strategic French army garrison at **Dien Bien Phu**. Although the United States provided France with plenty of aid to support its war in Indochina, Eisenhower refused to commit U.S. troops to the conflict.

THE ARMS RACE

The arms race continued to escalate during the 1950s. In 1957, advances in rocketry allowed the Soviet Union to launch an artificial satellite called *Sputnik* into orbit around the earth. This event sparked fears in the United States that Soviet science and technology had surpassed America. *Sputnik*'s flight also meant that the Soviets might soon be able to launch **intercontinental ballistic missiles (ICBMs)** that could travel from silos in the Soviet Union to destroy targets in the United States. Suddenly, the threat of nuclear attack became a real possibility for Americans.

The Space Race

In response, the Eisenhower administration accelerated its own space program. Soon, the United States had ICBMs of its own, while the **National Aeronautics and Space Administration (NASA)** blazed a trail in the exploration of space. Eisenhower soon became concerned about the increased militarization of American life. In his 1961 farewell address, he warned Americans to defend against the influence of the **military-industrial complex.** He feared that a powerful military linked to wealthy defense industries would negatively influence "every city, every state house, every office of the federal government."

During Eisenhower's term, the CIA developed a spy plane known as the U-2. The U-2 flew over the Soviet Union high enough to avoid Soviet fire but close enough to snap photos of a car's license plate. These flights angered the Soviets. As relations between the United States and Soviet Union warmed during the 1950s, Eisenhower hoped to stop the U-2 flights. But just before a meeting with Khrushchev in 1960, Eisenhower approved one final U-2 flight that Soviet defenses managed to destroy. When Eisenhower refused to apologize for the flight, Khrushchev called off the summit.

Kennedy and the Rise of Liberalism

Americans in the 1960s anticipated that the new decade would bring a sharp break with the past. A new generation came of age and attempted to distance itself from what it regarded as a stagnant 1950s. Instead of merely accumulating wealth, Americans began to envision using their wealth for something meaningful. During the 1960s, President John F. Kennedy established a powerful liberal state that extended some of the vast resources of the United States to people who needed them. At the same time, Kennedy promised a new approach to the Cold War.

THE ELECTION OF 1960

The election of 1960 featured many remarkable twists and turns. At first, many observers predicted Republican Vice President **Richard Nixon** would win because his Democratic opponent **John F. Kennedy** lacked Nixon's experience and national exposure. But Kennedy overcame these obstacles and narrowly won by just over 100,000 votes. Rather than challenge the results, Nixon gracefully accepted his surprising defeat.

Kennedy won the election of 1960 primarily thanks to television. In the nation's first televised debates, Kennedy projected a youthful confidence that contrasted sharply with Nixon's countenance. Although radio listeners judged the debates to be about even, television viewers believed Kennedy prevailed.

THE NEW FRONTIER

In his inaugural address, Kennedy challenged the American people to accept the nation's role as a world power and outlined his **New Frontier** program for the United States. "Ask not what your country can do for you," he stated. "Ask what you can do for your country." During his campaign, Kennedy promised changes toward economic equality and civil rights. With time, he grew increasingly frustrated as Republicans and southern Democrats joined together to defeat most of his domestic programs. As a result, Kennedy abandoned the New Frontier at home and refocused his attention on foreign policy.

Many of the liberal reforms of the 1960s originated from the Supreme Court, still led by Chief Justice Earl Warren. For example, the Warren Court:

- Forced states to redefine electoral districts to match the population
- Provided the right to counsel for accused criminals who could not afford lawyers
- Required law-enforcement officials to read suspected criminals their rights
- Worked to limit religion in schools

KENNEDY AND "FLEXIBLE RESPONSE"

At first, Kennedy's foreign policy appeared to share the same idealism as his domestic agenda. He founded the **Peace Corps**, which sent volunteers on humanitarian missions in underdeveloped countries. But the centerpiece of Kennedy's foreign policy was on anticommunism.

Whereas Truman had fought communism by giving money to fight communist insurgents and Eisenhower had threatened the USSR with "massive retaliation," the Kennedy administration devised the doctrine of **"flexible response."** Developed by Defense and State Department officials like Robert S. McNamara, the containment doctrine of "flexible response" gave Kennedy a variety of military and political options to use depending on the situation.

The Bay of Pigs Invasion

Kennedy chose to fight **Fidel Castro**'s revolutionary army in Cuba by allowing the CIA to train an anticommunist invasion force comprising 1,500 Cuban expatriates. The small invasion army landed at the Bay of Pigs in Cuba in spring 1961 only to find the Cuban revolutionaries waiting for them. The failed **Bay of Pigs Invasion** evolved into a major political embarrassment for the United States, and it ruined American-Cuban relations.

Commitment in Southeast Asia

Kennedy also sent approximately 30,000 troops to South Vietnam in 1961 as "military advisors" to prevent South Vietnamese from toppling **Ngo Dinh Diem**'s corrupt regime in Saigon. These troops served as the first American ground forces in Vietnam and thus marked the beginning of American military commitment in the region that would plague future administrations.

The Berlin Crisis

Relations between Kennedy and Khrushchev proved to be just as difficult. In 1961, Khrushchev erected the **Berlin Wall** between the eastern and western sections of Berlin. The wall quickly became a symbol of Cold War divisions.

The Cuban Missile Crisis

The most intense confrontation between the two leaders occurred in October 1962 when Kennedy learned that Khrushchev had sent nuclear missiles to Cuba. The drama of the **Cuban Missile Crisis** played out as follows over thirteen days:

*   U.S. intelligence photos showed Soviet workers constructing nuclear missile silos in Cuba on October 14, 1962.

*   Kennedy then announced a blockade of Cuba on October 22. He stated that U.S. forces would fire on any ships that attempted to pass through the blockade.

*   Soviet ships approached the blockade, but stopped just short of entering Cuban waters on October 24.

*   Kennedy and Khrushchev finally reached an agreement on October 28 in which Khrushchev agreed to remove the missiles in exchange for Kennedy's promise not to invade Cuba.

Never before had the Cold War powers come so close to nuclear war. In 1963, the United States and the Soviet Union agreed to the first arms control measure of the Cold War, when they signed the **Nuclear Test Ban Treaty**, limiting the testing of nuclear weapons.

JFK'S ASSASSINATION

On November 22, 1963, a gunman shot and killed President Kennedy in Dallas, Texas, as he was riding in an open car. The Kennedy assassination continues to puzzle Americans to this day. Soon after the assassination in November 1963, authorities arrested **Lee Harvey Oswald** for the murder. Days later, during transport between jails, Dallas nightclub owner **Jack Ruby** murdered Oswald. An investigation headed by Supreme Court Chief Justice Earl Warren concluded that Oswald had acted alone, but the mysterious circumstances surrounding his death have left some questions unanswered. Books, films, and other media have kept different conspiracy theories alive.

Timeline

1945	Roosevelt, Churchill, and Stalin discuss the postwar world at the Yalta Conference.
	The Potsdam Conference ends with an ultimatum for Japan to unconditionally surrender.
	The United Nations is formed.
1947	Truman announces his Truman Doctrine.
	Congress sends $400 million to Greece and Turkey.
	The United States gives Europe aid under the Marshall Plan.
	Congress passes the Taft-Hartley Act.
	Congress passes the National Security Act.
	House Un-American Committee hunts for communists.
1948	Israel is founded.
	Truman orders the Berlin Airlift.
	Truman is elected.
1949	North Atlantic Treaty Organization is created.
1950	Senator McCarthy begins hunting for communists.
	NSC-68 is put into effect.
	The Korean War begins.
	Congress passes the McCarran Act.
1951	Truman fires General MacArthur.
1952	Dwight D. Eisenhower is elected president.
1953	Julius and Ethel Rosenberg are executed.
1954	The Army-McCarthy Hearings are aired on national television.
	Segregated education is struck down in *Brown v. Board of Education*.
1955	The Warsaw Pact is created.
	Montgomery Bus Boycott begins.
1956	Eisenhower is reelected.

1957	USSR launches *Sputnik*.
	Southern Christian Leadership Coalition (SCLC) forms.
1960	The U-2 Incident angers the Soviets.
	John F. Kennedy is elected president.
	The Student Nonviolent Coordinating Committee (SNCC) forms.
1961	Bay of Pigs Invasion tarnishes Kennedy's image.
	Freedom Rides occur throughout the South.
1962	The Cuban Missile Crisis brings the Cold War powers close to war.
1963	The Nuclear Test Ban Treaty is signed.
	Martin Luther King, Jr. leads the March on Washington.
	Kennedy is assassinated.

CHAPTER 17

Civil Rights and Vietnam: 1963–1975

||||||||||||||||||||||||||||||||||||||||||||||||||||||||

Protest, defeat, and progress defined the United States in the 1960s and 1970s. While the civil rights movement and the war on poverty dominated the agenda at home, President Lyndon B. Johnson drastically escalated the Vietnam War to prevent the spread of communism. Nixon's administration further expanded the war in Vietnam in 1973.

Liberal and conservative critics alike expressed their disappointment with the government and the war, and this distress fueled the American public's growing distrust of the government, spurring the development of the counterculture that rose to prominence in the late 1960s and 1970s. Americans were starting to question the values and norms of the previous generation and challenge the social and political structure of the nation. For the first time, the youth of America began to emerge as a significant culture, a voice that rebelled against the regularity of the 1950s mentality. Ultimately, this backlash against rigidity would give birth to one of the country's most fascinating eras and a new generation of innocents with a utopian vision of universal brotherhood.

The Civil Rights Movement

Across the South, African Americans waged campaigns of civil disobedience that often proved effective enough to bring about social change. As the movement gained momentum, however, white racists increased their efforts to stop it. The conflict between social change and hatred drew national attention to civil rights.

STUDENT ACTIVISM

Students, including the **Student Nonviolent Coordinating Committee (SNCC),** waged some of the more powerful campaigns of the civil rights movement. SNCC organized a number of events that had far-reaching consequences. In 1960, African-American college students and other activists seated themselves at white-only lunch counters, refusing to leave until served. The demonstrators frequently suffered abuse from white onlookers and ended up in jail. Additionally, members of SNCC and the **Congress of Racial Equality** embarked on a series of bus rides across the South in 1961. The rides aimed to integrate traveling facilities across the South. White mobs greeted the riders with violence in Alabama. Finally, in 1964, northern college students went to Mississippi to register African Americans to vote. By the end of the summer, many activists had been severely beaten by the police, and a few lost their lives.

Major Civil Rights Organizations

Acronym	Name	Major Accomplishments
CORE	Congress of Racial Equality	Freedom Rides
NAACP	National Association for the Advancement of Colored People	*Brown v. Board of Education*
SCLC	Southern Christian Leadership Conference	Birmingham, Alabama, civil rights campaign; March on Washington
SNCC	Student Nonviolent Coordinating Committee	Freedom Summer

THE KING CAMPAIGNS

In 1963, **Martin Luther King, Jr.,** began a civil rights campaign in Birmingham, Alabama, to pressure the municipal government to end segregation in the city. King and his fellow activists staged sit-ins and marches. When authorities arrested demonstrators, including King himself, more demonstrators simply took their places. The city jail soon filled up and the city's bureaucracy became overwhelmed. A series of economic boycotts of downtown businesses also brought the city's economy to a halt.

As demonstrations grew in number and power, white resistance to the movement increased. Vigilante bombers attempted to kill King and his family and city police attacked demonstrators with fierce dogs and fire hoses. Pictures of the violence ended up in newspapers across the country, turning public opinion in favor of the civil rights activists. Eventually, city officials capitulated and ended segregation.

The March on Washington

Months after the successful Birmingham campaign, King led more than 200,000 civil rights activists in a **March on Washington**, D.C. Standing in front of the Lincoln Memorial, King gave his **"I Have a Dream"** speech, one of the key speeches of his career.

Selma

The next major civil rights campaign occurred in Selma, Alabama, in 1965. Civil rights activists planned a march from Selma to Montgomery to publicize whites' disenfranchisement of Alabama blacks. But Alabama state troopers attacked the activists as soon as they began their march. When the protestors demonstrated their determination to march again a few days later, President **Lyndon Johnson** sent the Alabama National Guard to protect them.

GOVERNMENT ACTION

Johnson supported the civil rights movement and succeeded in getting Congress to pass the **Civil Rights Act of 1964**. The act effectively ended legal segregation and discrimination. Racial dis-

1963-1975

crimination in all public places, including hotels, restaurants, and schools was outlawed. The Equal Employment Opportunity Commission was also created, which prevented racial and gender discrimination in the workplace.

After the Selma campaign demonstrated the degree of disenfranchisement among southern blacks, Johnson and Congress also passed the **Voting Rights Act of 1965**, which allowed African Americans to register to vote quickly and easily, without fear of violence.

THE MOVEMENT SPLITS

Most civil rights activism during the 1950s and 1960s occurred in the South. Racism existed in the North, of course, but ghettoes and urban poverty made civil disobedience far less effective there. Pent-up rage over black poverty and racial injustice eventually exploded across northern cities in the mid- to late-1960s.

Riots

For some African Americans, social change occurred too slowly. Outside the South, certain black Americans concerned themselves more with fighting poverty than with voting rights or desegregation. Beginning in 1964, riots erupted across major U.S. cities, the largest occurring in Watts, Detroit, and Washington, D.C. Rioters often had no specific goals other than expressing rage and frustration over the racial and economic inequality in American society.

Malcolm X

For decades, the **Nation of Islam** advocated black independence in the United States and drew a large African-American following in many northern cities. In the 1960s, **Malcolm X**, who promoted black pride and self-reliance, became one of the most eloquent and widely followed black Muslims. At times, he called for active self-defense against white violence. He was assassinated in 1965.

Black Power

Some African-American activists concluded that laws and speeches would not change the deep-rooted causes of racism and oppression. In the mid-1960s, these activists embraced a more radical approach to civil rights. SNCC leader **Stokely Carmichael** began to use the term **Black Power** to describe his cause. Black Power expressed many of the themes advocated by Malcolm X, and its supporters encouraged African Americans to become independent of white society.

Advocates of the movement formed all-Black schools, organizations, and political groups such as the **Black Panthers**. Above all, Black Power expressed pride in African-American culture. Mainstream press coverage of Black Power often emphasized its aggressive side, leading to a severe backlash among whites.

Johnson in the 1960s

After taking office in 1963, **Lyndon Johnson** pledged himself to righting the nation's social wrongs. In his State of the Union Address in January 1964, he informed Congress of his plans to build a **Great Society** by waging a **War on Poverty**.

THE GREAT SOCIETY

Author **Michael Harrington**'s 1962 national bestselling book, *The Other America,* exposed middle-class suburbanites to the hunger, poverty, homelessness, and disease that afflicted as many as 50 million Americans. In response, Johnson and Democrats in the House and Senate passed the **Economic Opportunity Act** in the summer of 1964 to help the poorest Americans, especially urban blacks. Johnson and the Democrats promised a revolution with over $2 billion in social welfare reform and hailed the Great Society as the beginning of a new tomorrow.

THE WAR ON POVERTY

The Economic Opportunity Act created the Office of Economic Opportunities to spearhead the various projects aimed at creating jobs, improving education and housing, and providing medical care to those who could not afford it. OEO Programs included:

- **The Job Corps,** which offered vocational training to thousands of young inner-city black men

- **Project Head Start,** which educated more than 2 million of the poorest preschool-age children

- **Medicaid,** which offered federally funded health benefits to the poor

- **Medicare,** which offered health benefits to the elderly

Johnson also helped immigrants by passing the **Immigration and Nationality Act of 1965** to eliminate the national quota system. As a result, the number of yearly immigrants, especially from East Asia, skyrocketed.

> *Eventually, the quest for civil rights became a quest for better housing and better jobs. In launching the War on Poverty, Johnson revived the belief that government had a responsibility to help the less fortunate. Not since Roosevelt's New Deal had Congress spent so much money on social welfare programs.*

The War on Poverty had only limited success in helping the poor. This was primarily because none of the new government programs tackled the root problem of enormous income inequality. Although the government did redistribute roughly $1 billion, most of this money went to Americans who already earned middle-class incomes—not those in poverty. Blacks in particular saw very little of this money, even though they had been among the first to demand more social welfare spending. The Job Corps, for example, taught obsolete skills and provided only temporary unskilled work that offered no future. The war in Vietnam also siphoned the most money away from the War on Poverty, because Congress simply couldn't afford to fund both an antipoverty campaign and a major war abroad. Johnson's semiutopian vision of a Great Society had all but died by the mid-1970s.

TONKIN GULF

As the War on Poverty moved forward, Johnson pledged to honor John F. Kennedy's limited troop commitments in Vietnam. More specifically, he promised not to send any more "American boys nine or ten thousand miles away from home to do what Asian boys ought to be doing for themselves." The president's policy changed dramatically, though, just a few months later when several **North Vietnamese Army (NVA)**, gunboats allegedly attacked two U.S. Navy destroyers in the **Gulf of Tonkin** off the coast of North Vietnam.

In response, Johnson requested from Congress the authority to take "all necessary steps" to protect U.S. servicemen in South Vietnam. Congress complied and passed the **Tonkin Gulf Resolution** in August 1964. Out of the 535 total members of Congress, only two voted against this resolution. Many policymakers considered this to be a de facto declaration of war.

THE ELECTION OF 1964

Johnson easily won the support of the Democratic nominating convention on a Great Society platform. The attack in the Gulf of Tonkin and the congressional resolution only helped him in his election bid. LBJ's Republican opponent **Barry M. Goldwater** argued that much more needed to be done in Vietnam to contain communism; he even advocated using nuclear weapons. A self-proclaimed extremist, he also denounced the Great Society, the War on Poverty, and the civil rights movement in favor of near-radical conservatism. Not surprisingly, Johnson won the presidency that year with more than 60 percent of the popular vote and with 486 electoral votes to Goldwater's fifty-two.

ESCALATION IN VIETNAM

In February 1965 procommunist **Viet Cong** guerillas in South Vietnam attacked Marine barracks on an American base in the hamlet of Pleiku. Eight soldiers died, and more than a hundred more suffered casualties. Newly endowed with a blank check from Congress, Johnson capitalized on the **Pleiku Raid** and immediately ordered the air force and navy to begin an intense series of air strikes called **Operation Rolling Thunder**. He hoped that the bombing campaign would demonstrate his commitment to the South Vietnamese and his resolve to halt the spread of communism. Ironically, the air raids seemed only to increase the number of NVA and Viet Cong attacks.

Operation Rolling Thunder

Operation Rolling Thunder set the gears in motion for a major escalation of the war. Johnson believed that he could convince the NVA to withdraw by slowly increasing the number of American troops in Vietnam. He ordered more and more troops to South Vietnam in the next two years, bringing the total number to a staggering 400,000 men by the end of 1966. By 1968, the total number of troops had further jumped to more than 500,000. Sadly, as the number of in-country troops increased, so too did the number of casualties. More than 100,000 American men were killed or wounded by 1968.

At the height of the Cold War, many believed that if the United States allowed one country to fall to communism, then many more would follow suit like a row of dominos. This **domino theory** led the United States to support anticommunist regimes throughout the world, whether or not they upheld democratic ideals. The domino theory also provided the primary rationale for Johnson's massive escalation of the conflict in Vietnam to full-scale war.

The Destruction of South Vietnam

Although Johnson hoped the 500,000 American troops would save South Vietnam, his policy of escalation effectively destroyed the country. By 1968 alone, the military had used 3 million tons' worth of bombs on Vietnam, more than all the bombs dropped in Europe during World War II. The United States also used **napalm**, a slow-burning chemical agent dropped with bombs to maximize destruction. The military also used 20 million gallons of another chemical weapon called **Agent Orange** to kill forest-lands and drive out the Viet Cong.

> *The Vietnam War was so destructive because neither Johnson nor the military leadership knew how to fight a* **guerilla war***. Having always fought professional armies in previous wars, Americans had no experience fighting an enemy like the Viet Cong. U.S. leaders failed to recognize that they had become involved in a civil war in which most civilians supported the NVA. As a result, American servicemen often found themselves fighting uncooperative or hostile civilians just as much as enemy forces.*

COLLEGE STUDENT ACTIVISM

By 1968, the war had drastically divided society. College students made up one of the more vocal segments of the antiwar movement. On campuses across the nation, students held teach-ins, marches, and other forms of civil disobedience in protest of the war. Some of the more radical activists initiated student strikes and violently occupied campus administration buildings. At the same time, many Americans continued to support the war. These **"hawks"** opposed the peace-advocating **"doves"** and tried to brand their antiwar activities as un-American.

The Tet Offensive

In 1968, the Vietnamese communists launched a major offensive against the South's major cities on the Vietnamese New Year, or Tet. Nightly news broadcasts showed the increasing violence and seemingly endless numbers of dead U.S. soldiers. Although American forces repelled the attackers and inflicted serious damage on the Viet Cong, most Americans at home interpreted the **Tet Offensive** as evidence that America was losing.

Consequently, criticism of the war increased sharply, and massive demonstrations occurred on college campuses and in Washington, D.C., while Johnson's popularity plummeted. With the situation in Vietnam becoming ever more hopeless, Johnson announced a bombing halt in March 1968. He then added that he would not seek reelection in the upcoming presidential election.

Johnson's request to send hundreds of thousands more troops to Vietnam while simultaneously declaring victory prompted many Americans to question the president's honesty in the late 1960s. This "credibility gap" widened further when Johnson authorized the CIA and FBI's "Cointelpro" (Counter Intelligence Program) to spy on antiwar activists. The credibility gap also made the president a political liability for the Democratic Party, ruining his chance to run for reelection in 1968.

The Assassinations of King and Robert F. Kennedy

As the war raged, tumultuous events continued to upset the nation. In April 1968, an assassin gunned down Martin Luther King, Jr., in Memphis, Tennessee. Riots broke out across America, an expression of tremendous rage and grief over the loss. Later that summer, an assassin killed **Robert F. Kennedy** at a California campaign rally. The younger brother of John F. Kennedy, Robert Kennedy had been running for president on a platform of opposition to the Vietnam War and support for civil rights.

The Election of 1968

In the summer of 1968, thousands of protestors traveled to Chicago for the Democratic National Convention. As the convention proceeded, massive demonstrations took place around the city. While most of the demonstrations remained peaceful, certain radical factions made more provocative statements. Chicago police forces started to attack the demonstrators, and a full-scale riot broke out.

The divisions in society caused by the war played out in the 1968 presidential election. Democrats nominated Vice President **Hubert Humphrey**, but Humphrey's refusal to denounce the Vietnam War divided the party. Republicans meanwhile nominated **Richard Nixon**, who campaigned on a platform of "law and order." **George Wallace** also ran on the third-party American Independent ticket. Nixon's campaign appealed to many Americans who believed in the war or thought that the antiwar and Black Power movements had gotten out of hand. Nixon won with 301 electoral votes to Humphrey's 191 and Wallace's 46.

Nixon Abroad

Soon after entering the White House, Nixon announced his new policy of **"Vietnamization"**—a slow withdrawal of the more than 500,000 American soldiers from Vietnam and a simultaneous return of control of the war to the South Vietnamese. He still intended to fund and train the South Vietnamese Army, but hoped that slow troop withdrawals would appease voters at home and reduce casualties in the field. He also announced the **Nixon Doctrine**: America would honor its current defense commitments but would not commit troops anywhere else to fight communism.

THE SECRET INVASION OF CAMBODIA

Nixon sought instead to defeat the North Vietnamese by destroying their supply lines and base camps in neighboring Cambodia. Although Cambodia officially remained neutral during the war, the NVA ran weapons and troops through the country to circumvent American bombers and raiding parties. In the spring of 1970, Nixon authorized the invasion of Cambodia. The order shocked Congress and the American public. Renewed public outcry and waves of protests convinced Nixon to renege the order later that summer.

> When criticized by antiwar protestors, Nixon and his vice president, **Spiro Agnew**, always responded that the **"silent majority"** of Americans still supported the war in Vietnam. In other words, the president claimed that noisy activists constituted only a small percentage of the American public.

MY LAI AND THE PENTAGON PAPERS

Other scandals sparked protest against the military and the president. In 1971, the U.S. Army court-martialed Lieutenant William Calley for ordering the rape, torture, and murder of more than 350 women and children in the 1968 **My Lai Massacre**. Other soldiers anonymously confessed that dozens of similar incidents had taken place over the course of the war. The military came under fire again that year when the *New York Times* published a series of leaked documents called the **Pentagon Papers**, which

1963–1975

accused the army, John F. Kennedy, and Lyndon Johnson of deceiving the public during the war.

CONGRESS CHECKS UNLIMITED POWER

Outraged by the unauthorized invasion of Cambodia and by the double scandal of the My Lai Massacre and the Pentagon Papers, many in Congress took steps to exert more control over the war and to appease an equally angry public. For example, the Senate (but not the House of Representatives) voted to repeal the Tonkin Gulf Resolution to reduce the military's unchecked spending power. Congress reduced the number of years drafted soldiers needed to serve in the army, and they also ratified the **Twenty-Sixth Amendment** in 1971 to lower the voting age from twenty-one to eighteen on the grounds that young soldiers in Vietnam should help elect the politicians who sent them to fight.

DÉTENTE

Nixon decided the only solution rested on improving relations with the Soviet Union; this policy came to be known as **détente**. He believed détente would divert attention from the growing failures in Vietnam and allow the United States to eventually withdraw on more graceful terms. Nixon's national security advisor **Henry Kissinger** supported the plan.

Nixon Goes to China

The president chose to approach Russia by opening relations with China in 1972. Although both communist countries, Maoist China and the Soviet Union were deeply suspicious of each other. Consequently, they had one of the most heavily fortified borders in the world. Nixon hoped dialogues with China would spark fear in Russia over a possible American-Chinese alliance. After visiting Beijing in 1972, Nixon and Kissinger then flew to Moscow, where they played their so-called **"China card"** to bring the Soviets to the negotiating table.

ABM and SALT I

Even though the tactic outraged liberals and conservatives alike back in the United States, Nixon's ploy worked. While in the U.S.S.R., Nixon managed to smooth tensions with Soviet leader **Leonid Brezhnev** and usher in a new era of "cooler" American-Soviet relations called détente. He agreed to sell the Soviets $1 billion worth of badly needed American grain. This arrangement both helped Brezhnev feed his starving people and boosted Nixon's popularity with farmers in the Midwest.

In 1972, Nixon signed the **Anti-Ballistic Missile (ABM) Treaty** to limit the missile defense system, and the **Strategic Arms Limitation Talks Treaty (SALT Treaty)** to prevent both sides from developing any more nuclear weapons for the next five years. Washington enjoyed improved relations with Beijing as an added benefit.

NIXON'S LANDSLIDE IN 1972

Nixon's successful trip to China and Russia gave him the advantage he needed in Vietnam. When the NVA crossed the demilitarized zone and invaded South Vietnam in 1972, Nixon authorized an intense bombing campaign of Hanoi without fear of retaliation from Moscow or Beijing. Nixon also secretly sent Kissinger to meet with North Vietnamese diplomats in Paris that year to discuss peace.

As the presidential elections of 1972 approached, Nixon clearly had the upper hand: he had initiated détente, reduced the number of American troops in Vietnam from 500,000 to 30,000, and had halted a major NVA advance. As a result, he easily defeated peace Democrat **George McGovern** in a landslide victory with 520 to thirteen electoral votes and nearly 20 million more popular votes.

THE CHRISTMAS DAY BOMBING AND CEASE-FIRE

Nixon authorized the **Christmas Day Bombing**, an intense two-week bombing campaign of North Vietnam that he hoped would end the war. Kissinger and North Vietnamese officials finally announced a cease-fire in January 1973. Nixon accepted and agreed

*Hoping to win reelection by a landslide in the election of 1972, Richard Nixon employed his **"southern strategy"** to make himself as appealing as possible to white voters in the South. He promised to take a hardliner's stance against civil rights and to oppose Great Society social welfare spending, even though he proved to be supportive to both causes during his tenure as president.*

to withdraw the remaining American troops, despite the fact that the NVA controlled more than a quarter of South Vietnamese territory. In exchange, the North Vietnamese promised that an election in Saigon would determine the fate of the country.

Nixon at Home

Although Nixon focused most of his attention on Vietnam and détente, he could not avoid contending with domestic issues, particularly the stagnant economy at home. Beginning in the early 1970s, both inflation and the cost of living crept skyward, while wages remained the same. Worker productivity was declining for the first time since before World War II. To make matters worse, cheaper and better foreign products from Japan started entering the market. On top of all this, Congress paid roughly $22 billion a year to fund Lyndon Johnson's social welfare programs and the war in Vietnam.

THE NEW LEFT

The war in Vietnam and continuing racial strife in the United States spurred the radicalization of American youth during the 1960s and 1970s. In the early 1960s, idealistic young white Americans involved in the civil rights movement and other liberal endeavors expanded their efforts to other issues, forming what collectively became known as the **New Left.**

COUNTERCULTURE

Students and other radical young people created a new **counterculture** in America. This counterculture flouted the values and conventions of middle-class society and embraced a new style that defied traditional standards. Many young Americans grew their hair long, wore shabby clothing, and exhibited rebellious disregard for the old manners and rules. Rock, folk music, and drugs, such as marijuana and LSD, came into vogue as well as new attitudes about sexuality. The ascendancy of the counterculture reflected wider currents in American society at large, as growing numbers of Americans became distrustful of the American government and official rhetoric during the Vietnam era.

> In the summer of 1969, about 400,000 people gathered on a farm in upstate New York for a three-day rock and folk music festival called the **Woodstock Music and Art Fair**. Performers included many who would become the most celebrated musicians of the counterculture movement, including Joan Baez, Janis Joplin, Jimi Hendrix, the Grateful Dead, and Carlos Santana.

NIXON AND RACE RELATIONS

Even in 1969, fifteen years after the Supreme Court ruled in favor of mandatory desegregation in *Brown v. Board of Education,* the majority of southern schools were not racially integrated. Backed by a supportive Supreme Court, civil rights advocates pushed through a number of policies that fostered integration in schools across the entire country. The Nixon administration placed severe limits on the methods schools used to achieve integration goals. One of the most controversial integration measures involved busing students across cities and school districts in order to achieve desegregation.

Some of Nixon's policies furthered the goals of the civil rights movement. He enacted several initiatives intended to motivate contractors and unions to hire more minorities, offered incentives to minority businesses, and expanded the power of the Equal Rights Employment Opportunity Commission. While Nixon never supported racial quotas in hiring or education, his administration did support certain forms of affirmative action.

WOMEN'S LIBERATION

The women's liberation movement gained new momentum in the 1970s. Engaging in peaceful protests for equality, these activists voiced their dissatisfaction with women's rights in the United States. Although women gained the right to vote in the 1920s, structural and cultural factors maintained inequality. The **National Organization for Women (NOW)** emerged as the primary group representing the concerns of mainstream feminists. NOW initiated strikes and protests to demand equality in employment, education, childcare, and reproductive control. Many smaller groups also fought for the passage of the **Equal Rights Amendment (ERA)** to the Constitution.

The ERA

The proposed Equal Rights Amendment to the Constitution would have required equal treatment of men and women in all domains. Although the amendment passed Congress and was ratified in a number of states, it failed to receive the three-fifths majority required to make it part of the Constitution. As a result, women continued to generally receive lower wages for comparable work in the ensuing decades.

> The Supreme Court's landmark decision in **Roe v. Wade** in 1973 granted constitutional protection to women seeking abortions. It also prohibited individual states from passing legislation that would ban abortions during the first three months of pregnancy.

NIXON AND THE ENVIRONMENT

Although the Nixon administration generally prioritized economic interests over environmental concerns, Congress passed several protective acts in the 1970s. The administration supported the **Occupational Safety and Health Act (OSHA)**, the **Clean Air Act,** and the **Endangered Species Act**. At the same time, Nixon also created the **Environmental Protection Agency (EPA)** to protect air and water quality and to monitor the use of pesticides.

NIXON'S SOCIAL WELFARE PROGRAMS

Nixon publicly advocated decreased government participation in social welfare. He cut key programs such as Medicare, Head Start, and legal services as part of his commitment to "Middle America." In spite of these cuts, Nixon also increased Social Security benefits, subsidized low-income housing, expanded the food stamp program, and established a government assistance program for low-income students.

ECONOMIC POLICY

The Arab oil embargo of 1973 combined with inflation at home created the nation's first energy crisis. Inflation rose steadily, as did the unemployment rate. The United States gradually lost its predominant place in the world economy as foreign countries such as Japan and Germany finally rebounded from post–World War II depressions. Nixon temporarily improved the economy by taking steps to increase exports while freezing wages and prices. Yet by 1974, the United States faced a severe economic crisis.

1963-1975

Several of the world's leading oil-producing countries formed the *Organization of Petroleum Exporting Countries (OPEC)* in 1960 to monopolize the sale of oil on the global market. OPEC began the *energy crisis* in the 1970s when it embargoed the sale of oil to the United States in retaliation for the defeat of several of its Arab members by the American-backed Israel in the 1973 Yom Kippur War. Throughout the 1970s, OPEC punished the United States and other Western powers that supported Israel with a combination of oil embargoes and unannounced rate hikes. These retaliatory *"oil shocks"* damaged the American economy by raising prices and aggravating inflation.

Watergate, Resignation, and Ford

On June 17, 1972, local police officers apprehended five men during an early-morning break-in at the national Democratic Party headquarters in the **Watergate** apartment and office complex. Police soon discovered that the men worked for the **Committee to Reelect the President (CREEP)**. The burglars had attempted to repair a bugging device that they had installed during a previous forced entry. Over the next two years, the investigation brought the Nixon administration's worst secrets to light.

THE NIXON TAPES

In April 1973, Nixon appeared on television to publicly accept responsibility for the Watergate events. He adamantly denied any direct knowledge of the break-in and cover-up and announced the resignations of several of his subordinates. The Senate investigative committee uncovered more incriminating evidence against the president and added charges concerning the misuse of federal funds and tax evasion. The committee subpoenaed some of the president's audiotapes of White House conversations, but Nixon refused to relinquish them.

NIXON'S RESIGNATION

In July 1974, the Supreme Court unanimously decided that the president had to present his White House tapes to congressional investigators. These tapes clearly established Nixon's guilt in the Watergate cover-up. Armed with damning evidence, the House Judiciary Committee gained majority support on three charges of impeachment against Nixon:

- Obstruction of justice
- Abuse of power
- Contempt of Congress

Faced with imminent impeachment, Nixon chose instead to resign. In a dramatic, nationally televised speech on August 8,

1974, he accepted responsibility for his poor judgment in the Watergate scandal but continued to defend his good intentions.

FORD: THE UNELECTED PRESIDENT

Following Nixon's resignation, Nixon's vice president, **Gerald Ford**, became president of the United States. Congress had recently appointed Ford to office after Vice President Agnew had resigned in the wake of a corruption scandal in 1973. As a result, Ford became the nation's first and only unelected president. Highlights of the Ford presidency include:

- **Nixon's presidential pardon**. Only a month into his presidency, Ford granted a formal pardon to Nixon for all his purported crimes, sparing the ex-president and the nation the embarrassment of a trial and likely conviction. The decision angered many Americans and ruined Ford's political and public credibility.

- **Evacuating Vietnam**. Ford pulled the last remaining troops out of Vietnam in 1975 which marked the end of American involvement in the Vietnam War. U.S. forces helped approximately 150,000 South Vietnamese flee the country.

- **The Continuing Economic Crisis**. Ford faced a number of liabilities during his brief term in office that proved insurmountable. He lacked the resources, knowledge, and political clout to tackle the stagnant economy. He also vetoed thirty-nine bills Congress had passed to improve domestic affairs and reduce taxes, and at the same time, he increased government spending. As a result, Americans faced the deepest recession since the Great Depression by the end of his two years in office.

Timeline

1963	Lyndon Johnson becomes president.
1964	Tonkin Gulf Resolution authorizes military action in Southeast Asia.
	Johnson launches War on Poverty.
	Freedom Summer marks the climax of intensive voter-registration activities in the South.
	Congress passes the Civil Rights Act of 1964.
1965	Johnson begins "escalation" in Vietnam.
	The Pleiku Raid sparks off an intense series of airstrikes called Operation Rolling Thunder.
	Peace protestors march on Washington D.C.
	Congress passes the Voting Rights Act.
1967	Rallies, riots, and protests erupt throughout the United States.
1968	The Tet Offensive incites massive demonstrations on college campuses throughout the United States.
	Paris peace talks begin.
	Robert Kennedy is assassinated.
	Martin Luther King, Jr., is assassinated.
	Riots erupt outside the Democratic convention in Chicago.
	Richard Nixon is elected president.
1969	The Woodstock Music and Art Fair attracts 400,000 people.
	Nixon begins "Vietnamization" withdrawl of U.S. troops.
1970	The United States bombs Cambodia.
	Student protests turn violent throughout the country.
1971	The *New York Times* publishes the Pentagon Papers.
	The Twenty-Sixth Amendment is ratified.
	Lieutenant William Calley is court-martialed for the My Lai Massacre.

1972	Nixon and Henry Kissinger visit China and the Soviet Union.
	Nixon signs the SALT and ABM treaties to reduce nuclear weapons.
	Nixon is reelected.
	Nixon authorizes the Christmas Day Bombing in North Vietnam.
1973	Congress passes the War Powers Act.
	The Watergate scandal erupts.
	Roe v. Wade gives women the right to an abortion.
	Arab oil embargo begins an oil/energy crisis.
1974	The House of Representatives prepares to impeach Nixon.
	Vice President Spiro T. Agnew resigns.
	Nixon resigns.
	Gerald Ford becomes president.
	Ford pardons Nixon.
1975	The Helsinki Accords reduces tension between Soviet and western blocs.
	Communists declare victory in South Vietnam.

1963-1975

CHAPTER 18

The Reagan Revolution to the Post-Cold War Era: 1976–2000

IIIIIIIIIIIIIIIIIIIIIIIIIIIIIIIIIIIIIIIIIIIIIIIIIIIIIIIIIIIIIIII

In spite of his honesty, faith, and good intentions, President Jimmy Carter appeared to lack the clout and political knowledge to resolve the numerous crises that plagued his presidency. A devout, born-again Christian, Carter hoped to humanize government with his southern style, humanitarian politics, and support for human rights. This left many cynics to proclaim that Carter was simply too nice to accomplish much in Washington. Carter's successor, the former actor Ronald Reagan, promised to shrink the government, slash taxes, and revitalize the military marked the end of the post–New Deal mainstream liberal consensus even as the Soviet Union was beginning to implode.

Reagan's more low-key vice president, George H. W. Bush, followed Reagan's two terms in office with less fanfare but a more practical approach to statesmanship. After twelve years of a Republican-controlled White House, Democratic President Bill Clinton used his deft touch with retail politics and an idealism tempered with realism to move the party to adopt less liberal positions. His eight years in office were marked by economic prosperity but also bitter political feuding and scandals.

The Presidency of Jimmy Carter

After defeating **Gerald Ford** in 1976, **Jimmy Carter** assumed the presidency with promises to improve the economy, strengthen education, and provide assistance to the aging and the poor. Carter began his term in office with confidence and enthusiasm. A variety of obstacles and unexpected events prevented the new president from achieving many of his goals.

THE ELECTION OF 1976

Gerald Ford received the Republican party's official nomination in the summer of 1976 and was desperate to win the presidency in his own right. Unfortunately for him, Americans had a tainted image of Washington politics, the White House, and anything even remotely tied to Richard Nixon. Instead, they turned to a surprise presidential contender, James "Jimmy" Carter. A Democrat, peanut farmer, and former governor of Georgia, Carter had almost no political experience in Washington, D.C., and was therefore "clean" in the eyes of many Americans. His down-to-earth demeanor and truthfulness only made him more likeable and refreshing to American voters.

During the campaign, Carter vowed to clean up Washington, cut taxes, and end the energy crisis. Thanks largely to enormous support from southern and black voters, Carter received slightly more than 50 percent of the popular vote and 297 electoral votes to Ford's 240.

DOMESTIC POLICY

Unlike most of his Democrat predecessors, Carter increased taxes for the lower and middle classes and cut taxes for wealthier individuals. In the face of soaring inflation, slow economic growth, and high levels of unemployment, Carter also made minimizing federal spending and preserving Social Security two of his top priorities. Additionally, he protected struggling big businesses by reducing capital gains taxes and deregulating the banking, airline, trucking, and railroad industries.

THE ENERGY CRISIS

Carter tried to reduce domestic oil consumption and American dependence on foreign crude oil, but he lacked the necessary support from consumers and Congress. As a result, none of the initiatives that Carter successfully launched had any real effect.

"Stagflation"

The president's inability to tackle the **energy crisis** damaged his reputation, especially considering voters had elected him to do just that. Americans were forced to wait in long lines or buy gasoline only on certain days, just as they had under Nixon and Ford. Moreover, soaring gas prices made it more expensive to transport goods across the country. Manufacturers and retailers compensated for the increased transportation costs by raising retail prices so that, on average, inflation increased by 10 percent *per year* between 1974 and 1980 without any economic growth or change in wages. In other words, a product that cost $100 in 1974 cost over $180 in 1980. It thus became more expensive to drive, buy a house, buy consumer goods, and even buy groceries.

> After a nearly two-week hiatus from any public appearances, Carter made a televised address to the nation in which he blamed inflation and the energy crisis on morally and spiritually bankrupt Americans concerned only with money and consumerism. This *"Malaise Speech"* shocked the nation and led many to question Carter's ability to lead.

CARTER'S FOREIGN POLICY

Carter made the protection of human rights through diplomacy his highest foreign policy priority. He slapped economic sanctions on countries like Argentina, Chile, and South Africa, infamous for rampant human rights violations. Critics argued that the president's human rights policies displayed inconsistencies. For example, he overlooked human rights violations in strategically important countries such as China, Iran, and South Korea. Others charged that Carter's human-rights-centered foreign policy distracted the United States from facing Cold War concerns, like the communist revolution in Nicaragua.

1976–2000

Outside of America, many leaders around the world lauded his morally grounded foreign policy.

Carter attempted to extend his moral principles to amend some of America's past imperialist actions. In 1977, Carter signed a new treaty with Panama regarding the control and use of the **Panama Canal**. Until this point, the United States enjoyed sole control of the isthmian canal, but the new treaty granted Panama joint control until the year 2000 (at which point Panama would assume complete control). Many Americans perceived this action as compensation for the "big stick" tactics the United States had utilized to secure the land to build the canal in the first place. At the same time, critics became concerned with Carter's willingness to forgo control of such an economically and strategically vital waterway.

Peace in the Middle East

Carter's successful leadership during negotiations between Egyptian president **Anwar el-Sadat** and Israeli prime minister **Menachem Begin** proved to be one of his greatest international achievements. After inviting the two men to the presidential retreat at Camp David, Maryland, Carter spent days guiding the discussion between the bitter rivals, who often refused to even meet face to face. Largely thanks to Carter, both men signed the **Camp David Accords** in 1978 to agree to end several decades of war. As a result, Egypt also became the first Arab nation to formally recognize Israel, and Israel agreed to withdraw from the Sinai Peninsula.

SALT II

Carter hoped to end his first term on a high note before the 1980 elections by reducing the threat of Soviet aggression and nuclear holocaust. In 1979, he met with Soviet premier Leonid Brezhnev to sign the **Second Strategic Arms Limitation Talks (SALT II Treaty)**, to reduce the number of both countries' nuclear warheads.

Although a treaty would have significantly eased American-Soviet relations, conservatives in the Senate bitterly opposed it out of fear that the treaty would leave Americans vulnerable to attack. They pointed to Russia's support of the Cuban interventions in Ethiopia and Angola and the Soviet invasion of Afghanistan in

December 1979. Carter denounced the invasion and stopped all grain shipments to the USSR, but party leaders in Moscow refused to withdraw.

The Iran Hostage Crisis

Carter's greatest international policy challenge came from Iran. Although the Shah of Iran, **Mohammad Reza Pahlavi**, had long been a U.S. ally, Carter criticized the shah's autocratic rule and refused to provide military aid to support him against an armed insurrection. In 1979, Carter allowed the shah to flee to the United States for medical treatment and political asylum. Iranian militants—who were enraged by American support of the ousted leader—broke into the U.S. embassy in Tehran and took fifty-three hostages.

The militants demanded that the United States return the shah for trial and possible execution in return for the release of the hostages. The new Iranian government, headed by the Shi'ite cleric **Ayatollah Khomeini**, actively participated in the hostage situation. Khomeini established a Shi'ite theocracy in Iran that remains in power.

Carter's attempts to deal with the hostage crisis were ineffective. After a year of failed negotiations, he authorized a military rescue operation. The rescue turned out to be a complete disaster, however, when eight American soldiers died in a helicopter crash in the Iranian desert. Khomeini refused to sign an agreement for the release of the hostages. Carter's inability to resolve the **Iran hostage crisis** weakened American confidence in the administration and contributed to his defeat in the election of 1980.

Carter's inability to curb inflation, prevent Soviet aggression, or save the American hostages in Iran damaged his reputation at home and abroad. The Malaise Speech worsened matters. Many people in the United States expressed outrage over the president's attempt to blame them for his own shortcomings. With so much controversy, anger, and resentment clouding Carter's four years, Reagan's victory in 1980 came as no surprise.

The Reagan Revolution

Americans elected **Ronald Reagan**, a former movie actor and governor of California, to the presidency in 1980. Reagan swept into the White House in 1981 on a mission to reduce the size of the federal government and shift the balance of political power back to the individual states. A die-hard conservative Republican, he abhorred most social welfare programs, hated affirmative action, and felt that policymakers in Washington had overstepped their mandate by exerting too much control over the lives of average Americans.

Reagan managed to overcome opposition and pass most items on his agenda by cajoling southern conservative Democrats in Congress to vote with his Republican allies. He also received support from the so-called **Religious Right**, a prominent group of conservative Protestant ministers who opposed homosexuality and abortion, among other things. More important, he had the support of the vast majority of Americans.

"REAGANOMICS"

Reagan immediately set out to balance the budget and curb the growing deficit that had plagued Jimmy Carter's administration. He proposed to slash social welfare programs in order to reduce the budget deficit to just under $40 billion a year. Then, he slashed tax rates across the board by nearly 25 percent. Corporations received even more benefits from Washington, D.C., in the hopes that their prosperity would "trickle down" to the average American worker. Although most conservatives praised Reagan's **"supply-side economics,"** a few Republicans dissented including Vice President **George H. W. Bush**, who had previously denounced Reagan's fiscal agenda as **"voodoo economics"** because it simply made no sense.

The Recession of 1982

By 1982, **"Reaganomics"** had taken its toll as several banks failed, the stock market plummeted, and unemployment soared in the worst economic recession since the Great Depression. Eventually the economy pulled out of the pit, thanks in part to sound policies from the Federal Reserve Board. Prosperity eventually came, but at a steep price as the gap between the very rich and the very poor widened considerably. With reduced government welfare programs to alleviate the hunger and homelessness, the poor had nowhere to turn for help. The recession hit women, children, and blacks especially hard.

> The Reagan administration angered many women by openly opposing the **Equal Rights Amendment** and abortion rights. Additionally, Reagan's social-spending cuts had a disproportionate effect on women, who often earned less than men and sometimes carried the burden of raising families alone. The women's movement worked hard to improve public knowledge of the needs of lower-income women and children, who outnumbered lower-income men.

Deficits and Debt

Although Reagan entered the White House promising to reduce government spending and return more power to the states, he ironically became the biggest spender in American history. Not even Roosevelt's New Deal during the Depression or Johnson's Great Society had dumped so much money into the economy as Reaganomics. Between 1980 and 1988, Congress overspent its budget by more than $200 billion every year, while the national debt soared from roughly $1 trillion to $2.5 trillion.

Moreover, almost all of Reagan's spending went into the military and defense; very little actually "trickled down" to the average American. Still, Americans continued to support the president. For many citizens, his charisma and his unwavering stance against Soviet aggression abroad translated to a sense of safety. In the wake of Vietnam, social unrest, the energy crisis, and the Iran hostage crisis, Americans sought strength and protection above all else.

> By raising the national debt to astonishing and unprecedented proportions, Reagan ensured that no future Congress, for at least several generations, would be able to afford major social welfare programs either. In this sense, the staggering deficit thus became an incredible, long-term political victory.

The Savings and Loan Crisis

Reagan also deregulated many aspects of the banking industry, which allowed the traditionally local, financially conservative **savings and loan** institutions to enter the arena of high-yield, high-risk corporate investments. As a result, hundreds of savings and loans across the country had gone bankrupt by the late 1980s. Congress's decision to rescue failing institutions saved many families from financial ruin, but it also further increased the federal budget deficit.

The Stock Market Crash of 1987

Though a bull market ruled for much of the decade, Americans indulged in several imprudent financial practices that ultimately caused a stock market crash. Following the cue of the federal government's increased deficit spending, both consumers and businesses ran up huge debts. The United States also had a very high trade deficit, importing much more than it exported. Again, borrowed money often paid for these imports.

A shaky stock market finally buckled on October 19, 1987, or **Black Monday**, when the Dow Jones Industrial Average lost nearly 23 percent of its value in a single day. $560 billion in paper assets disappeared. Reagan reassured the nation that the economy would remain stable and tried to help the economy by reducing some deficit spending and increasing some taxes. These measures could not prevent stock markets around the world from buckling.

CONSERVATISM IN THE COURT

Reagan's long presidency altered the composition of the federal courts. Reagan tended to appoint judges and justices who held politically conservative views and focused less on protecting individual rights. Reagan's most high-profile appointment was **Sandra Day O'Connor**, a middle-of-the-road conservative who became the first female Supreme Court justice.

While many critics expected Reagan's appointments to signal a profound change in the federal court system, the new conservative judges tended to maintain the status quo. Even when given the opportunity, they rarely overturned long-standing decisions on controversial issues (e.g., abortion). Instead, the justices began to defer to state-government decisions regarding rights issues.

LANDSLIDE REELECTION IN '84

Democrats prayed that the recession would ruin Reagan's chances for reelection in 1984. But the president's popularity held steady. Democrats nominated Jimmy Carter's former vice president **Walter Mondale**, who surprised everyone by choosing a woman, **Geraldine Ferraro**, as his vice-presidential running mate. In the end, Reagan and Bush easily defeated Mondale and Ferraro with approximately 17 million more popular votes and 525 electoral votes to their thirteen.

Reagan Abroad

A former "red" hunter in Hollywood during the McCarthy era, Reagan also took a hard stance against the "evil empire" of the Soviet Union. He believed that a **"window of vulnerability"** had temporarily weakened the United States.

STAR WARS

Tired of détente and outraged by Soviet aggression in Afghanistan, Regan proposed to dramatically boost defense spending based on the belief that a crippled Russian economy wouldn't be able to keep up with American military development. His plan culminated with the proposal of a futuristic orbital laser defense system called the **Strategic Defense Initiative (SDI)**. Most scientists agreed that **"Star Wars,"** as pundits called it, would never work. Still, Reagan hoped the proposal would strong-arm the Soviet Union to the bargaining table on American terms.

THE REAGAN DOCTRINE

The **Reagan Doctrine** stated that the United States had to combat any Marxist revolutions abroad in order to counter Soviet advances. The president employed this doctrine in several developing Latin American countries. For example, Reagan denounced the communist **Sandinista** revolutionaries in Nicaragua and gave tens of millions of dollars to the pro-American **"contra"** rebels to take back the country. He dumped even more money into neighboring El Salvador and sent military advisors to prevent a revolution there too. On top of this, Reagan ordered the invasion of the tiny island nation of Grenada in the Caribbean in 1983 to oust communist usurpers.

> *The Reagan Doctrine served as the principle tenet of Reagan's foreign policy. He incorrectly assumed that all instability in the third world stemmed from Marxist revolutionaries or Soviet aggression and committed the United States to preventing the spread of communism even in the farthest corners of the world. In doing so, he ended détente, reversed the Nixon Doctrine, and revived the policy of containment. In other words, the United States would do and spend whatever it took to maintain the status quo and keep communism contained. Reagan's pledge and the renewed Cold War cost Americans hundreds of millions of dollars for very little gain.*

THE IRAN-CONTRA AFFAIR

Even though the vast majority of Americans supported Reagan's tough stance against communism, Congress did not. This was primarily because upholding the Reagan Doctrine simply cost too much money. The United States had poured hundreds of millions of dollars into fighting communist revolutions abroad—most notably in Nicaragua, to help the "Contra" rebels fight the Marxist Sandinistas. Finally, the invasion of Grenada had proven that Reagan would not hesitate to use troops to fight these insurgents.

The Boland Amendment

Hoping to avert a Vietnam-esque war in Nicaragua, Congress passed the **Boland Amendment** in 1983, which forbade the federal government from further assisting the Contras with either troops or money.

Illegal Arms Sales

Scandal erupted when journalists discovered that the White House had ignored the amendment and funneled secret money raised from arms sales in Iran and other Middle Eastern countries into Nicaragua. After a lengthy investigation, a congressional committee indicted several officials on the president's National Security Council, including Admiral Poindexter and Marine Corps colonel **Oliver North**. Both Poindexter and North claimed they acted in the interests of national security. Essentially, they argued that the ends justified the illegal means. The investigation implicated Reagan and Bush, but their involvement was never proven.

REFORM IN RUSSIA

Although Reagan had taken an incredibly harsh stance against the Soviet Union, he actually played a key role in ending the Cold War. In 1985, reform-minded **Mikhail Gorbachev** came to power in the Soviet Union with some radical new ideas about politics, the economy, and society as a whole. Soon after taking office, he initiated **glasnost**, or "openness," to relax some political controls, including restrictions on the press, and **perestroika**, or "restructuring," to slowly convert the Soviet Union into a more capitalist economy.

In order to transition to capitalism, Gorbachev drastically reduced the amount the USSR spent on its military, which effectively meant ending the Cold War. He met with Reagan at four different summit meetings between 1985 and 1988 and signed the **INF Treaty** at the final summit in Washington, D.C., to remove all nuclear weapons aimed at Europe and effectively end the Cold War.

George H. W. Bush and the End of the Cold War

George H. W. Bush took office as president in 1989. An establishment Republican, he had held several high-level government positions, including ambassador to the United Nations and director of the Central Intelligence Agency, before serving as Reagan's two-term vice president. Bush would lead the country into the dizzying complexities of the post–Cold War era as well as its first major land war since Vietnam.

Bush's election signaled an attempt to keep the Reagan Revolution going even as the world was undergoing dramatic changes. In November 1989, the Berlin Wall was torn down, symbolizing an end to the Cold War. Then, in August 1991, Bush and Mikhail Gorbachev agreed to reduce their nuclear arsenals by one quarter. With the USSR tottering on the brink of economic collapse, hard-line communists attempted to oust Gorbachev to prevent the fall of the Soviet Union. Their efforts, however, were blocked by **Boris Yeltsin**, the president of the new Russian federation, who led the drive to dissolve the USSR.

After the fall of the Soviet Union in December 1991, U.S. foreign relations radically transformed around the globe as the Bush administration extended economic support to the former Soviet republics. China, however, remained staunchly communist. (Relations between China and the U.S. had soured in 1989 when the Chinese army violently crushed a pro-democracy protest in **Tiananmen Square**.)

The Gulf War

Led by **Saddam Hussein**, Iraq invaded its tiny neighbor, Kuwait, in August 1990. President Bush rallied the U.S. Congress and the American people, as well as the United Nations, in support of a counterattack to force the Iraqis out. In January 1991, the **Gulf War** began. The military campaign, led by Army General H. Norman Schwarzkopf, was called **"Operation Desert Storm."** The American people watched the attacks on TV in carefully edited clips that emphasized the military's vaunted new "pushbutton warfare"—a great contrast to the rawer, bloodier combat footage that helped turn public opinion against the Vietnam War.

In late February, U.S. ground troops began an attack on Kuwait City, driving out the defending Iraqis in under a week. The U.S. decided not to press on to Baghdad or to occupy any Iraqi territory, leaving Hussein in power. Victory was achieved with only 148 American deaths. However, more than 100,000 Iraqis, military and civilian, died.

In September 1990, after Iraq's invasion of Kuwait, Bush gave a speech to Congress on the Persian Gulf crisis and the federal deficit problem. In it, he laid out not just a plan for containing Hussein's aggression but also a vigorously Wilsonian view of a *"new world order"* that would be "freer from the threat of terror, stronger in the pursuit of justice, and more secure in the quest for peace. An era in which the nations of the world, East and West, North and South, can prosper and live in harmony." Although Bush's vision of a post–Cold War world free from war and strife would not come to pass, the term "new world order" would live on in the 1990s and early 2000s as catchphrase for activists of many kinds who chalked it up as nothing more than another form of American imperialism.

Although Bush's popularity soared after the public's rapturous response to the quick American victory—which included ticker-tape parades for soldiers, a spectacle that hadn't been seen since the end of World War II—it quickly plunged again. Having shown himself to be more adept at handling international crises than those at home, Bush was caught flatfooted by a stubbornly stagnant economy and a growing liberalization of the culture as pronounced as anything seen during the 1960s. Economic realities—including massive deficits run up in large part by his predecessor's military spending—forced him to break his famed 1988 campaign promise, **"Read my lips: no new taxes."** In terms of social issues, Bush was strongly criticized for his reaction to the April 1992 riots that erupted in Los Angeles following the acquittal of several white policemen who had been caught on videotape beating an unarmed black man named **Rodney King**.

In 1992, Bush overcame a primary challenge from longtime Republican presidential speechwriter Pat Buchanan. But Buchanan's insurgency highlighted the growing intraparty divide between moderate establishment Republicans like Bush and the burgeoning groundswell of stridently anti-government, isolationist, and overtly religious conservatives.

The 1990s and President Bill Clinton

A Rhodes scholar and former Arkansas governor, Democrat **Bill Clinton** was initially considered a long-shot for the presidential race. He beat a crowded 1992 primary field with a strategically centrist message that left behind the party's more populist policies and targeted the middle class's economic woes. Clinton won the presidency in a three-way race with Bush and Texas businessman **Ross Perot**, who ran on the Independent ticket. Clinton's presidency included some notable successes, as well as Congressional gridlock and scandals of a personal nature.

Perhaps the most important achievements of Bill Clinton's presidency were the balancing of the federal budget and the return to economic prosperity. Clinton's economic policies at home were mirrored by efforts to strengthen the U.S. economy through integration in the global economy. In November 1993, the House passed the **North American Free Trade Agreement** (NAFTA), eliminating most trade barriers with Mexico and Canada. During Clinton's eight years in office, the United States experienced the most powerful economic expansion in the history of the United States.

His most noted failure came in the realm of healthcare, when Congress blocked his 1993 effort to create a national system that would have replaced the increasingly expensive and ineffective ad-hoc employer-supplied private insurance system that several presidents going back to Truman had been trying to reform. Clinton also struggled to push his domestic reform package through an antagonistic Congress, which was controlled by Republicans after the midterm elections of 1994. Despite these problems, Clinton's Reagan-esque ability to emotionally connect with voters, along with a steadily improving economy, ensured an easy victory over his 1996 Republican opponent, Senator Bob Dole.

> In the landmark midterm election of 1994, Republicans took control of the House of Representatives for the first time in forty years. The "Republican Revolution" was led in part by Georgia congressman Newt Gingrich, who was named Speaker of the House. Gingrich was an intellectual firebrand who frequently played to the previously little-noticed cameras of the C-SPAN network with vituperative speeches. He and his colleagues published their objectives in a broadside called the **"Contract with America,"** which outlined a number of staunch fiscally conservative policies (including tax cuts and a balanced budget amendment) that would influence the party for years afterward. Although Gingrich and Clinton would eventually learn to work together, the sudden influx of aggressively reactionary Republicans uninterested in bipartisan compromise both inflamed the period's culture wars and the atmosphere of antagonism that would only grow in the nation's capital in the decades to follow.

CLINTON ABROAD

Foreign policy proved somewhat of a struggle for Clinton. Years of diplomatic effort and a great deal of personal involvement brought Clinton close—but not close enough—to securing an Israeli-Palestinian peace deal. After attacks by the burgeoning Islamic terrorist group Al-Qaeda on American embassies in Tanzania and Kenya (1998) and the USS *Cole* in Yemen (2000), the highly mobile and secretive perpetrators proved difficult to track down.

The swift victory of the Gulf War, the rapid spread of democratic governments, the collapse of the U.S.S.R., and its replacement by a militarily weaker Russia gave many Americans the false sense that the 1990s would be marked by a global consensus benignly watched over by the U.S. Although the American military still had no conventional rival, the spread of terrorist organizations and the specter of failed states made the post-détente era more complicated for Clinton's administration than many foreign policy experts would have thought.

A perfect example of the new chaotic era was the U.N. humanitarian mission in Mogadishu, Somalia, that led to the so-called "**Black Hawk Down**" battle. In October 1993, American special forces were ambushed by Somali militiamen, losing eighteen men in the process. Clinton withdrew troops early the following year. With the exception of an unopposed 1994 American military mission to support Haiti's deposed president Jean-Bertrand Aristide, Clinton would be very reluctant thereafter to commit troops again throughout the remainder of a restive decade. This led to criticisms that the West (still used to taking its lead from the U.S.) did nothing to avert the 1994 genocide in Rwanda and was late to use military air power to end to the vicious ethnic-cleansing conflicts in the Balkans following the breakup of Yugoslavia.

SCANDALS AND TABLOID CULTURE

Although earlier political scandals and firestorms revolved mostly around the abuse of power and money (i.e., Watergate and Teapot Dome), those that typified the American landscape in the 1990s were of a different nature. At the end of George H. W. Bush's presidency in October 1991, the nomination of **Clarence Thomas** to be the first black Supreme Court justice turned into a media firestorm after Thomas's former subordinate **Anita Hill**, an Oklahoma law professor, accused him of sexual harrassment. The televised hearings in which Hill was grilled by the Senate Judiciary Committee about the frequently obscene particulars of her charges, not only changed the boundaries of public discourse but also brought the issue of workplace sexual harrassment into the open.

Frequent accusations of sexual misconduct by President Clinton provided more grist for the increasingly tabloid-focused media culture that was spawned during the early 1990s—in part by the spread of twenty-four-hour news channels eager for salacious rating-boosting stories. These charges came to a head in August 1998, when Clinton testified in front of a grand jury that he had not engaged in inappropriate relations with White House intern **Monica Lewinsky**. Later, he was forced to admit that he had. In December 1998, the House of Representatives approved articles of impeachment for perjury and obstruction of justice. In February 1999, the Senate defeated both articles.

Clinton remained in office, but the Lewinsky scandal—as well as a number of other White House scandals of a more dubious nature pursued tirelessly by a new crop of conservative publications—overshadowed the rest of his presidency.

Timeline

1976	James "Jimmy" Carter is elected president.
1979	The Iran hostage crisis begins.
1980	Ronald Reagan is elected president.
1981	The Iran Hostage crisis ends.
	Reagan slashes taxes but increases government spending.
1982	Recession hits.
1984	Reagan is reelected.
1985	Mikhail Gorbachev initiates reform in the USSR.
	Nuclear disarmament is discussed at the first Reagan-Gorbachev summit meeting.
1986	The Iran-Contra Affair erupts.
	Congress passes the Immigration Reform and Control Act.
	The second Reagan-Gorbachev summit meeting is held.
1987	The third Reagan-Gorbachev summit meeting is held.
	Reagan signs the INF Treaty at the fourth Reagan-Gorbachev summit meeting in Washington, D.C., to remove all nuclear weapons.
1988	George H. W. Bush is elected president.
1989	The Berlin Wall is torn down, symbolizing the end of the Cold War.
1991	In Operation Desert Storm, the U.S. and its allies drive Iraqi forces out of Kuwait.
	Anita Hill testifies before the Senate Judiciary Committee.
1992	Bill Clinton is elected president.
1993	The North American Free Trade Agreement (NAFTA) is signed.
1996	Clinton is reelected.
1998	Al-Qaeda truck-bombings of U.S. embassies in Tanzania and Kenya kill over 200 people, including 12 Americans.
	Monica Lewinsky scandal.

CHAPTER 19

9/11 to the Great Recession: 2001–2014

||||||||||||||||||||||||||||||||||||||||||||||||||||||||||

The first years of the twenty-first century presented a complicated new landscape for America to navigate, both overseas and at home. The first president of the new millennium, George W. Bush, had to confront the challenges posed by the terrorist attacks of 9/11. The country's allies and even Bush's domestic adversaries all agreed the attacks were a grave threat, but the president's response, pushed by more hawkish members of his administration was wildly divisive.

Matters proved no less complicated for Barack Obama, who followed Bush's two terms to become the nation's first black president. Obama's soaring oratory and optimism were quickly overshadowed by a devastating financial crisis that began not long before he took office and by the ongoing wars in Iraq and Afghanistan. In 2010 Obama pushed through a landmark reform of the nation's health insurance system, and in 2012 he won reelection by a healthy margin. But the increasing polarization of the political class and the electorate meant that often even the most basic operations of government struggled to function during his presidency.

September 11, 2001, and Its Aftermath

George H. W. Bush's son, former governor of Texas George W. Bush, was nine months into an initially uneventful first term as president when, on the morning of **September 11, 2001**, two airliners hijacked by the terrorist group **Al-Qaeda** were flown into the World Trade Center in New York. A third hijacked airliner crashed into the Pentagon, while a fourth crashed into a field in rural Pennsylvania. It was the most devastating attack on American soil since Pearl Harbor.

Bush and his vice president, Dick Cheney, pursued an aggressive strategy of combating the threat from Al-Qaeda and its affiliates. The United States quickly began airstrikes in Afghanistan, because the Taliban, an extremist Islamic regime that had sheltered Al-Qaeda and its leader, **Osama bin Laden**, refused to turn over the terrorist leader. By December, the United States and its allies had toppled the Taliban, but had not captured bin Laden.

HOMELAND SECURITY

On the home front, a massive realignment of government agencies created the **Department of Homeland Security**. In October 2001, the **Patriot Act** became law. Its broad expansion of surveillance and information-sharing between government agencies (previously restricted following abuses during the Cold War) was considered by some to be a threat to constitutional freedoms. The Act was defended as being essential to fighting terror threats. This argument was made in particular by several members of the Bush administration, such as Cheney and Secretary of Defense Donald Rumsfeld, who were longtime stalwarts of the more hawkish wing of the Republican infrastructure in Washington.

Overseas, the Bush administration pursued an international campaign against terrorist groups and their allies. In addition to massive increases in the defense budget, the size of intelligence agencies like the CIA and the **National Security Agency (NSA)** expanded dramatically. There would be a vigorous debate throughout Bush's presidency not only over whether expanded surveillance programs were unconstitutional invasions of privacy, but also whether the CIA's campaign of detaining suspects in secret "black site" prisons for "enhanced interrogations" was in fact simply torture. The controversy about balancing security against traditional American values would prove to be one of society's key issues at the start of the twenty-first century.

The 2000 presidential campaign between George W. Bush and former Clinton vice president Al Gore was one of the closest in American history. In Florida, because Bush led Gore by only 1,800 votes out of some six million, state election laws dictated a manual recount. The tangled legal process that resulted generated a firestorm of controversy and charges of political favoritism (Florida's secretary of state in charge of the recount, Kathryn Harris, was also co-chair of Bush's campaign in the state). On December 12, 2000, the Supreme Court ultimately decided, in **Bush v. Gore***, that the recount should be ended, and Gore conceded to Bush. Later counts by multiple news organizations determined that Gore had in fact received more votes in Florida than Bush.*

THE IRAQ AND AFGHANISTAN WARS

Arguing that Saddam Hussein was concealing a program of **weapons of mass destruction (WMD)**, the Bush administration brushed aside massive international opposition and domestic protests to launch **Operation Iraqi Freedom** in March 2003. Notably, even though NATO participated in the U.S.'s use of miltary force in Afghanistan, the only American ally who joined the Iraq invasion was the United Kingdom. The Iraqi army was swiftly defeated and a democratic government installed in 2005. However, a bloody guerrilla war was fought by Saddam loyalists and Shiite militias (long suppressed by the Sunni minority) against allied troops and forces of the new Iraqi government.

The fighting dragged on for years, characterized by suicide and roadside bombings and civilian massacres. In 2004, a scandal erupted over charges that Iraqi prisoners at the American-run **Abu Ghraib** complex had been abused. In 2007, a so-called "surge" of American troops and unconventional counterinsurgency tactics were credited with keeping the fragile Iraqi government from collapse. An estimated 100,000 Iraqis and nearly 5,000 allied soldiers were dead by the time American troops withdrew in 2010, leaving behind a very fragile peace.

Meanwhile, another long-running guerrilla war raged in Afghanistan, where anti-Taliban forces had retaken their country with American and NATO assistance. Yet even with massive amounts of aid, popular antipathy toward the Taliban, and tens of thousands of Western troops on the ground, the new government in Kabul had only tenuous control over most of the country. The American military footprint remained comparatively small until 2009, when force levels were ramped up to combat increased Taliban activity. Eventually, more security duties were passed off to the new Afghan military, but coalition forces remained on the ground for support. By mid-2010, the Afghanistan War surpassed the Vietnam War to become **America's longest conflict**. Although casualties were much lower, both the Afghanistan and Iraq wars were frequently compared to Vietnam because of their long, grinding nature and ultimately inconclusive endings.

THE GREAT RECESSION

Starting in late 2007, signs of economic trouble began accumulating. While the stock market reached ever-higher levels, a growing number of financial institutions looked dangerously close to collapse because of their overexposure to dizzyingly complex investment and trading strategies that took advantage of a bullish real estate market. It became clear that the housing market was a bubble about to collapse, and several large institutions failed along with it. While Wall Street began to panic, homeowners across the country who had been assured that their houses would never depreciate in value saw their net worth plummet. This was the start of the **Great Recession**.

Brokerage firm Bear Stearns collapsed in March 2008. In September Lehman Brothers filed the largest bankruptcy case in American history. Insurance giant AIG was rescued by the federal government to avert a near-complete economic meltdown. That October, the **Troubled Asset Relief Program (TARP)** provided $700 billion in emergency aid to financial institutions. In February 2009, a "**stimulus package**" of nearly $800 billion was rushed out in order to prop up the teetering economy.

The unemployment rate, which had hovered between 4.5 and 6 percent since 2003, spiked to 10 percent in late 2009 and remained persistently above 7 percent for the next several years.

Barack Obama

Illinois senator **Barack Obama** won the presidential election in 2008. With a white mother and black father, Obama became the first person of non-white descent to hold the office. He defeated first his primary opponent Hillary Clinton (Bill Clinton's wife, who was elected to the Senate in 2000) and then Republican senator John McCain in the general election. He succeeded in part by marshalling a campaign whose ability to harness the Internet for fundraising and targeted advertising was unprecedented. Obama had a relatively thin political resume, but it was in part balanced out by McCain's unpolished and divisive running mate, Alaska governor **Sarah Palin**.

The election's euphoria was tempered by the country's most pressing problems: the Great Recession and two ongoing wars. Obama's first term was marked by strident Republican opposition, particularly to his stimulus package and an ambitious overhaul of the nation's healthcare system.

THE TEA PARTY AND A "POST-RACIAL" AMERICA

In the years that followed Obama's historic election, much of American political discourse centered around what was seen as an increasingly polarized atmosphere in the nation's capital. Part of this was believed to be due to the rise of the **"Tea Party"** movement in 2009. Initially the Tea Party was viewed as a nonpartisan call for fiscal restraint and deficit reduction following the financial crash and the attendant government bailout. But the network of grassroots groups quickly morphed into a hardline reactionary backlash that made the anti-government rhetoric of the Reagan era seem tame by comparison. 2011 would see some liberal groups, operating under the **"Occupy Wall Street"** banner, protesting the failure of the government to enact serious regulatory changes in the financial sector following the fiscal crisis. But large-scale protest movements during Obama's time in office would remain a mostly conservative affair.

2001-2014

Some had hoped that the election of Obama would prove America was entering a "post-racial" age. But the tendency of the electorate to still separate along old racial lines—with older white voters supporting the Republicans, and younger and minority voters going Democrat—seemed as strong as it had ever been.

Obamacare

The **Affordable Care Act (ACA),** popularly known as "**Obamacare**," became law in 2010. Among other things, it mandated that all American citizens would have to obtain health insurance or pay a penalty; Medicare was expanded and subsidies were provided for low-income citizens. As one of the biggest social programs put forward in America since LBJ's Great Society, the ACA was the perfect target for Tea Party activists who wanted to dramatically shrink government, not expand it. Partisan fights over the shape and constitutionality of the ACA consumed much of the Obama presidency's efforts on the domestic front.

OBAMA'S WARS, ABROAD AND AT HOME

Although Obama's election was seen in part as a repudiation of George W. Bush's actions in the "War on Terror," the new president continued many of his predecessor's policies, sometimes even more aggressively. Obama's foreign policy was carried out in part by his former rival, Hillary Clinton, who he appointed secretary of state. The killing of suspected terrorists by remote-controlled **drone strikes** and special forces increased under Obama, most dramatically with the May 2011 raid by Navy SEALs on a compound in Pakistan that killed Osama bin Laden. The public mostly favored this brand of targeted conflict over large deployments of troops overseas. But concerns were raised about the strikes' extrajudicial nature, particularly after **Anwar al-Awlaki**, an American citizen who preached a fiery brand of fundamentalist Islam and was believed to have links to Al-Qaeda, was killed by a U.S. drone in Yemen in 2011.

The NSA's **warrantless surveillance** of domestic and foreign targets also expanded to a degree that worried many civil rights and privacy advocates—not to mention foreign heads of allied states who discovered that they were being watched as well. The extent of the surveillance was exposed in a massive leak of clas-sified information in 2013 by CIA contractor **Edward Snowden**, the biggest such leak since the Pentagon Papers. The Obama administration would eventually agree to scale back some of the NSA's surveillance but in general it kept the programs in place.

Although American struggles abroad were primarily against terrorist threats, the specter of new military rivals continued to grow in the second decade of the twenty-first century. While remaining far behind America in terms of its defense capabili-ties, China dramatically increased its military spending and stoked conflict with neighboring countries like the Philippines and Japan. Under its intensely nationalistic leader, former KGB agent Vladimir Putin, Russia also pushed at its traditional boundaries, annexing small neighboring regions like Crimea and South Ossetia. Without the specter of communism to rally the country, and more limited non-military "soft power" options available, Obama's administration faced many challenges in keeping the international balance of power in America's favor.

Polarization

After a drawn-out Republican primary almost unprecedented for its sharp infighting, Obama handily won reelection in 2012 against Republican **Mitt Romney,** the first Mormon candidate for the office. Ironically, although he campaigned hard against Obamacare, Romney had put in place a statewide health insur-ance program that closely resembled the ACA during his term as Massachusetts governor.

Partisan strife between the administration and the Democrat-controlled Senate and the Republican-majority House continued unabated after Obama's reelection. Numerous fractious stale-mates over spending and revenue levels brought the government to the brink of shutdown on multiple occasions. Increasing dismay over the widening gap of income inequality amidst a stubbornly sluggish economy, and wildly divergent beliefs about how to best deal with those problems, meant that the admin-istration would have no shortage of issues to contend with during the rest of its time in office.

Timeline

2000	In *Bush v. Gore*, Supreme Courts ends recounts, George W. Bush wins presidency.
2001	George W. Bush takes office as president.
	9/11 terrorist attacks on the World Trade Center and the Pentagon.
	The Afghanistan War begins.
2002	No Child Left Behind educational act signed into law.
2003	Sweeping tax cuts enacted.
	The Iraq War begins.
2004	Bush wins reelection.
2005	Hurricane Katrina devastates Gulf Coast.
2007	Troop surge in Iraq begins.
2008	Barack Obama elected president.
2010	Affordable Care Act becomes law.
2011	U.S. citizen Anwar al-Awlaki killed by American drone strike in Yemen.
2012	U.S. forces withdrawn from Iraq.
	Obama wins reelection.
2013	Edward Snowden leaks expose NSA surveillance programs.

Contributors

Anaxos, Inc.

Timothy Buckner
Teaching Assistant, Department of History, University of Texas at
Austin

Gregg Cantrell, Ph.D.
Professor of History and Erma and Ralph Lowe Chair in Texas History,
Texas Christian University

Josh Cracaft
A.B., Government, Harvard University

Andrew Jones
B.A., International Studies, Oglethorpe University; M.A., Slavic
Languages and Literature, Ohio State University; M.S., Journalism,
Boston University

Ashley Laumen
Teaching Assistant, Department of History, Texas Christian University

Christian Lorentzen
A.B., Classics, Harvard University

Kelly McMichael-Stott, Ph.D.
Professor of History, Texas Christian University

Paul Rubinson
Teaching Assistant, Department of History, University of Texas at
Austin

Sean Taylor, Ph.D.
Visiting Assistant Professor of History, Minnesota State University
Moorhead

Index